The Politics of Ethnicity in Central Europe

The Politics of Ethnicity in Central Europe

Edited by

Karl Cordell
Senior Lecturer in Politics
University of Plymouth

First published in Great Britain 2000 by
MACMILLAN PRESS LTD
Houndmills, Basingstoke, Hampshire RG21 6XS and London
Companies and representatives throughout the world

A catalogue record for this book is available from the British Library.

ISBN 0–333–73171–9

First published in the United States of America 2000 by
ST. MARTIN'S PRESS, INC.,
Scholarly and Reference Division,
175 Fifth Avenue, New York, N.Y. 10010

ISBN 0–312–22790–6

Library of Congress Cataloging-in-Publication Data
The politics of ethnicity in Central Europe / edited by Karl Cordell.
p. cm.
Includes bibliographical references and index.
ISBN 0–312–22790–6 (cloth)
1. Silesia—Ethnic relations—Political aspects. 2. Silesia–
–Politics and government. 3. Europe, Central—Ethnic relations–
–Political aspects. 4. Europe, Central—Politics and government.
I. Cordell, Karl, 1956– .
DK4600.S4242P65 1999
305.8'009438'5—dc21 99–39505
CIP

This book is printed on paper suitable for recycling and made from fully managed and sustained forest sources.

10 9 8 7 6 5 4 3 2 1
09 08 07 06 05 04 03 02 01 00

Printed and bound in Great Britain by
Antony Rowe Ltd, Chippenham, Wiltshire

For Sophia

Contents

Acknowledgements

There are many people who in one way or the other have helped in the preparation of this book and deserve a mention. For reasons of space I will unfortunately have to limit it to a select band. First of all, I would like to thank my Head of Department, Adrian Lee, for having put up with me all these years and for having provided me with every means of support above and beyond the call of duty. I should also like to thank Vit Novony, Angelika Gutmann, and Catherine Johnson-Gerkes for their translations, without which this work could not have appeared. Thanks also goes to my sister, Julie Cordell-Szczurek, for arranging translation services in Germany. Thanks are also due to Karl Martin Born for stepping into the breach at a moment's notice. Many thanks are also due to everyone at Macmillan who helped in the preparation of the volume, and especially to Sunder Katwala, Alison Howson and Sarah Barrett for her patience and diligence with the manuscript. Also, I should also like to thank the Leverhulme Trust for their generous financial support, without which the book would not have appeared. Finally, a big vote of thanks to everyone who in various ways has supported me over the years; you know who you are.

Prefatory Remarks

Place-names in Central Europe change according to political circumstances. In order to prevent the reader drowning in a sea of parentheses, place-names used in the text are, unless specifically indicated, those which are appropriate to the period under examination. The accompanying list of place-names is designed to achieve two things. The first is to illustrate the point made in the introductory sentence. The second is to familiarize the reader with the historical equivalents of contemporary Silesian place-names. Given that the large majority of Silesia is today Polish, the general rule used is that Polish names appear first and traditional German names second. Czech names are also used where appropriate, and in addition 'pre-national' and where appropriate National Socialist place-names are also given.

Place-Names

Source: Snoch B. (ed.), *Ilustrowany Slownik Dziejow Slaska* (Katowice, Wydawnictwo 'Slask', 1991).

Official Polish place-names given first; alternatives follow the key below.

cz.	Czech names used in Opava and Tesin Silesia
n.	German names
n.d.	names cited in documents, usually Latin forms
n.n.	German names introduced after 1933
n.pw.	temporary Polish names used shortly after 1945
obocz.	names used in parallel to the official Polish names

Baborow	n.d. Baurow; n.Bauerwitz; n.pw. Bawaorow
Bardo	n.d. Gradice Barda, Brido; Wartha; n.pw. Warta
Biala Prudnicka	n.d. Bela; n. Zülz
Bielawa	n.d. Belsco, Belzco; n. Bielitz
Bierun Stary	n.d. Berun, Byerun; n. Alt Berun
Bierutow	n.d. Berolstadt, Bernhardtsdorf; n. Bernstadt
Bogumin	n. Oderberg; cz. Bohumin
Boguszow	n. Gottesberg; n.pw.Boza Gora
Boleslawiec	n.d. Bolezlaucz, Bolisslaw, Bonzlavia; n. Bunzlau
Bolkow	n. Bolkenhain; n.pw. Bolkowice
Borow	n.d. Boriow, Boraw, Borouw; n. Bohrau
Brochow	n.d. Prochow, Brockow; n. Brockau; n.pw. Prochow
Bruntal	n. Freudenthal; cz. Bruntal
Brzeg	n.d. Visoke Breg, Alta Ripa, Breg; n. Brieg
Brzeg Dolny	n.d. Breg, Brega; n.Dyhernfurth
Byczyna	n.d. Byscina, Biczina; n. Pitschen

Bystrzyca Klodzka	n.d.Weistritz, Hawelswerd; n. Habelschwerdt
Bytom	n.d. Bitom; n. Beuthen/OS
Bytom Odrzanski	n.d. Bitom; n. Beuthen and der Oder; n.pw. Bialobrzezie
Cerekwica	n.d. Circutce; n. Zirkwitz
Chelmsko Slaskie	n. Schömberg; n.pw. Szymrych
Chobienia	n.d. Chobena, Hobena. Kobin; n. Koben and der Oder
Chocianow	n.d. Choczenow; n. Kotzenau; n.pw. Kaczanow
Chojnow	n.d. Haynowia; n. Haynau
Chorzow	n.d. Charzow, Chorzow, Krolewsa Huta; n. Königshutte
Ciechanowice	n.d. Tschechanowecz; n. Rudelstadt
Cieplice Slaskie	n.d. Calidus fons, Warmenborn; n. Warmbrunn
Cieszkow	n.d. Freyno; n. Freyhan
Cieszyn	n.d. Tescin, Tessin; n. Teschen; cz. Cesky Tesin
Czarnowasy	n.d. Charnowoz, Czarnowaz; n. Czarnowanz; n.n. Klosterbruck
Czechowice-Dziedzice	n.d. Cechowitz, Ciechowicz; Dziedzicz; n. Czechowitz-Dzieditz
Czernina	n. Tschirnau
Czerwiensk	n.d. Netka, Nettkow; n. Rotenburg
Dobrodzien	n.d. Dobrodyn, Dobradin, Dobrodzyn; n. Guttentag
Dobromierz	n.d. Vrideberch, Fredeberg; n. Hohenfriedeberg
Dobroszyce	n.d. Dobra, Treskin; n. Juliusburg; n.pw. Julianowo
Duszniki	n.d. Dussnik, Rynarcz; n. Reinerz
Dzierzoniow	n.d. Richinbach, Richenbach; obocz. Rychbach; n. Reichenbach; n.pw. Rychbach
Frydek-Mistek	n. Friedek, Mistek; cz. Frydek-Mistek
Frysztat	n.d. Fristat; n. Freistadt; cz. Frystat (Karvina I Frystat)
Gliwice	n.d. Gliwicz, Glywycz, Glewicz; n. Gleiwitz
Glogow	n.d. Glogua, Glogav, Glogavia; n. Glogau

Glogowek	n.d. Glogov, Minor Glogovia; n. Oberglogau
Glubczyce	n.d. Glupcici, Glubchiz, Hlupchyzhe, Lybschutz; n. Leobschütz; n.pw. Glabczyce
Glucholazy	n.d. Capricollum, Cygenhals; n. Ziegenhals, obocz. Kozia Szyja
Gluszyca	n.d. Wustemdorph; n. Wustegiersdorf; n.pw. Gierzcze Puste
Gogolin	n.d. Gogolino; n. Gogolin
Gora	n.d. Antiqua Gora, Goravia; n. Guhrau
Gora Sw. Anny	n.d. monte Helm, M. Sancta Anna; n. Sankt Annaberg, Annaberg; obocz. Swieta Anna
Gorzow Slaski	n.d. Gorczow, Landisberg; n. Landsberg
Grodkow	n.d. Grodkovichi, Grodchov, Grodcov; n. Grottkau; n.pw. Grotkow
Gryfow Slaski	n.d. Griphenberch; n. Greiffenberg; n.pw. Gryfogora
Gubin	n.d. Gubyn; n. Guben
Henrykow	n.d. Heinrichow; n. Heinrichau
Hulczyn	n. Hultschin; cz. Hlucin
Ilowa	n.d. Ilua, Ilwa; n. Halbau; n.pw. Ilwa
Jablonkow	n. Jablunkau; cz. Jablunkow
Jawor	n.d. Javor; n. Jauer, obocz. Jaworz; n.pw. Jaworow
Jawornik	n. Jauernig; cz. Javornik
Jedlina Zdroj	n. Charlottenbrunn; n.pw. Zdrojowice
Jelenia Gora	n.d. Hyrzberc, Hersberg; n. Hirschberg
Jesienik	n.d. Frywaldov; n. Freiwaldau; cz. Jesenik
Kamienna Gora	n.d. Camena Gora, Landishute; n. Landeshut, obocz. Lancut; n.pw. Kamienio-gora
Karniow	n. Jagersdorf; cz. Krnov
Karpacz	n. Krummhübel
Karwina	n. Karwin; cz. Karvina
Katowice	n.d. Katowicze; n. Kattowitz
Katy Wroclawskie	n. Kanth
Kietrz	n.d. Ketscher, Kacer, Keczir; n. Katscher
Kluzbork	n.d. Cruceburch, Kluzbork, Krucibork; n. Kreuzburg

Klodzko	n.d. Kladsko, Cladsco, Klotsko; n. Glatz; n.pw. Kladzko
Korfantow Ferlat, Fyrlat	n.d. Fredland, Hurtland; n. Friedland; obocz. gwarowo
Kostomloty	n.d. Costomlot; n. Kostenblat
Kowary	n.d. Smedewerk; n. Schmiedeberg; n.pw. Krzyzatka
Kozle	n.d. Coszle, Kosle; n. Cosel
Kozuchow	n.d. Cosuchow, Cosuchovia; n. Freystadt, obocz. Frysztat
Krapkowice	n.d. Crapiez, Crapkowitz; n. Krappitz, obocz. Chrapkowice
Krosno Odrzanskie	n.d. Crosno, Chrosno; n. Crossen a.d. Oder
Krzeszow	n.d. Grissebor, Cresowbor, Grysovia; n. Grussau
Ksiaz	n. Furstenstein; n.pw. Ksiazno
Kudowa Zdroj	n.d. Chudoba; n. Bad Kudowa; n.pw. Chudoba
Kuznia Raciborska	n.d. Ferrocudina, Kuznicza; n. Ratiborhammer
Ladek Zdroj	n.d. Landecke; n. Bad Landeck
Legnica	n.d. Legnice, Legniz; n. Liegnitz, obocz. i n.pw. Lignica
Legnickie Pole	n.d. Legnichezke; n. Wahlastatt, obocz. Dobrepole
Lesna	n.d. Lesna, Lessa, Marglissa; n. Marklissa
Lesnica (Opole)	n.d. Lesniscie; n. Leschnitz; n.n. Bergstadt
Lesnica (Wroclaw)	n.d. Lesnicza, Lesnicz, Lesna; n. Lissa
Lewin Brzeski	n.d. Lewin; n. Löwen; n.pw. Lubien
Lewin Klodzki	n.d. Levinci, Lewyn; n. Hummelstadt
Lipa	n.d. Lypa; n. Leippe
Luban	n.d. Luban; n. Lauban
Lubawka	n.d. Liubavia, Lubavia; n. Liebau; n.pw. Lubawa
Lubiaz	n.d. Lubens; n. Leubus
Lubin	Lubin, Lubyn; n. Lüben
Lubliniec	n.d. Lublynecz, Lublinicz; n. Lublinitz; n.n. Lobau
Lubomierz	n.d. Lybental; n. Liebenthal; n.pw. Milosna
Lubsko	n. Sommerfeld; n.pw. Zems

Lutynia	n.d. Luthyna; n. Leuthen
Lwowek Slaski	n.d. Lewenberc, Leoberga; n. Löwenberg
Malujowice	n.d. Malewicz, Molwicz; n. Mollwitz
Miasteczko Slaskie	n. Georgenberg
Miedzianka	n.d. Cupri fodina; n. Kupferberg
Miedzyborz	n.d. Meczibor; n. Naumittelwalde; n.pw. Miedzybor
Miedzylesie	n.d. Medilese; n. Mittewalde
Mieroszow	n.d. I n. Friedland; n.pw. Frydland, Fyrlad
Mikolow	n.d. Miculow, Micolaw; n. Nikolai
Milicz	n.d. Milich, Miliche; n. Militsch
Mirsk	n.d. Fridberge; n. Friedeberg; n.pw. Spokojna Gora
Myslowice	n.d. Myslowicze, Mislowicze; n. Myslowitz
Namyslow	n.d. Namslauia, Namizlov; n. Namslau
Niemcza	n.d. Nemechi; n. Nimptsch
Niemodlin	n.d. Nemodlin, Falkenberch; n. Falkenberg
Nowa Cerckwia	n.d. Nova Ecclesia, Nowoczerkwie; n. Neukirsch
Nowa Ruda	n.d. Neuwenrode, Neunrod; n. Neurode
Nowa Sol	n.d. Nova Sal; n. Neusalz
Nowogrodziec	n.d. Novum Castrum, Nauburg; n. Naumburg a. Queis
Nowogrod Bobrzanski	n.d. Novum Castrum, Nuborch, Numburch; n. Naumburg a. Bober
Nowy Bytom	n.d. Czarny Las; n. Friedenshutte; to 1922 Nowy Bytom
Nysa	n.d. Nisa, Nysa; n. Neisse; n.pw. Nisa
Olawa	n.d. Olaua, Olavia; n. Ohlau
Olesnica	n.d. Olesnich, Olesnic, Olezniza; n. Oels
Olesno	n.d. Oleszno, Olesno; n. Rosenberg
Opawa	n.d. Opavia; n. Troppau; cz. Opava
Opole	n.d. Opol, Opole; n. Oppeln
Orlowa	n. Orlau; cz. Orlova
Ostrawa	n.d. Moravska O., Polska O., Slezska O.; Ostrau; cz. Ostrava
Oswiecim	n.d. Osswyanczim, Osswencin, Auswinczyn; n. Auschwitz

Otmuchow	n.d. Otomochov, Otmuchaw, Otemachaw; n. Ottmachau
Paczkow	n.d. Paczchow, Paczcow; n. Patschkau
Piechowice	n. Petersdorf
Piekary Slaskie	n.d. Pecare, Peccari, Wielkie Piekary; n. Deutsch Piekar
Pieszyce	n.d. Petirswalde; n. Peterswaldau; n.pw. Piotrolesie
Pobiedna	n. Ullersdorf
Polanica Zdroj	n. Altheide; n.pw. Puszczykow Zdroj
Polkowice	n.d. Polcowitz; n. Polkwitz; n.n. Heernlegen
Prochowice	n.d. Parchouici; n. Parchwitz; n.pw. Parchowice, Parchwice
Proszkow	n.d. Proscow, Proskow; n. Proskau
Prudnik	n.d. Prudnic; n. Neustadt; n.pw. Pradnik
Prusice	n.d. Prusicz, Prusin; Prausnitz
Przemkow	n.d. Primkenaw, Prymkenowe; n. Primkenau; n.pw. Przemkowo, Prymka
Psie Pole	n.d. Pze Pole; n. Hundsfeld (przejsciowo; Friedrichsfeld)
Pszczyna	n.d. Plisschyn, Plessina, Plschina, Plszczyna, Blasczina; n.Pless
Pyskowice	n.d. Pyzkuwicz; n. Peiskretscham
Raciborz	n.d. Ratibor; n. Ratibor
Radkow	n.d. Hradek; n. Wunschelburg; n.pw. Grodek, Hradek
Ruda Slaska	n.d. Ruda; n. Ruda
Rudna	n.d. Rudna; n. Raudten
Rudy Wielkie	n.d. Ruda, Rudno; n. Gross Rauden
Rybnik	n.d. Ribnich, Rebnic, Rybniki; n. Rybnik
Ryczyn	n.d. Rechen; n. Retschen
Scinawa	n.d. Scinauia, Stinava, Stinav; n. Steinau
Siedlecin	n. Boberröhrsdorf
Siemianowice Slaskie	n.d. Simanovici, Semenowitze; obocz. Huta Laura, n. Laurahütte, Siemianowitz
Siewierz	n.d. Siewior, Sewior
Skoczow	n.d. Zchotschow; n. Skotschau
Skorogoszcz	n.d. Scorogostov Most; n. Schurgast

Slawiecice	n.d. Slauecici, Slavientisz; n. Slawentzitz; n.n.Ehrenforst
Sobotka	n.d. Sobota, Sabat, Zabothus; n. Zobten
Sosnicowice	n.d. Sosnessowitz, Sosniessowitze; n. Kieferstadtel
Srebrna Gora	n. Silberberg
Sroda Slaska	n.d. Novoforo, Neumarch, Schoroda; n. Neumarkt
Strumien	n.d. Strumien; n. Schwarzwasser
Strzegom	n.d. Ztrigom, Ztregom; n. Striegau
Strzelce Opolskie	n.d. Strelci; n. Strehlitz, Groß Strehlitz, obocz. Strzelce
Sulikow	n.d. Newesschonburg, Schoninberch; n. Schonberg Oberlausitz, obocz. Szynbark
Swidnica	n.d. Zuidniza; n. Schweidnitz
Swieradow Zdroj	n.d. Flinssberg; n. Bad Flinsberg; n.pw. Wieniec Zdroj
Swierzawa	n.d. Sonowe, Schenow; n. Schönau; n.pw. Szunow
Swietochlowice	n.d. Swentochlewicz, Szwentochlovice; n. Schwientochlowitz
Sycow	n.d. Syczowe, Syczow, Syzow; n. Groß Wartenberg
Szczawno Zdroj	n.d. Salzborn, Salzborne; n. Salzbrunn, obocz. I n.pw. Solice
Szklarska Poreba	n.d. I n. Schoppinitz
Szprotawa	n.d. Sprottava, Sprotavia; n. Sprottau
Tarnowskie Gory	n.d. Tarnowice; n. Tarnowitz
Toszek	n.d. Tossech, Thosech; n. Tost
Tryniec	n. Trzynietz; cz. Trinec
Trzebnica	n.d. Trebnicha, Trebnice; n. Trebnitz
Twardogora	n.d. Vestenberg; n. Festenberg; n.pw. Twarda Gora
Ujazd	n.d. Uiazd; n. Ujest; n.n. Bitchofstal
Uraz	n.d. Uradz, Urac, Vraz; n. Auras
Walbrzych	n.d. Waldenberc; n. Waldenburg
Wambierzyce	n.d. Wamberic; n. Albendorf, HI. Gottesstadt
Wasosz	n.d. Wansose, Wanschosch; n. Herrnstadt

Wiazow	n.d. Venzouici, Wanzow; n. Wansen; n.pw. Wiezow
Widnawa	n. Weidenau; cz. Vidnava
Wielkie Strzelin	n.d. Strelyn, Strelin; n.Strehlen
Winsko	n.d. Vin, Vinzk; n. Winzig
Wisla	n.d. Vizla, Wisla; n.n. Weichsel
Wlen	n.d. Valan, Wlen; n.Lahn; n.pw. Lenno
Wodzislaw Slaski	n.d. Wlodislav, Wlodzislaw; n. Loslau
Wolczyn	n.d. Czunczo, Czunczenstadt; n. Konstadt, obocz. Walczyn
Wolow	n.d. Wolow, Wolouo; n. Wohlau
Wozniki	n.d. Woznik, Uoznici; n. Woischnik
Wroclaw	n.d. Wortizlav, Wrotizlaw, Wratislavia; n. Breslau
Wschowa	n.d. Veschow, Vrovinstat; n. Fraustadt
Zabkowice Slaskie	n.d. Sambowitz; n. Zembowitz; n.n. Fohrendorf
Zabrze	n.d. Zadbrze (Sadbre); n. Zabrze, n.n. Hindenburg
Zagan	n.d. Sagan, Zagan; n. Sagan; n.pw. Zegan
Zary	n.d. Zara, Zoraw; n. Sorau; n.pw. Zarow, Zoraw
Zawidow	n.d. Syden, Sydenberg; n. Seidenber
Zawonia	n.d. Sawona, Sawon, Zawon; n. Sawona
Zgorzelec	n.d. Gorlicz, Zgorlic; n. Görlitz; n.pw. Zgorzelice
Ziebice	n.d. Sambiz, Sambice; n. Münsterberg; n.pw. Ziembice
Zielona Gora	n.d. Viridis Mons, Grünberg; n. Grunberg
Zlote Gory	n.d. Cukmantl; n. Zuckmantel; cz. Zlate Hory
Zlotniki Lubanskie	n. Goldentraum
Zlotoryja	n.d. Aureo Monte; n. Goldberg; n.pw. Zlotoria
Zloty Stok	n.d. Richinstein; n. Reichenstein; n.pw. Rowne
Zmigrod	n.d. Smigrod, Zmingrod; n. Trachenberg
Zory	n.d. Sari, Zary; n. Sohrau

Notes on Contributors

Karl Martin Born is Research Fellow in the Department of Politics at the University of Plymouth, Great Britain, working with Karl Cordell on the implications for Poland of membership of the European Union. He obtained his PhD in 1995 on completion of research into the impact of spatial administrations, landscape architects, and historical societies in Germany and New England. Between 1994 and 1997 he was Research Fellow in the Department of Geographical Sciences, researching into the transformation of legal services in east Germany after *Die Wende*.

Karl Cordell is Senior Lecturer in Politics at the University of Plymouth, Great Britain. Over the years he has published extensively on a various aspects of German politics, Polish politics, German–Polish relations and the politics of ethnic identity. He is currently researching into the implications of membership of the European Union for domestic Polish politics.

Petr Kacir was until 1997 employed by the Zemsky Archive in Opava in the Czech Republic. He has published extensively on Czech Silesia in both the Czech Republic and Poland. He is currently working in the commercial sector.

Tomasz Kamusella combines teaching duties at the University of Opole, Poland, with his post in the provincial administration in Opole, where he is particularly concerned with Poland's entry into the European Union. He is currently completing his doctoral thesis on the politics of identity in Silesia, and has published on this and related themes in German and English.

Bernard Linek is a Research Officer at the Silesian Institute Opole, Poland. He recently completed his doctoral research on the Polonization and re-Polonization of Upper Silesia between 1945 and 1950 at the University of Opole. He has published books on related themes and topics, and has previously been published in German and Polish.

Kai Struve is currently employed as a Research Fellow at the Herder-Institut Marburg, Germany. He is currently completing his doctoral programme on the emergence of Polish and Ukrainian national identity at the Free University, Berlin. He has published in this and related areas in both Germany and Poland.

Terry Sullivan recently completed his doctoral research into the German minority in Poland at the University of Plymouth, Great Britain. He has also published on that theme and on the politics of nation and state-building.

Philipp Ther completed his doctoral research on Polish and German expellees between 1945 and 1956 at the Free University of Berlin Germany in 1997. The thesis was subsequently produced in published form in Germany. He spent the academic year 1997/98 at Harvard University, USA, as a John F. Kennedy Fellow, and currently works at the Center for the Comparative History of Europe at the Free University of Berlin.

A Chronology of Silesia

10th c.	Silesia contested by Premyslids and Piasts
900	Foundation of Wroclaw by Prince Wratislav I of Bohemia
989–92	Mieszko I, Prince of Poland, acquires Silesia from Boleslav II, Prince of Bohemia
1000	Emperor Otto III founds the bishopric of Wroclaw
1163	Division into Lower and Upper Silesia, each ruled by a Piast Prince
1203	Creation of a third Silesia principiality
1205–	Calls for German settlers and colonists
1217	Foundation of Opole
9 Apr. 1241	Battle of Legnica: Defeat of the joint Polish and German knights by the Mongols
1335/39	Treaties of Trentschin and Cracow: Charles I of Hungary assigned all Silesia to the Bohemian Crown
1425–35	Hussite Wars
1469–90	Hungarian rule over Silesia
1526	Silesia became part of the Habsburg Lands with the accession of Ferdinand I to the Bohemian throne
1740–48	Wars of the Austrian Succession between Frederick II the Great of Prussia and Empress Maria Theresa of Austria: Silesia became Prussian; only Kronow, Opava, and Cieszyn remained with Austria
1919	Treaty of Versailles and creation of Poland and Czechoslovakia
28 July 1920	Ciesyn Silesia divided between Poland and Czechoslovakia
16–24 Aug. 1919	First Polish Rising in Silesia
19–25 Aug. 1920	Second Polish Rising in Silesia
20 Mar. 1921	Plebiscite in Silesia
2 May–5 July 1921	Third Polish Rising in Silesia

20 Oct. 1921	Silesian Convention: integration of the south-eastern part of Upper Silesia into Poland
1939	Re-occupation of Silesia by Germany
17 July–2 Aug. 1945	Potsdam Conference declared Oder–Neiße line to constitute the boundary of Poland's western border and approved the expulsion of the bulk of the German population from Silesia
1945	Occupation of the former German parts of Silesia by Poland
1945–50	Expulsion of the Germans
Jan. 1990	Foundation of the first *Deutscher Freundschaftskreis* in Katowice
1991	Foundation of the first German Society in Czech Opava
1991	Final confirmation of the border between unified German and Poland
1993	Establishment of the Neiße-Euroregion between Germany, Poland, and the Czech Republic

Map 1 Polish Lands in the time of Casimir the Great

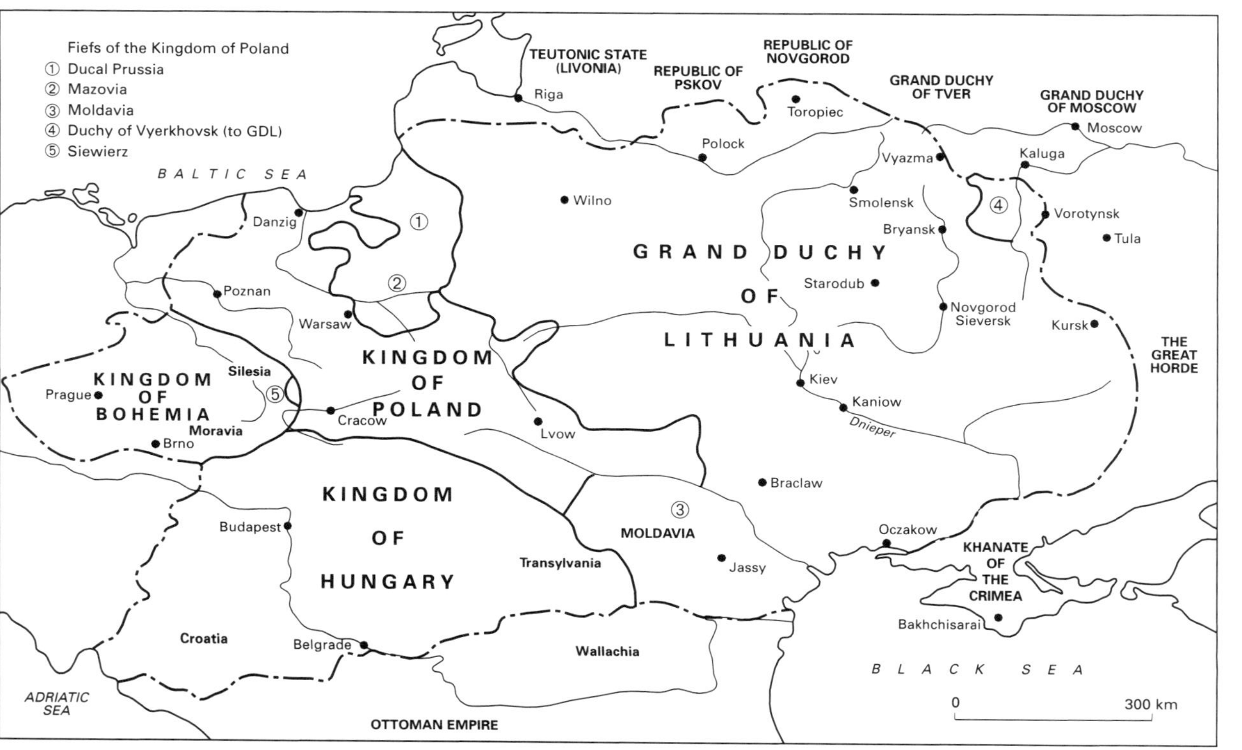

Map 2 Polish-Lithuanian Commonwealth c1500

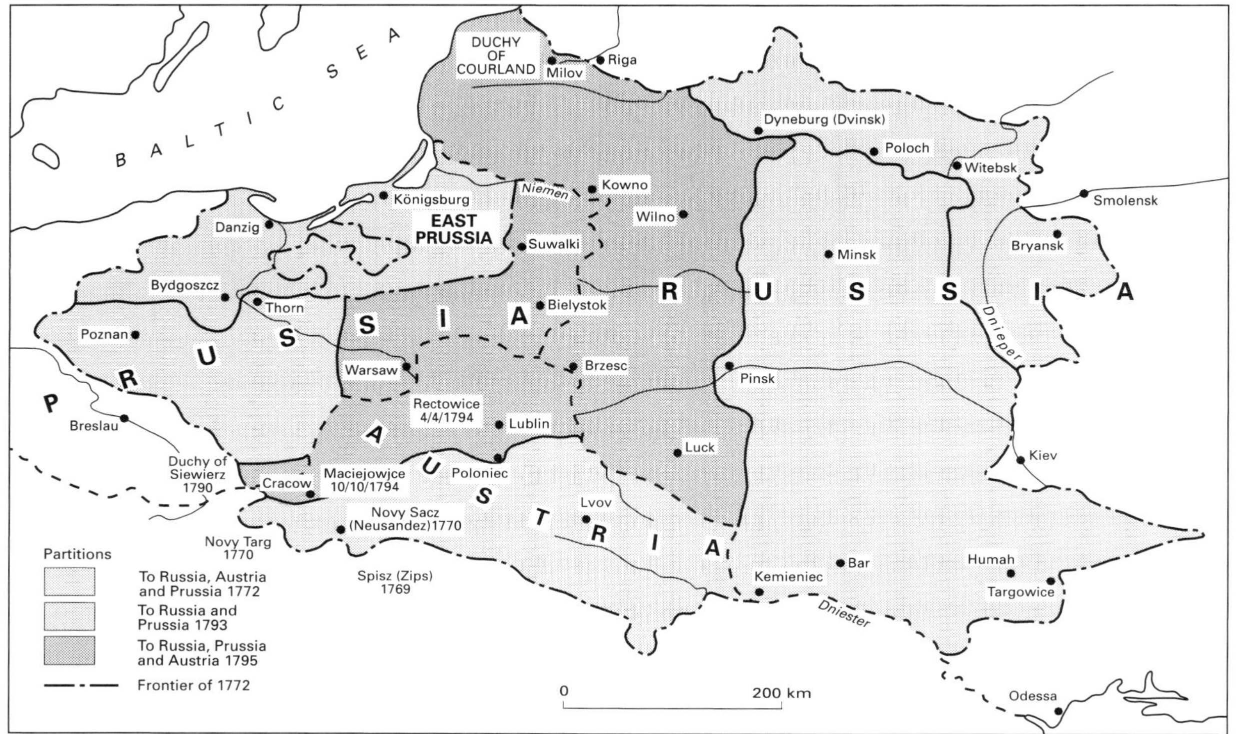

Map 3 Partitions of 1772, 1793 and 1795

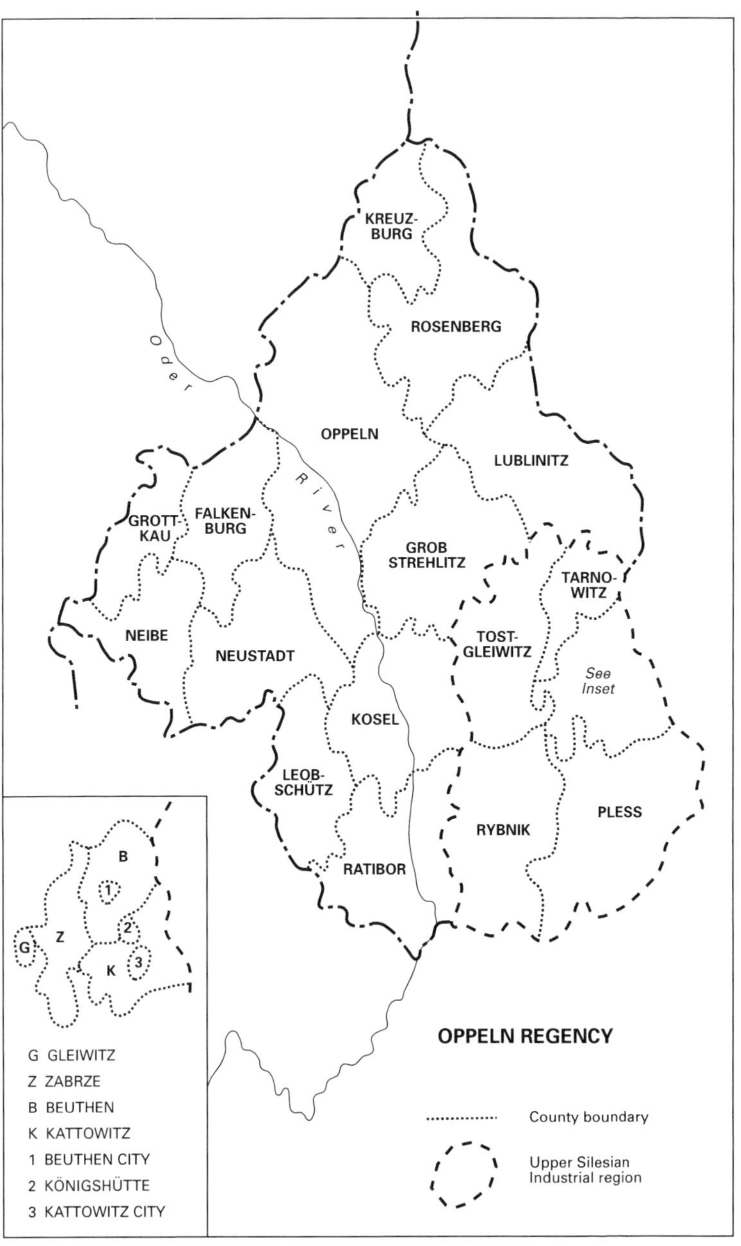

Map 4 Oppeln Regency

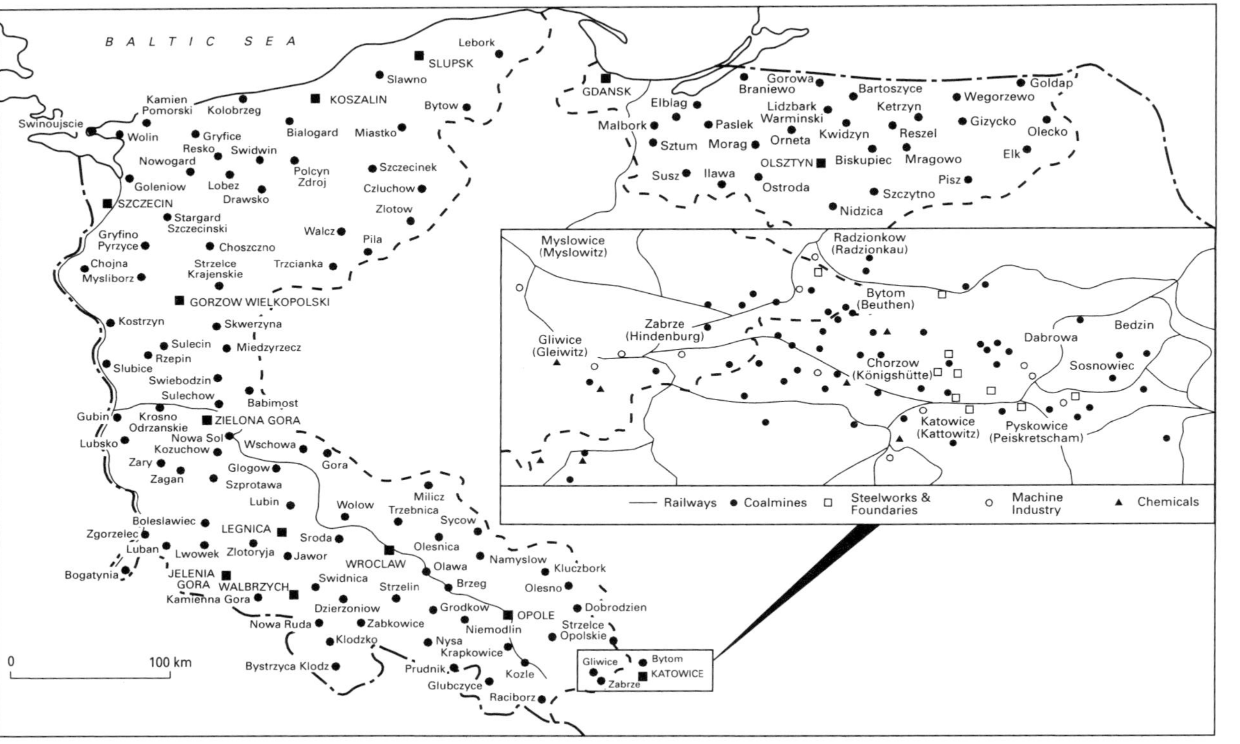

Map 5 Poland's Changing Borders 1918-45

Map 6 The Polish People's Republic 1975

Map 7 Silesia and Environs

Introduction

During the years 1985 to 1990 Central Europe bore witness to some truly remarkable changes. As the Gorbachev reform process gathered pace it gradually became clear to ruling elites, ordinary citizens, and dissidents as well as to seasoned foreign observers of politics in this part of Europe, that Mikhail Gorbachev was intent upon re-inventing Marxist socialism. As we know he was unable to accomplish this mammoth task, and from the summer of 1989 one by one the states of Central Europe began to leave the Soviet orbit. The question then became one of what would replace the old order? The most optimistic of commentators predicted a painless transition to politics based upon the value systems extant in the western part of Europe. The more gloomy prophesied a return to the authoritarian values of the pre-World War Two era. Unsurprisingly neither forecast was correct, and instead we have seen the establishment of a variety of regimes, none of which exactly replicates either the image of past experience in Central Europe, or the West European model. This state of affairs is due to the combination of inter-state relations, historical memory, economic performance, value systems, and cleavage patterns which govern the conduct of domestic politics in this part of Europe.

This volume deals with politics in Central Europe. It is composed of two distinct but never the less interrelated parts, with the chapter on Germany's relationship with the area taking the form of a bridge between the two sections. The initial focus lies with ideas of nation and nation-building processes in those states which by and large come from what was once referred to as the northern tier of the former Soviet bloc; Poland, Czechoslovakia/The Czech Republic/Slovakia and Hungary. These states have many similarities apart from their former geopolitical status. Although after their foundation as putative nation-states none of them can be claimed to have experienced fully functioning liberal democracy during the interwar period, they all possess a liberal and democratic tradition which marks them out from their erstwhile allies in the aforementioned Soviet bloc. These states also share another characteristic. Since the fall of 'really existing socialism' with the partial exception of Slovakia, they have made the most effective transition to both an economic system which allows for some expression of market principles and the construction of a polity which can be described as approximating to the civic democratic type.

That said, this volume is not designed to act as a guide to the political systems of each of these countries. Instead, its purpose is to focus upon one aspect of politics in each of these countries, namely the politics of ethnicity, and then to further the reader's understanding of the complexities of such politics through an examination of that area of Central Europe known as Silesia. Through our macro-analysis in the early part of the volume we will explore the dimensions of nationalist/ethnic conflict in the region. We have adopted this approach for a number of reasons. First, most of all we wish to inform the interested reader who may possess no specialist knowledge of the subject. Secondly, in all the states under examination, such conflicts have been of importance in shaping the nature of contemporary politics and indeed the current inter-state borders and ethnographic composition of each of these countries. Thirdly, we wish to dispel the myth that this part of Europe is some kind of dormant ethnic volcano which may erupt at any moment. This is not to deny that such problems exist. Rather it is to say that such problems are often magnified out of all proportion; sometimes out of ignorance, and on occasion because political capital can be accrued by exploiting historical grievance and a sense of the 'Other'. It is for such reasons that special attention is paid to Germany's historical involvement both in Central Europe as a whole and especially in Silesia in order to provide the reader with a deeper understanding of the background to the contemporary situation. Finally – and herein lies the key to understanding why Silesia has been selected as our primary case study – in their various historical incarnations, various sovereigns of the countries under examination have either laid claim to or exercised sovereignty over Silesia, and attitudes toward Silesia and its population remain on the political agenda, particularly in Poland, in which country by far the greater part of Silesia now lies.

These then are some of the reasons for a micro-study of the politics of ethnicity in Silesia. Another reason for engaging in such a study is because the story of Silesia epitomizes the conflict concerning ethnic provenance and identity which has dogged politics in this area of Europe since the dawning of the age of nationalism at the end of the eighteenth century. Despite the claims of primordial nationalists, Silesia never has been, and to this day is not an 'ethnic monolith.' Neither has it despite the wishes of some Silesians, ever succeeded in constituting itself as a nation-state. Instead in the modern era, it and more importantly its population has been, the object of Polish, German and Czech(oslovak) nationalism. As the reader will discover, Silesia has had a bewildering variety of rulers over the centuries, all of whom have left their mark. At various times during the medieval era it found itself to be part of the Bohemian, Polish and Czech kingdoms. In 1526 it was incorporated within the Habsburg Empire. At various times as part of that empire and its successor, the Austro-Hungarian Empire, it fell under the Czech, Hungarian or Viennese crowns, and at one time even formed part of the estate of the House of Luxembourg.

We should not fall into the trap of thinking that each of these rulers sort to fashion the inhabitants of Silesia in their own national image. The rulers of medieval kingdoms cared little about the bundle of factors which constitute the modern notion of ethnicity, any more than did imperial rulers until Napoleon's armies and Herder's ideas on nationhood ignited the continent. However, once the spark of nationalist doctrine had been lit, so nationalist movements appeared among peoples who previously in terms of collective identities had by and large only identified themselves as members of Christendom, the vassals of their aristocratic masters, or as the residents of a fairly narrowly defined locality. With the spread of such a doctrine and its ally, industrial society, it became possible, and perhaps necessary, to construct what Benedict Anderson has so memorably described as 'imagined communities'. With the growth of mass industrialization, came the need for mass literacy. As rural pre-capitalist forms appeared ever more redundant, so political activists sought to render the new world intelligible. The doctrine of self-determination and the emulation of the French, British, and American models of modern state organization increasingly became an object of desire.

In the case of Silesia, the Prussians, who had wrested possession of Silesia from Vienna in the 1740s, sought to turn the population into Prussian Germans. In the case of Lower Silesia this was not particularly problematic, as Slav inhabitants of the area had long since been assimilated into the Germanic culture of the migrants and settlers who had been invited to settle the area in the Middle Ages. As will become clear in the volume, in Upper Silesia the situation was different. This was a true cultural borderland, and until the onset of industrialization in the latter part of the eighteenth century, a distant backwater about which Berlin cared little. However, as Upper Silesia was transformed into an industrial powerhouse so migrants from other parts of Germany, as well as from the Russian and Austro-Hungarian empires, gravitated toward the area. Together with migrants to the cities from rural Upper Silesia, these Slav groups began to lose the trappings of their culture and acquire a German identity and culture.

Yet the passage of Upper Silesia into the *Deutschtum* did not go uncontested. Those who remained in the villages often remained largely unaffected by these processes right up until the early part of the present century. As we shall see, the nascent Czech and most especially the Polish national movements also laid claim to the territory, its growing wealth and its indigenous population. The Upper Silesian population, and gradually the entire territory of Silesia, became the object of nationalist aspirations and agendas. In essence, the second part of this volume deals with the antecedents to, and the nature of this contest, the conflicting claims put forward by each of the parties, and the nature of politics and in particular ethno-politics in (Upper) Silesia today. The chapters which pertain directly to Silesia seek to elucidate key themes and issues which have affected each part of Silesia in the national era, and careful attention is paid to the historical role of Germany, precisely because although only a small fragment of Silesia today lies within Germany, it was German culture and Silesia's relationship with Germany that was the most important factor in Silesian politics from the early part of the nineteenth century until the end of the Second World War.

This volume does not seek to vindicate the position of one or the other of the various protagonists in the battle for Silesia. Rather what it seeks to do, as dispassionately as possible, is to analyse and describe the events and processes by which Silesia and its population exist in the form they do today. In so doing, material which may be uncomfortable to nationalist partisans from all countries which have laid claim to Silesia is presented. The authors make no apology for adopting this stance. There would be little point in producing a volume which merely seeks to re-tell the partisan claims of one side or the other, and which in effect does nothing to aid our understanding of the area and its people.

Through the prism of Silesia the volume seeks to explain to the new reader just why ethnicity has been the focus of so much conflict in

Central Europe. In so doing it seeks to make clear that ethnicity is not some kind of biologically determined phenomenon, but rather that it is a social construct, albeit a deeply seated one. By virtue of a seeming paradox, ethnicity can be and often is fluid, as the case of Upper Silesia, and the competing nationalist claims over its population, together with the response of that population to such claims, shows. Rather than being determined by genetic make-up, ethnicity is as often as not determined by economic progress and political expediency, and indeed sometimes by the sheer need to survive.

In the latter stages of the volume, we examine the nature of ethno-politics in Silesia today. It is to be hoped that after having read this book, the reader will come away disabused of the idea that Silesia and other parts of Central Europe are some kind of perpetually ticking ethnic time bomb. On the contrary it is suggested that national-ethnic conflicts are by no means inevitable and as much as anything else the products of specific ideological and socio-economic tensions and forces. We make no predictions for the future, save to say that Polish accession to the European Union may provide a long-term solution to residual tensions over Silesia, and finally extinguish the embers of previous conflicts. Above all, we hope that having read our work, the reader will come away informed and enlightened about the nature of ethno-politics in Central Europe, both at the macro and micro levels.

1
Nationalism and the Nation-State in Central Europe

Establishing the parameters

This chapter has a dual purpose. The initial objective is to familiarize the reader with the ideas which from the late eighteenth century provided the stimulus for nation-building in the European continent. Within that the differences between the West European and East European experiences are made clear, as are the factors which caused such a contrast to come about. The second objective is to chart the growth of both the idea of nation and the doctrine of nationalism in Central Europe, the response of the imperial powers to this phenomenon, and finally to make some observations on the politics of ethnicity in Central Europe following the collapse of empire and the establishment of titular nation-states upon the ruins of the old order. As we shall see, the Versailles system contained the seeds of its own destruction and in order to appreciate why this system was so fundamentally flawed, we must first establish the intellectual propositions upon which ideas of nation and national self-determination in Central Europe were based.

The chapter is also designed to facilitate understanding of some of the phenomena and events which are covered elsewhere in the volume. It is not designed to serve as a historical narrative. Rather it seeks to explain why in Central Europe ideas of nation and routes to national self-determination have been different from those traditionally employed in Western Europe. Although reference to past events is unavoidable just as it is necessary, it is more important that we understand the intellectual and other forces which influenced the growth of the national idea. As a result a straightforward narrational style has deliberately been avoided. Similarly, given that Chapter 3 deals exclusively with the impact of Germany in Central Europe, in the early part of this chapter the empirical focus lies primarily with developments in the Russian and Austro-Hungarian empires, and not with Prussia or the Wilhelmine Reich.

The role of ideas

Putative nation-states first emerged in the west of Europe more specifically in England, the Netherlands and France between the sixteenth and eighteenth centuries. An historically shared territory, legal-political community, legal-political equality of members, and a common civic culture and ideology are the components of the standard western model of the nation-state (Smith, 1991: 11). However, the conditions under which nations were forged in Western Europe differed significantly from those prevailing in the east of Europe at the dawn of the nineteenth century as Napoleon's armies spread the doctrine of self-determination throughout the continent. Put simply, in Western Europe the process of nation-building was state led, whereas in the eastern part of the continent, nationalist ideologues attempted to carve nation-states from among a patchwork of territories which were generally subervient to one of the various European/Eurasian empires.

The growth of the bureaucratic centralized state in Western Europe tended to precede the construction of the 'nation'. The comparatively stable environment provided by fully-fledged feudalism in England and France fostered the growth of the state, which in turn became the primary agency of nation building in the aforementioned countries. Consequently, allegiance to the state, residence therein, and submission to its jurisdiction are the hallmarks of the western idea of nationality. So much so that the use of the terms 'citizen' and 'national' are virtually interchangeable. An individual's place of residence and their passport are the primary determinants of nationality, and it is these territorial and juridical criteria (*jus soli*) in part, that confuse and conflate the terms 'state' and 'nation', and lead to the misnomer 'nation-state' (Ra'anan et al., 1991: 11).

Outside the western world, or in our case Central and Eastern Europe, nationalism arose not only later, but also generally at an 'earlier' stage of social and political development. The frontiers of an existing state and of nascent nationalism rarely coincided, and so it was that nationalism grew as a protest against and in conflict with the existing state pattern-not primarily to transform it into a citizens' state, but to redraw the political boundaries in conformity with ethnographic demands (Kohn, 1945). These 'revived' nations, deprived as they were of the chance to engage in state-building according to the West European model, endeavored to recreate the nation, primarily in the cultural field. Nationalists in Central Europe often created an idealized picture of the 'promised land', which was simultaneously based on a romanticized version of the past and devoid of any immediate connection with the present, or indeed in some instances any connection with what might pass for reality.

The reinterpretation of western notions of nationality in the east necessitated the incorporation of pre-national modes of thought within the nascent national consciousness, which were then reinforced by a vigorous process of ethnic homogenization. Perhaps the pivotal pre-national concept prevalent in the east was that of *jus sanguinis,* literally 'issues of blood'. In contrast to the western concept of *jus solis,* it is not *where* an individual resides or indeed was born which determines their nationality, but rather *who* they are, their cultural, religious and historic identity and from whom they are descended i.e. their ethnicity. In part the concept of *jus sanguinis* was the product of the historic experience of different cultural groups residing side by side on the same territory yet maintaining distinct identities both in a cultural and a legal sense. Consequently one is dealing here with the *personal* concept of nationality as opposed to the western *territorial* concept, and as we have just seen, this difference between western and eastern notions of nationality, or the territorial and ethnic interpretations of identity is by no means new (Kohn, 1945; Smith, 1971; Kellas, 1991; Ra'anan, 1991).

So membership of the nation is affected both by philosophical/ideological principles and the political circumstance upon which the nation has been built. In Western Europe, where statehood preceded nation-building, membership of the nation has traditionally been open and inclusive in a legal-political sense. Legal-political membership however, is not the same as cultural membership of a nation. Full acceptance into the national community does not rest solely upon the fulfilment of legal and political criteria, there is also a cultural threshold which has to be met. Deviation from the cultural norm may be tolerated but is not necessarily welcomed. The newcomer is generally encouraged, either formally or informally, to conform to a certain standard of cultural homogeneity. Cosmopolitanism is attractive in theory, but does tend to have its limits in practice, even in states whose national community is founded upon the principle of *jus solis.*

In a state which employs the notion of *jus sanguinis* it is even more difficult for outsiders to become members of the titular nation. As identity is constituted largely around the ancestry and cultural inheritance of the individual, no amount of legal or constitutional mechanisms can fully ensure equality of participation in the national community. In fact, some states utilize legal and constitutional means to deny 'others' equal citizenship, an outstanding case until recently being the difficulties encountered by German-born descendants of non-ethnic German immigrants to Germany in obtaining German nationality.

Indeed, Germanic notions of identity were crucial for the nationalist movements of nineteenth century Central Europe, as they came under the countervailing influences of French and German nationalism. The revolutionary decade of 1789–99 in France saw dramatic changes in the notion of sovereignty. Power was transferred from the monarchy to the citizenry, at least in theory. The state was no longer identified with the king but with the nation, and the nation was then forged in the image of the state. Thus, the idea that the sovereignty of the state could be equated with the will of the nation was born. However the notion that citizenry equaled nation was a hotly contested one. In principle, membership of the nation was based upon citizenship, and citizenship required the individual to adhere to a common set of laws, rights and obligations. In practice the acquisition of French citizenship became inextricable from the acquisition of the French language. The logic being that in order fully to participate in the affairs of the state an individual must speak the language of the state (Hobsbawm, 1992: 22).

Whereas the organizational structures of the French state served as a role model for nationalist elites in Central Europe, French notions of citizenship were treated with more caution. With regard to notions of who could constitute a member of the national community, of more importance in the long run was the German notion of cultural nationalism as developed in the eighteenth century above all by Johann Gottfried von Herder. For Herder, the nation was an organic entity, as natural as the family or other forms of social organization. This was because he saw humans as social animals for whom gregariousness and communication are the foundations of existence. Human society developed in relation to its environment, and thus the diversity of nations could be explained by their relationship to their surroundings. Cultural markers such as language, customs and character were defined by geographic boundaries. Hence, nations were natural and each was endowed with a distinctive national spirit, shaped by its environment and expressed through culture and language (Llobera, 1994: 167). For Herder, the Germans formed but a single Volk by virtue of their use of a common German language. For Herder, states as constituted during his lifetime were in and of themselves artificial creations, and served only to divide nations or constrain different nations to live uneasily side by side. The only natural state was the nation-state: one people speaking the same language, in its own territory, governing itself. For Herder this was a universal principle, which applied not only to Germany but also to the nations of Central Europe to whom empires denied the natural right of self-determination and individual and collective cultural expression.

A further impulse to such ideas was occasioned when Johann Gottlieb Fichte, in his 'Addresses to the German Nation', written in the aftermath of Prussia's defeat at the hands of Napoleon at Jena in 1806, sought to harness the 'power of the soul' to aid in the revitalization of the Prussian state, the creation of a German nation-state which would surpass the achievements of Jacobin France and one which would be a community of individuals linked by descent and culture rather than residence. To this end the will of society, and especially that of the young as the inheritors of the nation, should be bent to the collective will of the nation. For Fichte, a nation could only be constituted by a group of people who were possessed of a common language. In turn such a nation could preserve itself only if it constituted its own state. Moreover he claimed that those political frontiers which separate the members of a nation had to be overturned on the grounds they were arbitrary, unnatural and unjust. The diversity of political institutions in the German-speaking world at the time was for many an impediment to the development of a modern German nation-state. What Fichte and his contemporaries succeeded in doing was to foster the revolutionary idea that the boundaries of states should in some way be 'natural', and correspond with apparently equally 'natural' discrete ethno-linguistic boundaries (Kedourie, 1960: 63). One can only surmise that had Fichte had the benefit of modern transportation and telecommunication links, he may have been forced to reconsider the extent to which such theories corresponded to everyday reality.

Such a comment is not as dismissive as it appears at first sight. Perhaps the most striking contrast between Western and Eastern Europe is that although they are of a comparable size, even today the ethnic composition of Eastern Europe is some three times as diverse as that of Western Europe, despite the carnage wrought by two world wars, accompanying campaigns of genocide, and the forcible expulsion of millions of people from their places of birth. Neither diversity nor war and its attendant consequences is the overriding cause of the dominant form of nationalism in this area, but when that diversity is overlaid by the intermingled patterns of settlement the difficulty of providing clear-cut analysis of and/or solutions to the 'nationalities problem' is vividly illustrated. Some groups are relatively compact, such as the Czechs and Poles, whilst others such as the Jews and Roma, and until 1945–49 the Germans, exhibit a more diasporic pattern. In the main given that many groups reside predominantly within certain areas the pattern can best be described as mixed.

The contemporary arrangement of ethnic groups in Central Europe although largely having been shaped during the years 1919–49, has its origins in the centuries of colonization and conquest of Europe from Asia in the first millennium AD. Population movement and pressure from Asia saw older established population groups either pushed to the geographical peripheries of Europe, or submerged within the newcomers as they surged through the Eurasian plains. Initially the acquisition of land was due as much to demographic swamping as pitched battles and armed conflict only came about as land ceased to be available. Although successive migrations disrupted what we now label Eastern Europe and Russia, Western Europe settled down into a relatively more stable and sedentary condition. The last significant period of eastern invasion in the thirteenth century saw the East Slavs fall under the dominance of the Mongols, precisely at that time when groups such as the Poles, Czechs and Magyars, themselves descended from earlier waves of Asiatic migrants, were becoming ever more exposed to western ideas and influences. After this turbulent era the pattern of settlement became more stable, the eventual extension of the Holy Roman Empire and its various offshoots and imitators affecting it through programmes of 'ethnic management' (Pearson, 1983), and significantly by virtue of German colonization.

The importance of territory in the precarious environment of Eastern Europe cannot be overestimated. It is the claim to territory that counts for nationalists, almost as much as the demand that it then be populated by the 'rightful' owners. Claims to land can be roughly divided into demographic and historic, the majority settlement of an area and its past ownership respectively. Frequently, the two claims clash as in the case of Transylvania. Ruled by the Magyars until the twentieth century, the Romanians claimed to be the larger population from the eighteenth century. The selective use of history generally enables both sides to present a positive case. Moreover, demographic claims are no more free from bias than historical ones. Statistics, elections and plebiscites can all be rigged and interpreted to taste, and in the checkered history of the region generally have been. A large proportion of population statistics from the pre-1919 empires and their interwar successors tend to exaggerate the dominance of the majority population and underestimate the numbers of minorities. In between the two world wars the Polish state invented a new nationality, *tutejszi* or 'people from here', for the inhabitants of certain areas in which Byelorussans predominated. The result was to considerably reduce the number of regions in which Byelorussans constituted the majority.

The degree to which an appeal to nationalism found a popular response within a given population also rested upon territorial considerations. Those who enjoy daily proximity with the borders of the state tend to have much stronger feelings of national identity than those who inhabit the more insulated regions of a territory. Awareness of the alternatives and the greater relevance of territorial readjustment contrasts with the near complacency of the 'core dwellers'. This 'castle and border' model (Ardrey, 1967) corresponds with the idea that identity becomes more pronounced as the level of threat to that identity increases (Larrain, 1994: 143). However, because territory and nation did not always coincide, spontaneous nationalism could not always be counted upon to secure the land. In the absence of the imperial notions of tradition and ancestral right, nation-builders downplayed regional identities and a more artificial legitimacy that of 'nationism' was invoked (Pearson, 1983). The superiority of the fatherland or motherland came to be espoused, and the corrupt and unnatural character of neighboring states was taken for granted. The national territory became a sacrosanct and living organic entity, the partitioning of which was viewed as a blasphemous defilement of the very soul of the nation.

The metaphor of the soul is quite apt as nationalism took on the aura of a secular religion. Its relationship with the more traditional forms of religion was ambiguous. Established religions were generally supportive of nationalism in a situation where a different faith was introduced by a conquering power. In some cases the respective churches even took it upon themselves to act as the guardians of the nation when no other means of protection was available. When the Polish nation found itself partitioned between the Catholic Austrians, Protestant Prussians and Orthodox Russians, the Roman Catholic Church in the Polish lands succeeded in both securing the future of the Polish nation and extending its authority over the Poles to such an extent that by the mid-nineteenth century it was unthinkable to be a non-Catholic Pole, unless you were Jewish, in which case your standing as a Pole, or otherwise, depended upon the needs of the governing power at the time. However, when nationalism came to fulfill a similar function to that of religion in the life of a significant section of the population, or became too radical or anti-clerical, then the traditional/conservative face of the church would surface.

For some groups religion acted as the primary identifier in demarcating themselves from another group. In the case of the Jews it generally served to separate them from everyone else, but was also needed as a surrogate for a lack of territory. For the Roma the weaker bond of the Romani language had to suffice. The Uniate Ruthenes clung to their Orthodox rituals under papal auspices in order to differentiate themselves from Orthodox Ukrainians. However, language tended to play the decisive role in the identification of ethnic and national groups in Central Europe. Broadly speaking, in Central Europe during the imperial era two types of language were in use, the lower-class parochial vernaculars, and the upper-class cosmopolitan *lingua franca*. Despite the fact that it had never had wide currency in the eastern part of Europe, there were attempts to replace German and French with Latin as the international language of communication. Under the influence of German Romanticism it had become popular for the upper-classes and educated elites to unearth the folklore and traditions of the peasantry, including the vernacular languages, and it gradually became apparent that there was a linguistic fragmentation in Eastern Europe to match its ethnic heterogeneity. Clearly the nationalist doctrine that every linguistic group should constitute itself as a nation was not as straightforward as it might seem. A possible reason for this is that it was a totally unsuitable criterion to apply. For example *Hochdeutsch* was just about the only factor that all the Germanic peoples had in common, and even then it was primarily the preserve of an educated elite. As protégés of German nationalist philosophy, nationalists in Central Europe attempted to apply a model developed in conditions that did not match their own, and indeed barely existed in Germany, with wildly varying results.

The hypersensitivity of nationalists over language was institutionalized by almost every emergent nation of Eastern Europe. Fervent nationalists objected not only to foreign semantic intrusions but even to foreigners attempting to speak their language: interpreting such attempts as infringements of the nation's monopoly of access to its sacred inheritance. Thus the obvious pragmatic advantages of language to nationalism, such as promoting linguistic solidarity within the national territory and asserting the separate identity and high status of the nation before an international audience, were soon overlaid by a mystical, semi-religious aura. With communion reserved for the chosen people and deliberately withheld from outsiders, language became the sacrament of nationalism.

As the nineteenth century wore on a new phenomenon became apparent. It was at first unimportant, yet as we shall see later in the volume, it came to define the nature of inter-ethnic relations in Central Europe. We are speaking of the politics of race, and ideas of a hierarchical arrangement of the races, with all that such a statement implies. From the middle of the nineteenth century, such undercurrents became observable among certain quarters of the Magyar, German and Czech national movements. Pan-Slavism also existed but it was generally only when an isolated Slav group was menaced by neighbors of another race that a sense of 'racial community' surfaced among Slavs. Non-Slavic groups however, were more aware of the demographic weakness of their position. The notion of beleaguered 'ethnic islands' provided a breeding ground for issues of race to appear in the cause of ethnic survival, and a portent of what was to follow in the twentieth century. Bohemian Germans in particular began to develop a siege mentality which, over the course of time made them more receptive to the ideas of Spencer and Social Darwinism, especially as the agencies and instruments of mass social control which made such philosophies feasible became more widespread (Pearson, 1983).

The experience of empire

The merging of racist with nationalist doctrine was still some way off. Despite the creation of the short-lived and ill-fated Second German Empire in 1871, throughout the course of the nineteenth century it became more apparent that the imperial order was under threat. This was especially true of the Ottoman Empire, or at least its European possessions, and the Habsburg Empire, or Austro-Hungarian Empire, as it became known after the *Ausgleich* of 1867. External intervention in the Habsburg Empire played a virtually negligible role in the activities of the national minorities, rather it was the efforts of the monarchy to manage the multi-national problem that contributed in large part to the shape of the subsequent national regimes in the inter-war years. In the Habsburg Monarchy the nationality problem dominated the domestic political agenda. A total of eleven recognized distinct territorial groups existed within the empire's boundaries; Germans, Magyars, Czechs, Poles, Ruthenians (Carpatho-Ukrainians), Romanians, Croats, Slovaks, Serbs, Slovenes and Italians. 1848 marked the point at which liberal and national claims erupted throughout Europe, and within the empire transformed an administrative headache into a political nightmare. The danger for the Danubian Monarchy was that claims for national self-determination took precedence over demands for the democratization of society. The events of 1848 were successfully contained by the establishment's counterrevolution but nevertheless set in motion a process that was to change the territorial face of Central Europe. Unsurprisingly, the strongest challenge to Habsburg rule came from the second largest national group, the Magyars.

A revival of Magyar culture had begun in the 1820s, in part as a response to the Germanization efforts of Emperor Josef II in the late eighteenth century (Pearson, 1983). The Magyar nobility were concerned with maintaining their feudal rights and privileges, but as romantic nationalism spread, fueled by the writings of intellectuals such as Sandor Petöfi (himself a Magyarized Serb), the need to widen the base of the nation was recognized. In the absence of a strong middle class, radical nationalism became associated with intellectuals and the impoverished gentry. An individual from the latter group who was to take a leading part in the events of 1848–49 was Lajos Kossuth, who represented the populist side of Magyar nationalism that saw the Magyar nation as under threat from the demographically superior Slavs (Taylor, 1948). For the romantics the Magyars had sacrificed themselves in the wars against the Turks, and had been taken advantage of by their neighbors in their moment of weakness. In the face of this strident appeal to blood the smaller minorities within the Magyar lands inevitably sided with the Habsburgs, who with the aid of Russia, eventually subdued the new Hungary in 1849. Savage reprisals served only to furnish the nationalist cause with martyrs, and the Hungarian lands were administratively re-divided deliberately cutting across historic boundaries.

Actions on both sides in the conflict clearly illustrate how minority nationalism in the empire came to be associated with blood and land. The Magyar reaction against Austro-German dominance and their own repressive treatment of their minorities inevitably divided groups along ethnic lines. This policy was further exacerbated by the imperial policy of pitting differing national groups against one another in order to restore imperial control. After the Magyars had been subjugated the recourse to territorial re-division emphasized the importance of territory as a resource, and inflamed the minority's sense of injustice and determination to win it back. Such strategies of ethnic management were applied throughout the empire and generated a common response: the burgeoning of ethnically based nationalist movements (Pearson, 1983).

Between 1849 and 1867 Hungarian nationalists, under the leadership of more liberal individuals such as Ferenc Deak, followed a concerted program of passive resistance and public protest toward Vienna. Not only did this gain the respect of the imperial authorities, but it also allowed the Hungarians to make the most of any changes in the fortunes of the empire. This opportunity arose in 1866 with the defeat of Austria by Prussia at Sadowa, which simultaneously ended Austrian involvement in and signaled Prussian ascendancy over Germany. The consequent slump in morale in Vienna was effectively exploited by the Hungarians, who were able to negotiate the compromise or *Ausgleich* of 1867. The division of the empire into Austrian and Hungarian spheres of influence had major repercussions for nationality policy in both halves of the empire. For the Austro-Germans political liberalization in 1860 meant that an accord had to be reached with the Czechs and the Poles as the two next largest groups. In Hungary, continued Magyarization deeply affected the tone of inter-ethnic relations, especially with the emergent Slovaks.

Although dominant within the Viennese empire, Germans still only made up just over a third of the population as a whole (Kann, 1974). In order to retain control of the parliament in Vienna they needed the support of one of the smaller groups. Entering into coalition with the Polish Conservative Party of Galicia had a number of advantages. First, such a coalition possessed a parliamentary majority. Secondly, unlike the Czechs, all Poles did not live within the empire. Thirdly, once again unlike the Czechs, the Poles had not been alienated by the *Ausgleich* with Hungary, and furthermore Galicia was geographically remote. In return for their support the Poles were granted a good deal of autonomy. The process of Germanization in Galicia was halted, Polish became an official language, and the universities of Cracow and Lwow were turned into centers of Polish learning. Such a compromise with the Czechs would have entailed far more risks for Vienna. As the third largest national minority the Czechs had been aggrieved by concessions made to the Magyars, and considered themselves next in line for promotion to power-sharing. The proximity of the Czech and German populations to one another in Bohemia and Moravia made the granting of the sort of privileges the Poles enjoyed virtually impossible. Nevertheless, the Czechs continued to press for some sort of recognition, but despite their persistence, both the Hohenwart federalist plan of 1871, and the Badeni scheme to grant the Czech language equality with German foundered before German and Magyar opposition. The Germans, alarmed by the growth of the Czech economy and bourgeoisie, were determined to maintain their superior social position. Meanwhile, the Magyars refused to countenance any alteration of the dualist system to include a third partner. Fortunately for the Germans, there was no significant Czech movement willing to risk their economic prosperity for the elusive goal of national sovereignty. In Galicia the Polish nobility were only too happy to maintain their status through cooperation with the empire, having already been reminded of their precarious position when imperial forces rescued them from the peasant *jacquerie* of 1846 (Davies, 1986).

Within Hungary the picture was far more uniform. Croats, Romanians and Slovaks were subject to Magyarization policies on a comprehensive scale (Taylor, 1948). Having all supported the Habsburgs against the Magyars in 1848–49, the removal of Austrian protection in 1867 left them at the mercy of Hungarian assimilationist policies. Despite the passing of a Nationalities Law in 1868 granting recognition of minority language, education and cultural rights, the reality was that as far as the Hungarians were concerned there were many nationalities in the kingdom but only one nation, the Magyars. Magyarization was forcefully imposed through education and the imposition of the Magyar language; those who assimilated would be treated as equals, those who chose to retain their distinctive cultures were fiercely repressed. Long-standing tension between Hungarians and Romanians over Transylvania further aggravated relations between the two groups. As for the Slovaks, their late-blooming national consciousness in the early nineteenth century suffered a major setback under the Hungarians. The only minority to fare reasonably well in the Hungarian Kingdom were the Serbs. This was primarily for two reasons; firstly, the existence of a strong Serbian state made the treatment of the Serbs a foreign policy issue as well as a domestic one; and secondly, the promotion of Serbs in Croatia-Slavonia helped to undermine Croat ascendancy (Pearson, 1983).

Given the mutually contradictory tensions that existed within all the European/Eurasian empires, and the burgeoning hostility of a vengeful France toward an increasingly more powerful and bellicose Germany, it was becoming increasingly likely that war would be employed as a means of providing some kind of 'resolution', to the problems of a state-system that was increasingly anachronistic and dysfunctional. It came in August 1914, and by November of that year the old order had completely collapsed in Central Europe. Before analysing the consequences of that debacle, let us first make some observations about Czardom. As we shall see an understanding of Poland's relationship with imperial Russia, and its successor the Soviet Union is crucial to understanding Polish attitudes toward nation, and the territory of Silesia with which the latter part of the volume is concerned.

The Russian empire in Europe

For the Romanovs the revolutions of 1848 were not so much an immediate threat to imperial authority, as a warning of possible future unrest. Curiously, the role played by the Third Department, the oppressive police apparatus set up by Nicholas I after the Decembrist Revolt of 1825, was minimal (Seton-Watson, 1967). The aggressive and arbitrary actions of the internal police were well known and feared, but the likelihood of this reputation being enough to dissuade minority groups from demanding greater autonomy from the Czar is improbable. Of the groups closest to the Russian heartlands, the largest ones, the Ukrainians and Byelorussans, were at a much earlier stage of national consciousness than subordinate minorities further west. As for the Poles, the disaster of the 1830 rising in the Russian controlled Congress Kingdom and the suppression of the 1846 *jacquerie* in Austrian Galicia, had taken the wind out of the sails of any resistance movement.

Many of the minorities within the empire proper had been subject to Russification since the first half of the nineteenth century. Prior to this, loyalty to the Czar had been the overwhelming consideration. However, the centralization processes beginning in the seventeenth century received a more nationalistic impulse after the defeat of Napoleon in 1812. Thus, by the nineteenth century the official attitude towards the Ukrainians and the Byelorussans was that they were in fact either Russians, or 'Little Russians' who could be incorporated quite easily within the wider Russian nation. This attitude became more pronounced from the 1840s. At the same time Ukrainian nationalism was receiving a considerable boost from the poetry of Taras Shevchenko, who wrote in Ukrainian and so helped to produce a standard literary Ukrainian. Linked to this was the belief amongst nationally aware Ukrainians that Muscovy had usurped the earlier foundation of Kievan Rus'. In the Baltic provinces the Czarist authorities attempted to minimize the influence of non-Russian cultures. With regard to the Poles, as Slavs they could theoretically have been included within the Greater Russian aspirations, under the guise of Pan-Slavism. Yet, as the Czarist authorities were to find out, most of their efforts in Russifying their European borderlands would confront the intractable problem of Polish national aspirations.

The establishment of Congress Poland in 1815 had allowed those Poles living under Czarist rule a certain amount of autonomy in domestic affairs. These limited constitutional rights had been suspended after the 1830 rising. By the 1860s some attempts were being made under Wielopolski to win Polish loyalty for the Czar through a program of reforms. Polish radicals were opposed to any policies any policies which might encourage Polish-Russian reconciliation and proceeded to agitate against them. They may well have been unsuccessful in this had not Wielopolski, in a misguided attempt to deprive the radicals of support, declared his intention to conscript young Poles into the Russian army, and in so doing helped to precipitate the rebellion of 1860, which differed from that of 1830 in two ways. First, it was a guerrilla war waged in the countryside rather than a frontal assault on the forces of the Czar. Secondly, after the Polish defeat Russian reprisals were savage and far-reaching. Deportations to Siberia, the confiscation of property, executions and imprisonment were not enough, the name of Poland was to be wiped off the map of Europe.

From 1864 onward the policy of Russification, including in the newly absorbed provinces of the Vistulaland, as the Congress Kingdom was now known, proceeded apace. Loyalty to the Czar was no longer sufficient, subjects of the Russian Empire would now be Russians or potential traitors. Throughout the nineteenth century reforms in administration and education sought to impose the Russian language upon minority groups. However, as these reforms consisted mainly of enforcing the use of Russian from above and closing indigenous educational establishments, not to mention the erection of Orthodox churches in Catholic and Protestant parishes, their effect was to arouse feelings of resentment rather than loyalty. Previously acquiescent groups asserted themselves in reaction to such measures. For those to whom the Russians already appeared as enemies it all served to add fuel to the nationalist fire.

In 1905 the domestic social and political situation of the Russian Empire reached crisis point. Waves of strikes and political protests, precipitated by the massacre of peaceful demonstrators outside the Czar's Winter Palace in St Petersburg, forced Nicholas II to concede the establishment of a Duma. In the non-Russian provinces the revolutionary situation was seized upon by the growing nationalist movements. The Finns recovered some of their former autonomy, the Poles made gains in the field of education in the Polish language, whilst other groups used the resultant instability as an opportunity to gather more support for their various national causes. This period of relative freedom was however brief. By 1907, under the prime ministership of Stolypin, Russian nationalism had begun to reassert itself. In its effort to become a modern state, at least in Europe, the Czarist authorities attempted to impose the sovereignty of the Russian nation upon its subject peoples. Yet just as Magyarization failed in Hungary after 1867, so Russification was unsuccessful in its mission to convert the Poles, Ukrainians and others, all of whom were beginning to assume collective political identities of their own. In short the concessions of 1905 solved nothing.

We have already noted that in the summer of 1914 the pressures upon the imperial system caused the First World War. The factors that precipitated the outbreak of hostilities are well known, as is the course of the war itself (Taylor, 1948). The collapse of the Romanov Empire through internal revolution did not immediately affect either the Austro-Hungarian or the German empires. However, the end was not long in coming. In a bid to divert such a nationalist revolution a late effort was made to transform the Austro-Hungarian Empire into a federation in October 1918, but it was too late. The armistice, President Wilson's Fourteen Points and the recognition of the general right to self-determination ended the long-running multi-national experiment that had been the Habsburg Empire.

National independence and interdependence

Space does not permit us to go into any detail on the negotiations which surrounded the establishment of the new state system in Europe in 1918 and 1919. Suffice it to say that in Central Europe politics was greatly influenced by the experience of imperial rule, whether it had emanated from Berlin, Vienna or Moscow. Previous policies of ethnic and territorial divide and rule coupled with memories of aggressive assimilationism set the tone for inter-ethnic relations in the interwar years. The examples of Germany and Italy in the 1860s demonstrated the effectiveness of military action in order to strengthen the territorial base of the state, and the need for a strong center. The imperial legacy also undermined the notion of self-determination. States were based on particular national ascendancies, and as such the right of different nationalities to equal treatment was denied, as was the principle of equal participation of minority nationalities in the new states' political institutions. In general, where assimilation was the goal of state centres, the states of Western Europe encouraged it through inclusion in the political process, whilst the governments of East-Central European states pursued it through exclusion and the implementation of discriminatory policies against minority groups. The elites of the newly independent states were now in a position to either accept or ignore external ideas and influences upon nation-and state-building policy. Despite the declarations of good intent and the activities of the new-born League of Nations, in Central Europe, nation-building policy invariably followed the ethnic rather than civic path.

In effect the Treaties of Versailles and Trianon did nothing to solve the nationality problem of Central Europe. What they did succeed in doing was to reduce the preponderance of minority populations by about half. Under the empires, approximately half their populations constituted 'minorities', under the new state system the proportion still stood at around one quarter, many of whom were bewildered by the failure of the victorious allies to bestow the gift of self-determination upon them. The dominant minority system had been replaced by one of dominant majorities (Pearson, 1983). This was especially true for the Magyars and Poles. In Czechoslovakia, the Czechs constituted but a dominant minority. Prior experience of imperial treatment and the political realities of the new states would inevitably define contemporary inter-communal relations. For the Germans and Magyars the loss of their formerly dominant positions made the prospects of reconciliation to the new situation particularly problematic. The Bohemian Germans, who for so long had resisted attempts by the Czechs to gain equal status, now found themselves incorporated into a Czech dominated state. For Slovaks, national self-determination meant junior status within a new state.

In Czechoslovakia (the Slovaks even denied the recognition granted by a capital letter), the Pittsburgh Agreement negotiated by Masaryk with the émigré Slovak population in the United States in return for financial and political support was never implemented. The agreement had proposed the establishment of an autonomous diet for Slovakia within a federal Czecho-Slovak state. In reality Slovakia became a virtual dependency of the Czech Lands, a unitary state structure was imposed from Prague, and Czech administrators occupied the vast majority of senior positions within Slovakia itself. The Czech claim that this was for the good of the Slovaks after their suppression by the Magyars was hardly borne out by the widening economic and social gap between the two groups over the course of the 1920s and 1930s. Territorial autonomy was also to have been extended to the Ruthenian population, but this too was withheld. The Czech attitude is perhaps understandable given that the German, Magyar and Ruthene minorities could all look to patron states across the border, and that the Germans in particular were unreconciled to their inclusion in Czechoslovakia, but the Czech policy of strengthening the center merely served to increase the alienation of the non-Czech periphery. As we shall see later in the volume, these tensions were eventually to be 'solved' by a number of measures: the Munich Agreement of 1938; independence in 1939 for Slovakia with German backing, and the absorption in the same year of the remaining Czech Lands by Germany, without any reference to the wishes of the Czechs themselves.

Turning to Hungary, we find that the Magyars, although in possession of their own state, were particularly aggrieved by the loss of two-thirds of their territory and the inclusion of one third of the Magyar population in surrounding 'foreign' states. Hungary's former position as the junior partner in the empire meant that it was a loser in the territorial readjustment that followed the war. The hasty establishment of a government by liberal politicians in September 1918 was not enough to divert the wrath of the Allies, nor placate the minorities (Pearson, 1983: 170). The government could not withstand the national trauma of Trianon and the loss of Transylvania, Croatia and Vojvodina. The communist party rushed to fill the vacuum and a proletarian republic under Bela Kun was proclaimed (Bideleux and Jeffries, 1998: 423). The collapse of the new republic in the face of internal resistance and external threat meant that the left had forfeited its legitimacy to govern in interwar Hungary. The swing to the right under Admiral Horthy would lead inexorably to alliance with Nazi Germany.

To the north, the new Polish state was proclaimed on Armistice Day 1918. The incoming authorities had to somehow rationalize and unify six separate currencies, five distinct regional administrations, the four languages of command used in the army, three legal codes and two incompatible rail gauges. Not only was there a proliferation of political groupings with varying programs seeking to perform these tasks, there were also three different state-building traditions to draw upon. The diverse ethnic make-up of the new Poland would also put additional strains upon the fledgling territorial structure.

In addition to over three million Jews, there were also large numbers of Ukrainians, Byelorussans, Germans and Lithuanians. Accommodation of smaller groups, such as Czechs, Slovaks and Greeks was not particularly problematic. This was not the case for the larger groups. Accusations of discrimination against the Lithuanians in the north-east of Poland were compounded by the dispute over the city of Wilno (Vilnius). Where Ukrainians and Byelorussans were in the majority claims of discrimination were expressed by sub-state nationalist movements (Leslie, 1980). In the west, territorial redistribution had been undertaken not only to restore former Polish land to the Poles, but also with an eye to constraining German power. The large numbers of ethnic Germans who remained unreconciled to the re-created Polish state were later to provide a focus for German revanchism, and, as we shall see in particular, the Polish–German dispute over Silesia and the ethnic provenance of its inhabitants was to prove to be of crucial importance in determining the fate of millions of people.

Theoretically, German–Polish and domestic tensions could have been overcome had Poland developed a political system that facilitated compromise, and a political elite willing to foster a spirit of accommodation. Unfortunately, as many of the post-Versailles regimes discovered, a stable political system is often dependent upon a stable economy. In Poland, a series of feeble governments was faced by a long list of intractable problems and a succession of economic crises. In an attempt to impose some sort of order, Marshall Pilsudski came out of retirement in 1926 and established the *Sanacja* (revitalization) regime. This military junta operated behind a parliamentary facade, democratic institutions being bypassed rather than abolished. Concerns over newly won national independence meant that the touchstone for any moderately successful national party was necessarily nationalism. The fragmentary nature of the Polish parliamentary system meant that no consistent national line was followed.

Despite his successful coup Pilsudski, who was himself partly of Lithuanian extraction and who strove no matter how haphazardly to create some notion of civic identity independent of ethnicity, and the *Sanacja* were unable to effect any improvement in inter-ethnic relations. Democratic and nationalistic opposition to the *Sanacja* regime was severely punished. When the parties of the centre-left published a democratic manifesto in June 1930, calling on Pilsudski to relinquish power, those responsible were summarily arrested, imprisoned and exiled. The National Democrats meanwhile had formed a broad right-wing opposition bloc titled the Camp of Great Poland (OWP).

Inevitably, this organisation slid towards nationalist xenophobia and was instrumental in driving the Bloc for Minorities into support for the Non-Party Bloc for Co-operation with the Government (BBWR). After the death of Pilsudski in 1935 the army continued to dominate political life under the 'regime of the colonels' within the Camp of National Unification (OZoN). This regime was fairly undistinguished except in one field. Although sandwiched between two hostile powers, namely Nazi Germany and the Soviet Union, rather than make tactical concessions to either of the parties in order to ensure that in the event of conflict Poland would not be fighting on two fronts, the colonels looked to France as the guarantor of Polish independence. The result of this 'policy' was the Molotov–Ribbentrop pact and the Fourth Partition.

Concluding remarks

As is clear from the above by the autumn of 1939 the whole edifice had crumbled. The post-Versailles state system had been flawed from its inception. The problems of economic slump merely served cruelly to expose just how illegitimate such structures were. Hypothetical answers to the crisis became increasingly radical and hysterical in their tone. Eventually, and particularly in Germany, hyper-nationalism became entwined with doctrines of racial superiority and a demand that a campaign of racial purification take place in order for once and for all to destroy the ancestral cause of this and all other crises of civilization.

In order to achieve their ends, the Nazis were determined to reshape Central Europe in their own image. Alongside programs of genocide directed against the Jews and other 'degenerate' groups, a campaign was launched which effectively sought to reduce Poles to the status of *Untermenschen*. Such policies were accompanied by some remarkable ideological gymnastics on the part of the regime in Berlin, which made common cause with the palpably non-Aryan governments in Budapest and Bratislava. In short one nation was pitted against the other, in a classic policy of divide and rule, and the inter-state boundaries were redrawn accordingly.

With the final defeat of Germany and its allies in 1945, so Stalin came to implement his plans for Central Europe. Once again this involved the redrawing of state borders and attempts to homogenize the population, this time through mass deportations, primarily although not exclusively of Germans, as opposed to by means of genocide. With the benefit of hindsight we can say that no matter how morally reprehensible such policies were, with regard to Poland, Hungary, Czechoslovakia and both of its successor states the policy seems largely to have achieved its desired ends.

Not only are these countries much more ethnically homogeneous today than they were in the 1930s, they have emerged as liberal democracies which are much more stable than many predicted they would be. Although it is true that to a certain extent the political cultures of these countries had remained frozen during the years of Soviet imperialism, the governments in Prague, Bratislava, Warsaw and Budapest are markedly different from their pre-war precursors. In the following chapter we shall focus upon how since 1989 successive governments in each of these four countries have sought to manage the process of ethnic accommodation. We will discover that areas of conflict and concern still do exist. More importantly perhaps, we shall find that predictions of an ethnic conflagration have proven to be wide of the mark.

Bibliography

Ardrey R., *The Territorial Imperative*. New York, Atheneum, 1967.

Bideleux, R. and Jeffries, I., *A History of Eastern Europe*. London, Routledge, 1998.

Davies, N., *God's Playground: A History of Poland*, ii: *1795 to the Present*. Oxford, Oxford University Press, 1986.

Hobsbawm, E. J., *Nations and Nationalism since 1780*. Cambridge, Cambridge University Press, 1992.

Kann, R., *A History of the Habsburg Empire 1526–1918*. Berkeley, University of California Press, 1974.

Kedourie, E., *Nationalism*. Oxford, Blackwell, 1960.

Kellas, J. G., *The Politics of Nationalism and Ethnicity*. Basingstoke, Macmillan, 1991.

Kohn, H., *The Idea of Nationalism*. New York, Macmillan, 1945.

Larrain, J., *Ideology and Cultural Identity*. Cambridge, Polity Press, 1994.

Leslie, R. F., *The History of Poland since 1863*. Cambridge, Cambridge University Press, 1980.

Llobera, J. R., *The God of Modernity*. Oxford, Berg, 1994.

Pearson, R., *National Minorities in Eastern Europe 1848–1945*. London, Macmillan, 1983.

Ra'anan, U. et al. (eds), *State and Nation in Multiethnic Societies*. Manchester, Manchester University Press, 1991.

Seton-Watson, H., *The Russian Empire 1801–1917*. Oxford, Clarendon Press, 1967.

Smith, A. D., *Theories of Nationalism*. London, Harper & Row, 1971.

Smith, A. D., *Nations and Nationalism in a Global Era*. Cambridge, Polity Press, 1991.

Taylor, A. J. P., *The Habsburg Monarchy 1809–1918*. London, Hamish Hamilton, 1948.

2
Ethnic Conflict and Conciliation in Central Europe Today

Having clarified the relevant theoretical issues concerning nations, nation-building and national identity in Chapter 1, and examined some of the pitfalls encountered by the post-Versailles state system in the relevant area, this chapter seeks to familiarise the reader with elements of the debate on national and ethnic identity in contemporary Central Europe. The intentions of the author are threefold: first, to familiarise the reader with the general contours of the debate in each of the four countries under consideration; secondly, to highlight indicative salient themes and issues concerning identity in the geopolitical area together with official policy toward indigenous ethnic minorities; and finally, to provide the reader with an appreciation of the sometimes amorphous nature of identity (in Central Europe), so that she or he is better equipped to understand the nature of identity both in the region as a whole and within Silesia in particular. Given that today Silesia itself lies almost wholly within Poland, it is appropriate that we commence with an examination of that country.

Poland reconstructed

As we have already seen, following its re-emergence as a state in 1918 one of the primary features of Polish politics was chronic instability. The causes of this state of affairs were many and varied. They included geopolitical factors, industrial underdevelopment, the absence of civil society, economic recession, unfulfilled territorial aspirations, and the presence of national minorities who were to varying degrees either dissatisfied with their treatment by the Polish government or quite simply not reconciled to their membership of the Polish state. Our focus lies of course with the politics of ethnicity, but we should not forget the role that all the above-mentioned factors play in provoking and exacerbating ethnic tensions.

Prior to the outbreak of war in 1939, the most numerous of Poland's minorities were Ukrainians, Byelorussians, and Germans. There were also smaller communities of, among others, Czechs, Lithuanians, Armenians and Tartars. As for the Jews, whereas they were classified as Poles of Jewish faith, their religion, lifestyle, patterns of spatial settlement and economic activities marked them as being clearly different from Polish Catholics. Despite fitful attempts to provide a degree of cultural autonomy for various of the minority groups, no satisfactory accommodation had been reached prior to the onset of war in 1939. The war itself was to change the ethnographic map of Poland for ever. The details of the Holocaust are well known. The vast majority of Poland's Jews were murdered by the German occupiers and their auxiliaries (Hirsch, 1998: 10). What is less well known outside of Poland and its neighbouring states is both the degree to which Poland became ethnically homogeneous in the aftermath of the German-Soviet invasion of 1939, and more especially the methods by which such homogeneity was achieved. If we turn first to former Polish territories seized by the Soviet Union in 1939, we see that the 'problem' of ethnicity was solved in a typically Stalinist manner. Through the forcible incorporation of these territories the number of Lithuanians, Belorussians and Ukrainians living in reconstituted Poland was to be drastically cut. As for Poles living in these areas the Soviet attitude was clear: the Polish bourgeoisie together with all anti-Soviet elements was deported *en masse* to the Gulag. Those who remained, i.e. communists, peasants, and industrial workers, were to be assimilated into Soviet society as *homo sovieticus* (Urban, 1994: 60–5).

However, this planned assimilation never took place to any significant degree and the decision to resettle Poles from former eastern Poland within the borders of the postwar Polish state, provides a prism for explaining how the Polish communists resolved to Polonize the territories gained from Germany at the end of the Second World War. Whilst having 'lost' the bulk of its Jewish, Lithuanian, Belorussian and Ukrainian populations, through war, genocide and the loss of eastern Poland, Poland had simultaneously acquired German territory east of the Oder-Neiße line, together with several million Germans, most of whom were unwanted. The solution chosen was to expel the vast majority of the newly acquired Germans together with those German prewar citizens of Poland whom the Poles saw fit to expel. Certain groups of 'indubitable' Germans, mainly skilled people, remained in the new Poland whether they liked it or not, but others namely Kashubes, Upper Silesians, Mazurs and Ermlanders, who were held to be Germanized Slavs, were 'encouraged' to remain in Poland on the basis that they were not really Germans (Urban, 1994: 11–24).

The end result was that the ethnic minority population of Poland, which before the war had totaled approximately one third of the whole, by the late 1940s amounted to about one tenth of the total. As we shall see, for various reasons this population was then subject to further depletion. Treatment of the minorities was as differentiated as far as it could be within the confines of an ideological programme that was as much ethno-nationalist as it was neo-Stalinist. Thus Jews, although officially granted the right to self-expression as Jews, found themselves once again subjected to both quasi- and unofficial discrimination and pogroms. The end result was that virtually all had emigrated by the late 1960s. With regard to the Ukrainian population which by 1945 was largely confined to the south-eastern corner of Poland, huge numbers were deported to newly acquired former German territory. The purpose of this was on the one hand to break armed nationalist resistance and on the other to promote the assimilation of as many Ukrainians as possible into Polish society. As a result, Ukrainian and for that matter Lithuanian and Byelorussian cultural autonomy was severely limited until the return of Gomulka to power in 1956. At that point such autonomy was enhanced and many Ukrainian deportees were allowed to return to their former areas of residence. However, we should note that at no point neither political autonomy nor the right to use minority languages in the public sphere was ever considered by the Polish government (*Schlesisches Wochenblatt*, 28 September 1998).

Turning to the German minority, as will be explained in more detail elsewhere in the volume, they were divided into two categories: those whom the Poles considered to be German, and those whom the government and wider society considered to be Poles. The former category was, after having initially being declared to be stateless, granted the right to acquire either Polish or German Democratic Republic (GDR) passports. They were permitted a degree of cultural and educational autonomy, and again the coming to power of Gomulka in 1956 had an impact upon their position in society. Although their cultural autonomy was increased, the thrust of this change was blunted by the greater ease of emigration to the Federal Republic of Germany (FRG) which the Gomulka thaw ushered in. As a result the officially recognised German minority dwindled to such an extent, that by the late

1980s only a few thousand remained, together with an unknown number of such Germans who had become fully assimilated into Polish society (Rogall, 1993: 31–48).

The fate of the Kashubes, Upper Silesians, Ermlanders and Mazurs was very different from that of the 'indubitable Germans'. The whole thrust of Polish policy was to turn those who did not consider themselves to be Poles into Poles. The results hovered between tragedy and farce. Given both the means, i.e. neo-Stalinist political and police methods, and the ends, i.e. forcible assimilation, what in fact happened was that many members of these groups who were previously either well disposed toward the Polish option or were open to persuasion, became alienated from both the Polish nation and state. Instead of adopting standard Polish language and customs, ever-increasing numbers clung onto their own customs and dialects (they were forbidden by law to speak *Hochdeutsch*) as a means of signifying their alienation from the Polish state. Of course the prosperity of the Federal Republic acted as a beacon, as did continuing familial links with those who had either emigrated (before the war), or who had fled or been expelled after the war. Yet the way in which Polonization was forced upon them clearly served to strengthen identification with Germany, and encouraged people to apply for emigration to Germany under the various post-1949 resettlement programmes. This was particularly true of the Ermlanders and Mazurs of former East Prussia, where today only a remnant of the prewar population remains. As for the Kashubes, those who elected to stay are today largely integrated into Polish society. The case of the much more numerous Upper Silesians is more complex, in that many had opted for Poland prior to 1939, and that a majority of those who had opted for Poland at this time subsequently retained their allegiance. However, the fact remains that the largest ethnic minority in Poland today is the German, and this minority is overwhelmingly made up of Upper Silesians who were either the victims of the policy of forcible assimilation or are the descendants of such people (Bartodziej, 1993: 1–8).

Changing perspectives

Thus we can see that from 1918 right through to the 1980s, ethnic minorities in Poland always faced difficulties, very often simply because they were different. What did change according to the overall political climate was the degree of difficulty encountered by the members of such groups who today make up no more than three per cent of the overall population. The first real improvement in their position of course came with the transition away from Marxism-Leninism in the late 1980s. Part of the rationale of Solidarity's project was to create both civil society and liberal democracy. To that end it was determined to break with past policies with regard to national minorities. This entailed creating a climate within which minorities would not be viewed as a putative enemy. In the case of Belorussians, Ukrainians and Lithuanians this was not especially problematic, as their existence had never been denied. Similarly with regard to the smaller population groups such as Slovaks, Greeks, Armenians, Macedonians and Tartars; their lack of presence meant that they carried no political weight except at best in isolated villages, and as such could be easily accommodated. For differing reasons, groups as the Lehmke, Kashubes and (Upper) Silesians presented a problem to both official public opinion. As for the former group, there is no common agreement (even among the Lehmke themselves) as to whether they are or are not part of a wider Ukrainian family. With regard to the other two groups, there is dispute as to whether they actually exist as collective entities separate from the Polish nation. Whereas the Kashubes have won limited recognition in that regard, the Silesians have not. In fact, as recently as 1997, the Polish Constitutional Court decreed that that there was no such thing as a Silesian nation, and that Silesians were in fact simply a branch of the greater Polish nation (*Frankfurter Allgemeine Zeitung*, 25 September 1998).

As for the Germans their demands for recognition were loudest, precisely because the overwhelming majority did not officially exist as Germans until 1988. Given the historical legacy, the fact that virtually no German under the age of 60 could speak German properly, if at all, due to the ban on use of the language in German-oriented parts of Upper Silesia, and years of propaganda which had insisted that 'only a few thousand' Germans lived in Poland, their sudden visibility came as something of a shock to most Poles. Despite an initial furore and spurred by a surge of interest in their existence in both Poland and Germany, the Germans succeeded in organising themselves and obtaining recognition as an ethnic minority (Weber, 1991: 2). The need to establish good bilateral interstate relations between Poland and Germany played a role here, as did the common sense of both governments who both appreciated the need for a new start and acted accordingly.

As indicated, the Germans, in common with all other ethnic minority groups, still face problems. Indeed, no one actually knows with any degree of certainty just how many Polish citizens belong to the ethnic minority groups. The three largest are the Germans, Ukrainians and Belorussians respectively. Most estimates reckon there may be as many as 500,000 Germans, 400,000 Ukrainians and 300,000 Byelorussians resident in Poland. However, as the census permits of no question concerning ethnic/national origin there are in fact no official figures. The minority organisations themselves offer estimates which tend to be on the wild side of optimistic (funding is linked to claimed adherents), and with regard to the German minority in particular, one still hears claims from ethnic Poles that most of them are Poles who for purely opportunistic reasons claim to be Germans, an argument which is often repeated in Germany itself.

With regard to constitutional and legal provisions, Poland is a signatory to all of the standard agreements guaranteeing both human rights in general and minority rights in particular. In addition, the preamble to the new 1997 constitution explicitly refers to 'We, the Polish Nation – all citizens of the Republic', and as such acknowledges that not every Polish citizen is ethnically Polish. Articles 5 and 13 guarantee basic civic rights and principles of non-discrimination. Article 27 establishes Polish as the national language, but acknowledges that this provision 'shall not infringe upon national minority rights resulting from ratified international agreements'. In turn Article 35 guarantees the minorities the right of free association and the collective and individual expression of their cultures.

Yet constitutional guarantees do not of themselves solve anything. For example, there is still no national minorities law in Poland, and one will not be presented to parliament until a separate piece of legislation guaranteeing Polish as the national language is passed. One of the main reasons for the lack of progress in this field is that for most Poles the issue of (official) bilingualism harks back to previous attempts to eradicate the state and nation. Despite the fact that Poland is signatory to international agreements which provide for bilingual signs and the public use of minority languages in areas in which significant numbers of such minorities are resident, such provisions in fact contradict Polish law, as well as to some extent impinging upon the national psyche. At the time of writing, a draft law which will allow bilingual signage under certain circumstances is ready to be laid before parliament. However, it remains to be seen when and in what form the law will be passed. Another bone of contention is the reorganisation of regional and local government which took place between 1998 and 1999. When the plans first appeared in 1997, the German minority claimed that planned abolition of the Opole voivodeship or province in Upper Silesia was a deliberate act of discrimination on the part of Warsaw. Whether Warsaw was really so anxious to dilute the regional power of the German minority in the Opole voivodeship of Upper Silesia is doubtful, especially as the legislation will affords the German and possibly the Ukrainian and Byelorussian minorities the chance to take control of several (new) county councils. Whatever the case, there was widespread opposition from within the voivodeship to its planned abolition. In the end the government, which was faced with a revolt from its own anti-devolutionary right-wing, was forced to agree to a proposal put forward by the president and Democratic Left Alliance (SLD) which among other things provided for the continued existence of the Opole voivodeship.

The contemporary debate

What rights, then, have been accorded to the various national minorities in Poland since 1989? If we turn first to the area of politics, we find that as ethnic minorities they can field candidates in all areas of electoral competition. Indeed, at national elections their candidates are exempted from the normal electoral thresholds. Ukrainian, Byelorussian, Lithuanian and especially German candidates have had success at the local level, but only the Germans have met with success at the national level, and it must be acknowledged that their success has waned with each successive general election (*Schlesisches Wochenblatt*, 5 June 1998).

With regard to educational rights, the right to be educated in the mother tongue has been established in principle if not in fact. A lack of both internal and external resources, coupled with a lack of demand, has meant that these provisions are not as far-reaching as some minority activists, particularly Germans, would like. On the other hand, they go a lot further than some Poles think is healthy. Access to the mass media has also improved. Magazines, journals and books are published in all the recognised vernaculars, but again there is dispute as to whether the supply is sufficient. Similar rows surface from time to time in over access to the broadcast media in areas of minority settlement (*Schlesisches Wochenblatt*, 12 December 1997).

It should, however, be stressed that for most Poles, the signage issue aside, these issues are of no particular importance. The issue of minority rights does not dominate either the national or the regional media. This itself is a sign that ethnic Poles are less concerned with the ethnic provenance of a relatively small number of their co-citizens and more preoccupied with either more prosaic or more important issues. As for the minorities themselves, whereas they acknowledge an improvement in their situation, their activists insist there is further scope for improvement. With these qualifications, we can say that on the whole, inter-ethnic relations in Poland indicate that Poland is progressing towards the construction of civil society. We do need, however, to add two caveats. The first is that anti-Semitism still rears its head from time to time, and is much more casually accepted than it is in either the United States or most West European societies. Secondly, as elsewhere in the region, the Roma remain total outsiders and show no signs of leaving the margins of Polish society. Given the gulf that exists between most Roma and a majority of Poles, this is an obvious area of concern, although governmental initiatives aimed at healing the breach appear to be rather sparse. Such caveats to one side, we can say that Poland's 'return to Europe', has not provided for the polarization of politics and society around ethnicity and the ghosts of history.

Minority rights in the Czech Republic

Czechoslovakia was formed in the aftermath of the First World War. It could actually be argued that, for a number of reasons, the name of the state was something of a misnomer: first, although Czechs and Slovaks are both members of the west Slav linguistic group and are culturally close to one another, the two languages whilst being mutually intelligible are distinct. Secondly, the Czech Lands of Bohemia and Moravia were much more heavily influenced by the German-speaking world than was Slovakia, which in turn had been subject to greater Hungarian influence. Thirdly, the Czech Lands were more heavily industrialized than was Slovakia. Fourthly, the new state contained sizeable numbers of Ruthenes, Hungarians and Germans, the majority of whom became progressively more alienated from their putative homeland. In addition, as with all states in the area, there was uncertainty over the status and place of Jews and Roma within the national fabric. Finally, we need also to acknowledge the fact that whereas the Czech strategic ethnie in effect proceeded from the basis that Slovaks were 'proto-Czechs', some Slovaks claim that their language has a written tradition going back to seventeenth century, which would indicate that, as is so often the case among fervent nationalists, Czech nationalists allowed dogma to substitute for observable evidence (Slovak Currents, 1998).

Given the lack of consensus as to whether Czechoslovakia should exist within its given boundaries, or indeed whether it should exist at all, it unsurprisingly became a hotbed of ethno-nationalist and ultimately racist agitation. Following the rise of Hitler to power in Germany, demands grew from both the German government and ethnic Germans living in Czechoslovakia for a revision of the Czechoslovak–German border. In 1938 in Munich, in their failed effort to placate Hitler; the French, Italian and British governments took it upon themselves to agree to German demands that German-speaking areas be detached from Czechoslovakia, and be united with Germany. For good measure, the Hungarians received parts of southern Slovakia, and Poland helped itself to the disputed Silesian town of Tecin together with its immediate hinterland. This decision, which was passively accepted by the Czechoslovak government, effectively spelled the end of the state. In March 1939 spurred on by Germany, Slovak nationalists declared the independence of Slovakia and the Germans occupied the remainder of the country (Steinacker, 1987: 12).

During the war the fate of Jews and Roma was no different to anywhere else in fascist Europe. Slovaks were redesignated as Aryan, and the Czechs were regarded as being suitable candidates for Aryanization. Despite the presence of an indigenous fascist regime in Slovakia, armed resistance was greater there than in the Czech Lands. As for Czech politicians in exile, they in turn resolved that in the wake of the defeat of Germany and its allies, the national question would be resolved by completing the job of ethnic homogenization begun by the Nazis. Thus when the Benes government returned from London, the overwhelming majority of the German-speaking population, including Jews who had survived the Holocaust, was forcibly evicted to Germany. Similarly, large numbers of Hungarians were also forcibly expelled, as were smaller numbers of Poles and Silesians of uncertain national provenance (Heinrich, 1997: 14 ff.). The Ruthene 'problem' was largely dealt with by the Soviet Union's annexation of western Ruthenia. Those Ruthenes who remained in Czechoslovakia were in turn reclassified as Ukrainians.

However, neither this short-lived 'liberal democratic' government nor its communist successor actually managed to create a primary, overarching sense of Czechoslovak national consciousness. Until the late 1960s Czechoslovakia remained an official national monolith, although after that time the existence of ethnic Germans, Hungarians and Ukrainians was acknowledged. Neither communist nor post-1989 attempts at federal solutions solved the problem of how the state should be organised. As is so often the case in such instances the uneven level of industrial development in one part of the country (Slovakia), and how to raise the Slovak standard of living and modernise Slovak industry, accentuated trends toward separation. This coupled with the unpopularity of economic liberalism in Slovakia, and the lack of a common party system was what precipitated the Velvet Divorce of 1992.

The remarkable features of this process were the lack of popular agitation to keep Czechoslovakia intact, and the corresponding lack of violence when the state did actually disintegrate. In the Czech Republic today a generally liberal attitude is taken toward national identification, although, as we shall see, obtaining a Czech passport is not necessarily easy. Unlike in Poland, the national census actually allows people to declare their nationality. Thus according to the census figures of 1993, in addition to 8,363,768 Czechs, there are also 1,362,319 Moravians, 314,877 Slovaks, 59,389 Poles, 48,556 Germans and 44,446 Silesians. There are also small communities of Magyars, Ukrainians, Russians and Ruthenes. Furthermore, according to the census figures there are 32,903 Roma (The Czech Population, 1998). However, it is generally reckoned that in the census the overwhelming majority of Roma who took part passed themselves of as either Czechs or Slovaks as was their entitlement. This was due to the level of antipathy that exists toward Roma, and their subsequent reluctance to reveal their true identity. In fact, the true figure for the Roma population is reckoned to be over 200,000. It is also possible that the number of Germans is higher, and that for similar reasons, an unknown number of Germans declared themselves to be Czech or Silesian. To complicate matters even further, Silesian identity tends to be amorphous, which raises the possibility that those who declared themselves to be Silesian could also lay claim to a Czech, Polish, Moravian or German identity; and that some although claiming adherence to the latter four categories could have declared themselves to be Silesians.

If we turn now to constitutional provisions, as we shall see the constitution itself does not pay the same amount of detail as the Hungarian equivalent to the position of national minorities, but the Preamble, and Articles 3, 6 10, and in particular Article 25, either directly or indirectly acknowledge the rights of ethnic minorities to freedom of expression. Various Council of Europe agreements have been acceded to, but ratification of the Framework Convention for the Protection of National Minorities, although signed, will not be ratified until the planned reorganisation of regional and local government has taken place. At the moment the legislative plans are stalled. In order to ensure that these stipulations and agreements are adhered to the Czech government established the post of Commissioner for Human Rights in 1998. The Commissioner in addition chairs the governmental committee on National Minorities and the Roma (*Frankfurter Allgemeine Zeitung*, 11 September 1998). As we shall see, and as the name of this committee suggests, the situation of the Roma in the Czech Republic is a source of contestation. Finally, within this context we should note that together with the Roma, those national minorities who possess a parent nation-state, such as the Germans, are permitted cultural and linguistic autonomy (Human Rights Watch Prague, 1996: 2–3).

With regard to the Germans, we should note that given the overall age of the community, and the lack of a working knowledge of the language on the part of younger Germans, their long-term future is uncertain. Having said that, by playing upon the intransigence of the Sudeten *Landsmannschaft* and the high level of German investment in the Czech Republic, the extreme right Republican Party has in recent years deliberately stoked up fears of a German takeover in the event of Czech accession to the European Union (EU).

The situation of the Roma is particularly acute. They have been subjected to an increasing spate of attacks on Roma by Czech neo-Nazis who themselves have been spurred by both the Republicans and groups to their right. The Roma have been particularly disadvantaged by the citizenship law introduced by Prague following the dissolution of Czechoslovakia. This law had the effect of denying Czech citizenship to certain groups of former Czechoslovak citizens who, within the five years prior to the coming into force of the law, had been convicted of a criminal offense. Given their higher crime rate, which is not unrelated to their socioeconomic status, the Roma have been particularly affected by this measure. The situation was made more complex by the fact that an estimated 95 per cent of all Roma resident in the Czech Republic when the new state was created, had in fact been born in Slovakia (Czech Helsinki Committee, 1996).

From 1968 Czechoslovakia had operated a system of internal dual Czech and Slovak citizenship. Most Roma had never bothered to take out Czech citizenship after the law of 1968 was passed. As a result, the post-Czechoslovak Czech authorities have regarded such people and their children as prima facie Slovaks. In fact it has been argued that this was the precise objective of the law, together with the corresponding intention of 'dumping' as many of the Roma into Slovakia as possible. In order to obtain Czech passports those affected have to obtain proof of their Slovak citizenship which is not cheap, and then apply for a Czech passport, which is also not cheap. Financial considerations aside, for poorly educated people, already alienated from authority, this whole process can be both confusing and intimidating; especially when officials from both sides make it clear that they would prefer it if the Roma went to live somewhere else. Additional problems include the aforementioned clean criminal record requirement, and the fact that in order to gain Czech citizenship applicants have to prove at least two years residence in the Czech Republic. All in all, a situation was created that could have been avoided if more straightforward criteria of citizenship were adopted, as they were for the few hundred Czechs who live in Ukraine, who were granted Czech passports on the grounds of ethnicity alone. In 1996, the Czech Interior Ministry claimed that only 200 former Czech citizens had been denied Czech citizenship as a result of this law, but human rights groups claim the figure is well wide of the mark, and that the real total could be as high as 25,000, with the large majority being Roma. The result is that many actually end up as stateless with all that entails. Since the spring of 1996 in partial acknowledgment of the difficulties created by the clean criminal record clause, the Ministry of the Interior has the right to waive it on behalf of applicants. The extent to which this measure has brought widespread relief is inevitably a matter of dispute.

With regard to employment practices, Roma employees have often been the first to be made redundant, they have correspondingly often been the last to be offered new jobs, and face widespread social exclusion. The results have been as inevitable as they have been pathetic. Over half of all adult Roma are unemployed, and the rate of criminal activity has increased. This in turn fuels the claims of the Czech right that the Roma are genetically disposed toward criminality. In short there appears to be a chasm of understanding between many Roma and their Czech fellow-citizens. In an effort to alleviate the situation, the Czech government recently announced a package of financial incentives for employers willing to employ Roma. It is of course far to early to tell whether such measures will have a positive effect.

To conclude this section, we shall offer a few observations on the situation of the Moravians and Silesians. They possess no special cultural or linguistic rights. Indeed the appearance of the former in particular is something of a curiosity. Linguistically Moravian is considered to be little more than a dialect of standard literary Czech. Having said that, self-designation as Moravian does not of itself necessarily translate into a demand for autonomy let alone independence. Although

Moravian and Silesian autonomists achieved some early success in the aftermath of communism, their electoral success has been limited since the break-up of the old state. The appearance of Poles and especially Silesians was even more surprising. Given the fluidity of national identification, especially in (Czech) Silesia this assertion of a non-Czech identity bears a striking resemblance to the sudden reappearance of Germans in Polish Upper Silesia. Thus people who have simultaneously been subjected to forcible assimilation and suffered economic disadvantage have rejected an identity which was foisted upon them and has brought no discernible benefit. Silesian or Polish identity being available to them through a combination of ancestry and historical precedent thus becomes a means of collective and individual self-assertion. The extent to which it has actually taken root, as opposed to being a mere badge of protest, is a question that can only be answered by analysis of the next census, and observation of the actors themselves. So far, the evidence would seem to indicate that assumption of Polish or Silesian identity has not led to any crisis either in Czech–Polish relations or within the Czech Republic itself.

Slovakia: a different route

With the accomplishment of the Velvet Divorce, Czech–Slovak relations have ceased to be a major issue in either country. This does not, however, mean that ethnicity does not operate as the basis of political cleavage in Slovakia. According to the Slovak government, 87.1 per cent of the population is ethnically Slovak. By far the biggest minority is the Magyar, who constitute a minimum 10.6 per cent of the population or about 400,000 individuals (Mandzak, 1998). The number of Magyars living in Czechoslovakia after the post-1945 population transfers expulsions with Hungary was always a matter of conjecture, as many ethnic Magyars passed themselves off as Slovaks in order to avoid either deportation or discrimination. As we shall see, there are particular tensions surrounding Slovak–Hungarian relations, and the issue of Slovakia´s Magyar minority cannot be separated from them. Matters are further complicated by claims from Budapest that although Articles 6, 12 and 34 of the Slovak constitution guarantee minority rights, other passages of the constitution which refer to territorial Slovak sovereignty, and the right of all citizens not to be treated in a discriminatory manner, contradict such assurances (Constitution of the Slovak Republic, 1996).

Magyars aside, the remainder of the ethnic minority population consists of small numbers of Czechs, Ruthenes, Ukrainians, Germans and

Poles. There is also an indeterminate number of Roma. Once again, there is an obvious reluctance on the part of many Roma to declare their identity. As we have noted, the position of the Roma in Slovakia has been complicated by the Czech citizenship law, and we might also observe that, if anything, the economic condition of the Roma is even worse in Slovakia than in the Czech Republic. In short, no one can be sure of just how many Roma are resident in Slovakia, but their number may be as high as 400,000, a figure which the Slovakian government would almost certainly contest.

The Roma community seems to exist completely on the margins of Slovak society. Unlike the Hungarian minority it possesses neither internal coherence nor external support. As a result it has become easy in recent years for unscrupulous Slovak politicians to scapegoat the Roma as and when the need arises. The consequence of this situation, which has been replicated to a lesser extent in the Czech Republic, has been to prompt migration on the part of many Roma to EU member states (and Canada) in the hope they may find greater tolerance. It is debatable as to whether or not they will find such tolerance other among officials or the general public in these countries. It is equally debatable as to whether the EU is capable of devising a common policy on the issue that will provide an effective means of resolution.

The degree of alienation from the Slovak state is also particularly acute among Magyars. The extent to which the situation has been deliberately manipulated by former Prime Minister Meciar is hotly debated. There is little doubt that the constant constitutional wrangling in Slovakia, and the various changes of government which have occurred there since 1993, have contributed to a situation in which the Magyar minority has been used as a political football. The Hungarian government is adamant that it will only sign bilateral treaties with foreign governments the terms of which in its opinion correspond to international norms. This has been interpreted by the Slovaks as an attempt by Budapest to dictate the nature of such treaties, and impinge upon the sovereign rights of Slovakia. The situation is further complicated by the fact that independent Slovakia has not repudiated the Benes decrees of 1945. It was as a result of these decrees that all sections of Czechoslovak society which were deemed to have collaborated with the Axis powers were forcibly expelled from the country. The fate of the German *Sudetenlanders* is well known. What is less well known is the fact that tens of thousands of ethnic Magyars were expelled to Hungary (The Magyar Millennium, 1997). Until the decrees are repudiated the victims of these expulsions, which were comprehensive rather than selective, are entitled neither to the right of return nor to any measure of compensation from either of the successor states to Czechoslovakia. There is also suspicion on the Slovak side, that international and bilateral agreements notwithstanding, Budapest's support for territorial autonomy for Slovakian Magyars, masks an desire to undo the results of the First World War as far as it can without causing alarm in the wider international community.

To make matters worse, the dispute over the Gabcikovo-Nagymaros hydroelectric dam has inevitably soured Hungarian–Slovak relations. In 1977 Czechoslovakia and Hungary signed an agreement to dam and divert the Danube in order better to harness the river's hydroelectric potential and promote the growth and modernization of industry especially on the Czechoslovak side of the border (*Daily Bulletin of the Hungarian News Agency*, 11 March 1998). In 1992 as a result of growing pressure from environmental campaigners within Hungary, the Hungarian government unilaterally withdrew from the project. For their part, the Slovaks carried on as best they could. The river was diverted, and on the Hungarian side it is claimed that valuable wetlands dried up, and that farmers and others lost their livelihoods. As of 1998, despite the International Court at The Hague having apportioned blame equally and having ordered the two countries to come to agreement over the issue, no accommodation had been reached. Once again we have an instance of economic factors impinging upon inter-ethnic relations, thereby creating an environment which facilitates the manipulation of grievance. In this instance such matters concern the issue of Slovakia's treatment of its Magyar minority. Whereas, the general rule can apply anywhere, our focus shall remain upon the fate and place of the Magyar minority in Slovakia which is a major issue in both countries.

Hungarian sources claim that the Magyar minority comprises some 600,000 and not 400,000 individuals (*Hungarian Quarterly*, 1995: 1). Either way, it constitutes a sizeable chunk of Slovakia's population. The fact is that ethnic Magyars do not vote for non-Hungarian parties to any discernible extent, and that despite Slovak adherence to the letter of its international obligations on minority rights, there is criticism of the behavior of the Slovak government from both domestic and foreign critics. Having said that, the linguistic rights accorded the Hungarian minority in Slovakia are in fact greater than those accorded to any minority in Poland, where for example the use of bilingual street signs is still anathema.

As a result of the aforementioned reservations over the Slovak constitution, uncertainties over the general nature of bilateral relations, and also (as we shall see in the next section) in order to fulfil wider domestic and foreign policy goals, Budapest considered the conclusion of a bilateral Hungarian–Slovak treaty to be of the utmost importance. Although the two began negotiations on such a treaty in 1992, the treaty itself was not in fact signed until 1995 because of objections from within the Slovak parliament toward provisions which granted territorial autonomy to areas with a substantial Hungarian minority. In turn, Hungarian political and community representatives claim that the Meciar government was systematically attempting to deprive Magyars of their culture (*Weekly Bulletin of the Hungarian News Agency*, 15 April 1995: 1). It is too early to tell whether increased support for the nationalist right in the Hungarian general election of 1998 will have an adverse effect on the situation, but the portents are not good.

Under the terms of the treaty, both sides agree to respect their bilateral border, and confirm that neither side harbors territorial claims on the other. For Slovakia this was of the utmost importance, given the residual concerns of the legacy of both world wars. Articles 14 and 15 of the treaty contain the usual provisions concerning the outlawing of all forms of discrimination. Most importantly, Article 15 lists in some detail the rights of both Hungary's Slovak minority and Slovakia's Magyar minority. It confirms, for example, the right of individual and collective expression, the right to free association, the use of mother tongue languages in the public sphere, the use of mother-tongue signage, and the right to receive education in the mother tongue. The two states also declare that in their opinion the treaty corresponds to the norms of international law, and the various Council of Europe, The Organization For Security and Cooperation in Europe (OSCE) and United Nations documents which cover both human rights in general and minority rights in particular (Preamble of the Hungarian–Slovak Treaty of 1995).

This is all well and good, but as with any other political decision, the terms of implementation are open to interpretation, there may be problems over resource allocation, and we also need to consider the aforementioned overall context. Despite the treaty, there is evidence to show that at the political level at least, ethnic Magyars are poorly integrated into Slovak society, as is evidenced by the continuing success of their political parties at national and local level. The three Magyar parties, The Hungarian Christian Democratic Movement, Coexistence, and The Hungarian Civic Party, poll a share of the vote which correlates extremely closely with the estimated percentage of Magyar citizens of Slovakia (Political Science in Slovakia, 1998). Moreover, the

Hungarian government has gone so far as to claim that the situation of the Magyar minority in Slovakia has actually grown worse since the treaty was signed. In the absence of any common ground between major political actors across the ethnic divide, this is a development that cannot be taken as being particularly healthy. The main disputes centre over the extent to which Hungarian may be used as an official language in areas in which there is a sizeable Hungarian population, and over education provision for ethnic Magyars. Under the Slovak language Law, which was passed in 1996, Magyars can theoretically be obliged to address officials in Slovakian as opposed to Hungarian. For the Hungarian side the implications are clear; the law may be used as a cover for the deliberate placement and promotion of Slovak public servants in Hungarian-speaking areas who have no knowledge of Hungarian in order to reduce the public use of Hungarian and thereby promote the assimilation of Magyars.

In the realm of education, the Hungarian minority has claimed that Hungarian-speaking headmasters have been removed from schools on purely political grounds and that attempts to introduce optional bilingual education in Hungarian schools are in fact an attempt to limit Hungarians' knowledge of their own language and in effect turn Magyars into Slovaks. Hungarian representatives also complain that there are 130 Hungarian populated villages where there is no provision for a Hungarian education, and that the Slovak government should afford ethnic Magyars greater opportunities to pursue further and higher education in the Hungarian language (*Weekly Bulletin of the Hungarian News Agency*, 6 October 1995: 2). Neither are they satisfied with the support given by Bratislava for cultural activities. There are claims that the publication of a Hungarian language daily paper, several journals, 36 hours a week of radio programmes and 25 minutes a week of Hungarian-language programming are insufficient for the communities' needs. Clearly the situation is not good, and an examination of the situation of ethnic and national minorities in Hungary itself, together with an examination of Budapest's foreign policy goals, will help us better to understand the reasons why.

The case of Hungary

Prior to the Second World War Hungary was not marked by the presence of any substantial ethnic cleavage, although once again both Jews and Roma faced difficulties in obtaining full equality. Yet the issue of ethnicity was present due to the large amount of territory which

Hungary lost at the end of the First World War and the fact that around one third of all Magyars found themselves assigned to other countries. Independent Hungary quickly found itself prey to both economic crisis and political polarisation and quickly succumbed to de facto dictatorship under Admiral Horthy. Irredentist desires led Hungary into a fateful embrace with the Nazi Germany which resulted in a temporary expansion of Hungary's borders at the expense of Czechoslovakia and Romania (Hobek, 1995: 46 ff).

In comparative terms for an Axis power, anti-Semitism was not particularly pronounced under the Horthy regime, but in late 1944 the Hungarian Arrow Cross movement seized power and increased the tempo of both more general anti-Semitism and the extermination campaign. Although tens of thousands of Hungarian Jews perished at the hands of the Germans and their Hungarian allies, Hungary alone of all Central European countries today boasts a Jewish community that can be numbered in the tens of thousands. However, as Jews are counted as Hungarians of Jewish faith, no separate provision is made for them under the provisions of Hungary's minorities legislation.

After the conclusion of hostilities, most ethnic Germans who had not fled were forcibly expelled from Hungary on grounds of collaboration with the Nazis. Although we should note that as a result of Allied pressure, such expulsion measures were by no means as comprehensive as they were in Czechoslovakia, Yugoslavia or Poland. With regard to other minorities and eventually also the Germans, the Hungarian communists trod carefully – as much as anything else because they were conscious of the position of the Hungarian diaspora in the Soviet Union, Romania and Czechoslovakia. No attempt was made forcibly to deny national self-expression as long as it did not contradict the prevailing ideological mores. On the other hand, by reducing self-expression to the preservation of folkloric customs, de facto assimilation was the result. It was the existence of similar policies in Romania which caused a deterioration of bilateral relations during the 1980s, and brought constant accusations from Hungary and international human rights groups that ethnic Magyars in Transylvania were subject to discrimination.

Since the transition from communism began, Hungary has presented itself as something of a role model in its treatment of ethnic minorities, which may constitute as much as 12 per cent of the overall population. In fact, since 1996 the Hungarian state has even gone so far as to declare 18 December to be National Minorities day. According to the census of 1990 there are a total of 213,111 non-Magyar Hungarian citizens, of whom 137,724 claimed to be able to communicate in their mother tongue. The largest group is the Roma, followed by the Germans, with an 'official' membership of 142,683 and 30,284 respectively (Fact Sheets on Hungary 2, 1995). However, a large caveat must be noted here. No one, including the Hungarian government, takes these figures seriously. First of all, all minorities were subject to assimilation during the period of communist rule. Secondly, in the aftermath of the Second World War most Germans who remained in Hungary hid their identity. Having said that, it is worth noting that, known Nazis aide, German expellees now have the right to return, and to reclaim their Hungarian passports. Thirdly, the Roma in particular have been subject to both official discrimination and popular antipathy. In Hungary as elsewhere, the Roma tend to find themselves toward the margins, suffering from disproportionately high rates of unemployment and poor prospects with regard to education. It is reckoned that their true number is upwards of 400,00, and that in addition there may be as many as 250,000 Hungarian citizens of German descent who in the light of their previous experiences pass themselves off as Magyars (Hungarian Government Report No. J/3670 n.d.). As for the other groups, minority activists estimate that the true membership of their communities is higher than the official statistics allow. Whereas that is probably true, it should also be noted that it is in the interests of activists to make such claims because the level of financial subvention from both the Hungarian and any ancestral state is largely determined by the number of the minority. In short, all such statistics must be treated with a degree of caution. Whatever the case, the Hungarian government acknowledges the existence of thirteen ethnic and national minorities and estimates that they total well over one million individuals.

All of the designated minorities also receive subsidised and largely generous access to the written and printed media. With the exception of the Roma, numbers determine access. For example the Germans, Croats and Romanians all have a weekly press, receive two hours a day of radio airtime and enjoy 25 minutes a week of TV airtime. At the other end of the spectrum, the tiny Greek, Armenian, Bulgarian and Polish communities only receive periodic publications, receive no radio airtime and have to share a monthly 30-minute TV programme (Hungarian Government Report No. J/3670, n.d.). The Roma, once again as much as anything else due to their marginal position in society, do not receive access to the media in proportion to their numbers. The relevant declarations, statutes, conventions and resolutions of the UN, Council of Europe and OSCE have been taken as providing the standards to which domestic Hungarian legislation should conform To achieve these ends, since 1990 a complex minority rights regime has been established.

The amended constitution of 1949 is the basis from which Hungarian minority rights legislation proceeds. Article 27 establishes the right of parliamentarians to submit questions to the Ombudsman for the Rights of National and Ethnic Minorities. Article 32/B establishes the mechanism by which the Ombudsman is elected, and defines the remit of the office. Article 68 explicitly acknowledges the existence of national and ethnic minorities in Hungary and goes on to outline the general terms and conditions of state policy towards such minorities. Finally, Article 70/A deals with the outlawing of all forms of discrimination.

In 1990, Government Decree No. 34 complemented these measures by establishing an Office for National and Ethnic Minorities with the brief of implementing such policy and maintaining direct links with minority organizations, and which is directly responsible to the prime minister's office. In 1993 the legal framework was further tightened by the passing of an Act on the Rights of National and Ethnic Minorities. The act specifies both individual and group rights in the sphere of local government, the use of mother-tongue languages in both the public and private spheres, education, culture, and access to the mass media. In addition under a ruling of the Constitutional Court in 1991 and under the terms of the previously mentioned law, each of the 13 designated minorities is supposed to be guaranteed representation in parliament. However, parliament has so far not approved the necessary enabling legislation, and by way of response in January 1998, representatives of the German, Czech and Croat communities came together to found the Nationality Forum in order to contest the elections of 1998 (the overall results of which showed a marked swing to the right) on behalf of those and other minority population members who cared to give them their votes (Daily Bulletin of the Hungarian News Agency, 10 March 1998: 1).

Perhaps the most novel aspect of the welter of minority rights legislation has been the 1994 Act on Self-Government Electoral Rights. This act established the right of ethnic minorities to establish 'self-governments'. These self-governments exist in parallel to territorially based local authorities. At the local level, their powers are considerable. In matters concerning local public education and culture, local media, the fostering of traditions, the collective use of language, the territorial administration can only pass bylaws if the relevant minority self-governments agree. Since 1994, a total of 681 such minority self-governments have come into existence. They represent every one of the 13 officially recognised minorities, except the Ruthenes, who were unable to reach any common agreement on how to take advantage of the legislation. The remaining 12 minorities possess a wide degree of group autonomy through the existence of self-governing councils which themselves perform a number of functions.

With regard to education, minority education is provided as and where demand exists, and finances allow, within the overall ambit of the national curriculum. By way of illustration we can cite the following examples: the Greeks are provided with a Greek-language education in a total of six schools. Croat education takes place in over 40 schools both at the level of kindergartens and within the primary school sector. There are also two secondary schools for ethnic Croats. As of 1996, the Germans had a total of 254 German-language schools catering for over 40,000 pupils. Once again, the Roma stand apart. There are no special Roma schools, and by all educational indices, the Roma have the lowest rate of achievement (*Budapest Week*, 24 October 1996). There is a special development programme in place, but the extent to which it has been successful is debatable. Indeed, despite the passing of a raft of resolutions and special ordinances to cater for the Roma, if anything their situation continues to deteriorate. Their lack of education has traditionally meant that they have been left to do the jobs no one else wants. With the post-communist industrial shake-out they have suffered from disproportionately high unemployment. The failure to implement policies which alleviate their position or reduce public hostility means that they remain as isolated as ever from the mainstream of Hungarian society.

It is important to note that Hungary is not acting purely for altruistic reasons in providing for such opportunities and guarantees. Once again the Hungarian diaspora plays a role, as does Hungary's desire to join the EU and NATO. Hungary presents itself as a model European citizen in order to promote its entry 'into Europe'. In part it does so as a means of drawing attention to the position of ethnic Hungarians who live in neighbouring states. In that way, in Budapest the Hungarian model has become the yardstick which is seen as appropriate for Ukraine, Slovakia, Yugoslavia (where ethnic Magyars have been treated less harshly than other minorities) and Romania. This is of particular importance given the delicate nature of relations between Hungary on the one hand and Romania, Yugoslavia and Slovakia on the other, and continued allegations that Magyars in each of these three countries are to some extent disadvantaged.

Although such a policy may seem somewhat Machiavellian it has brought benefits both to the Magyar diaspora and to non-Magyar Hungarian citizens. Also, given the general absence of ethnic tensions in the country, these policies have contributed to the growth of civil society. On the other hand, there have been criticisms that the elaborate system of ethnic councils does little to foster integration and has also resulted in the growth of ethnic elites who have become divorced from their wider constituencies. From this perspective, such an elaborate minority rights regime may inadvertently serve to create informal apartheid structures and eventually damage the fabric of society as a whole, precisely because ethnic bonds take precedence over civic values.

So we can see that the picture in Central Europe is mixed. Some groups have made real strides; others, particularly the Roma, face a whole range of problems. We have also seen that there is no common framework among the four states. It should also have become clear that from time to time people have changed identities, sometimes of their own will, sometimes not. From the comments we made concerning the identity of Silesians, there is evidence that there exists a unique situation, and one which is worthy of greater attention. This is important for two reasons: the first is that through an examination of Silesia we may learn more about the overall process of state and nation formation in Central Europe and elsewhere. The second is that Silesia and the provenance of Silesians have often been at the centre of disputes between kingdoms, empires and nation-states. An examination of the area will enable us to gain a better understanding of the nature of these disputes and of how they have been manipulated. Before we examine the case of Silesia, let us first turn to an examination of Germany's historical relationship with the wider region.

Accomplishing this task is important for a number of reasons. First, because German influence has been decisive in terms of state and nation formation in Central Europe. Secondly, Germanic notions of nationhood formed the basis for nation-building in the countries we have just examined. Thirdly, because to this day contemporary debates on nationality and citizenship in Central Europe are often stimulated by the past and continuing presence of German communities. Finally, and perhaps most importantly, because Silesia was for centuries firmly within the German orbit, and Upper Silesia still possesses a large German minority.

Bibliography

Bartodziej, G., 'Die Lage der deutschen Minderheit in Polen'. Unpublished discussion document, 10 Aug., 1993.

Budapest Week, 24 Oct. 1996.

Constitution of the Republic of Hungary: http://www.meh.hu.nekh?angol/6-1-1.html

Constitution of the Republic of Poland: http://www.uni-wuerzburg:de/law/p10001_.html#c001_

Constitution of the Slovak Republic: PRESSFOTO, Bratislava, 1996.

Czech Helsinki Committee, *Report on the State of Human Rights in The Czech Republic,* Prague, 1996.

Czech Republic-population: http://cech.cesnet.cz/insight/texts/CZ-Population:htm/

Daily Bulletin of the Hungarian News Agency, 10 Mar. 1998; 11 Mar. 1998.

Hirsch, H., *Die Rache der Opfer.* Rowohlt, Berlin, 1998.

Ministry of Foreign Affairs, *National and Ethnic Minorities in Hungary,* Fact Sheets on Hungary, Budapest, 1995.

Ministry of Foreign Affairs, *The Magyar Millennium,* Fact Sheets on Hungary, Budapest, 1997.

Frankfurter Allgemeine Zeitung, 25 Sept. 1997; 11 Sept. 1998.

Heinrich, R., *Vorlesungen über die Sudetendeutschen den Anfängen bis zur Gegenwart.* Universität Salzburg, 1997.

Hobek, M., *Die Geschichte der Ungarndeutschen.* Österreichische Landsmannschaft, Vienna, 1997.

Human Rights Watch/Helsinki, *The Czech Republic,* Human Rights Watch Prague, Prague, 1996.

Hungarian Quarterly 36, autumn 1995.

Krekeler, N., 'Die deutsche Minderheit in Polen und die Revisionspolitik des Deutschen reiches 1919–1939', in W. Benz (ed.), *Der Vertribung der Deutschen aus dem Osten.* Fischer, Frankfurt-am-Main, 1995.

Mandzak, P., http://www.math.uni.hamburg.de/home/mandzak/results:html

Political Science in Slovakia: htp://www.eunet.sk/slovakia/slovakia/history-politics/politics.html

Republic of Hungary, Report No. J/3670 of the Government of the Republic of Hungary to the National Assembly on the Situation of National and Ethnic Minorities Living in the Republic of Hungary: http://www.meh.hu/nekh/angol/htm

Rogall, J., 'Die deutschen Minderheit in Polen heute', *Aus Politik und Zeitgeschichte,* 26, Nov. 1993.

Schlesisches Wochenblatt, 5 June 1998; 28 Sept. 1998; 12 Dec. 1998.

Slovak Currents in the Seventeenth Century:htt://www.culture.gov.sk/ANGLICKY/2VIH/STOPPAGE/gov10.htm/

Steinacker, R., *Die Karpatendeutschen in der Slowakei.* Bund der Vertriebene, Bonn, 1987.

Treaty between the Republic of Hungary and the Slovak Republic on Good-Neighbourly Relations and Friendly Cooperation of 19 Mar. 1995, Ministry of Foreign Affairs, Budapest, 1995.

Urban, T., *Deutsche in Polen*. Munich, Beck'sche Reihe, 1994.
Weber, N., *Religiöse und ethnische Minderheiten im heutigen Polen*. Evangelische Akademie Berlin (West), Berlin, 1991.
Weekly Bulletin of the Hungarian News Agency, 6 Oct. 1995; 11 Mar. 1998

3
The Germans and Central Europe in the Pre-modern Era

Introduction

As indicated toward the end of the previous chapter, this contribution deals specifically with the relationship between the German-speaking world and Central Europe, from the early Middle Ages up to the third partition of Poland in 1795. As we shall discover, the terms of this relationship have often been of decisive importance to both parties. Hence the rationale for a chapter which deals with the role of 'Germany' in the region. We shall also discover that in the Middle Ages Central Europe emerged as a region which after an early period of sociocultural rapprochement eventually came to differ from Western Europe by virtue of its specific socioeconomic, political and cultural structures. In the main, as with the previous two chapters, we shall concentrate on territory which today comprises the states of Poland, the Czech Republic, Hungary and Slovakia.

The role of Germany and the Germans in this area of Europe has long been a matter of dispute. Whilst, from the nineteenth century especially, German historians tended to portray German migrants as bearers of culture, to whom the Eastern European peoples owed a debt for having raised their standard of technological and economic development, historians from Central Europe have tended to emphasize an aggressive German *Drang nach Osten*, which began in the Middle Ages and which reached its nadir between 1939 and 1945. Such perspectives became fully crystallized at the end of the nineteenth century. On the one hand Polish and Czech national activists saw their contemporary struggles for national self-determination as simply the latest phase of a thousand-year struggle against German aggression. On the other, for their German counterparts the theory of German *Kulturträgertum* in the

East provided a justification for the policy of Germanization *vis-à-vis* the Poles in Prussia and for German imperial aspirations towards the region until the close of the Second World War.

In other words, the history of German involvement in the area came to be viewed through a set of largely inappropriate, nationalistic principles. This chapter seeks to go some way beyond such national perspectives of history by focusing on specific features of the region and especially on how German history and the history of the Central European nations have been shaped by the mutual relationship between the nations and states of Central Europe on the one hand and the Germans and the German political entities on the other. By extension, the chapter will also illustrate how the history of Silesia, as a core region of Central Europe, has been fundamentally shaped by these relationships.

Christianity and the formation of Central Europe

The origins of Central Europe as a historical region can be located in the tenth century. The factors which gave the region common features include the gradual acceptance of Christianity, the formation of medieval kingdoms, the immigration of Germans and a series of improvements in agriculture and the economy. As a result of these processes, basic religious and national features of the region emerged. The kingdoms of Poland, Bohemia and Hungary originated during this period, in which the loyalty of elites emerged with not only respect to their feudal lord, i.e. the king, but also to the political entity, as symbolized by the crown. Thus the loyalty of the feudal elites went beyond their oath of allegiance to the king, and they began to identify with, for example, the 'Crown of the Kingdom of Poland' (*Corona Regni Poloniae*), a notion which incorporated ideas about a common history and territory. This identification was further strengthened by the adoption of patron saints as Christianity spread eastward. From this starting point a direct route which led to the creation of early modern 'political' nations in the region was commenced (Graus, 1980).

The pattern of settlement of the Slavic tribes who had first arrived in the area in the fourth century AD, and which extended in the west to the Elbe and Saale rivers and the eastern Alps and as far south as modern-day Greece, was shattered in 896 by the Magyar invasion. After the conquest of the Slavic inhabitants of what became known as the Hungarian Plain and the territories adjacent to it, the Magyars adopted a settled lifestyle, any thoughts of further territorial expansion having been dealt a mortal blow after their defeat by Emperor Otto I at the battle of Lechfeld in 955. A little less than a generation later, in 997, Prince Stephen, who was later to be canonized, adopted Christianity. In the year 1000 an archbishopric was established in Esztergom. Hungary had become a part of the Christian world.

The origins of Poland can be traced back to the rule of the Piast Duke Mieszko I, who was baptized in 966 and with that act introduced Christianity to Poland. In the year 1000 an archbishopric was founded in Gniezno. In the same year the integration of Poland into the Christian world found its most powerful symbolic expression in the joint pilgrimage to Gniezno of Emperor Otto III and the Polish Duke Boleslaw Chrobry to the grave of the martyred Czech missionary St. Adalbert. Otto recognized the independent status of the Polish duke, whom he proclaimed ruler over the *Sclavinia*, which granted Boleslaw Chrobry parity of esteem with the rulers of the *Italia*, *Francia* and *Germania*. Otto III sought the renovation of the Roman-Christian universal empire under pope and emperor. In this scheme of things, the Christianized Slavs would have equal status in Christendom. After Otto's death in 1002, Boleslaw Chrobry and Otto's successor, Heinrich II, quickly became involved in a long dispute over the terms of the relationship between Poland and the empire. Nevertheless, the political and cultural inclusion of Poland in the affairs of the Christian world continued to progress, although it retained its status as an equal and independent part of the Christian world (Ludat, 1995).

Unlike in Poland and Hungary, the Premyslids in Bohemia remained vassals of the German kings. Bohemia adopted Christianity before Poland and Hungary, but no ecclesiastical independence was obtained. The Prague bishopric remained subordinate to that of Mainz. Yet Bohemia retained greater autonomy and internal unity than did other territories of the German kingdom. Already since the beginning of the twelfth century Bohemian dukes, and subsequent Bohemian kings, belonged to the most distinguished nobles of the German kingdom. Indeed in the fourteenth century under the rule of the Bohemian king and emperor of the Holy Roman Empire Karl IV, Prague became the splendid centre of the empire. Bohemia itself was, more than other larger territories of the empire, a European power of considerable strength and intensive relationships with other European states.

Whilst during the tenth century, as Poland, Hungary and Bohemia emerged as medieval states, the eastern Franconian state consolidated itself and Otto I (936–73), drawing on Carolingian traditions, strengthened the authority of the king. The threat of the Magyar invasions, the challenge of the conversion of pagans to Christianity, combined with the emergence of stronger centres of power to the east in Bohemia, Poland and Hungary were important factors in deciding Otto on this course. Thus the mutual relationships between these emerging political entities laid the foundations for the later emergence of future Central European nations and states.

However, the Slavic tribes sandwiched between the German territories to the west, and Poland and Hungary to the east, and both to the north and south of Bohemia did not adopt the Christian faith voluntarily, and neither did they create comprehensive lasting political entities. One reason for that seems to have been that they lacked the cohesive power that the organization of the church could provide. The other reason was that no stable relations with the neighbouring Christian powers existed. The conversion of these peoples was promoted by Bavarian and Saxon feudal lords. The process of conquest and conversion did not proceed in a smooth uninterrupted fashion. In fact, it was halted by the great Slavic uprising of 983 and was not resumed until the middle of the twelfth century, when the resistance of pagan Slavs and Balts was broken after the Slavic Crusade.

Clearly, the process of Christianization had a different meaning in these areas than in Poland, Bohemia and Hungary. Here it did not mean the integration into the Christian world on the basis of equality. On the contrary, the local people were conquered, and their elites were either killed or suppressed. A combination of population depletion through war, migration of Germans from west of the river Elbe and the assimilation of the remaining Slav population meant that today in those territories between the Baltic sea and Bohemia and in the Eastern Alps once populated by Slav tribes, only the Sorbs of the Lausitz in east Germany and the more numerous Slovenes to the south retain their Slavic language and identity.

After the heathen Balts of Livonia and Estonia, who had been subjugated by Germans and Danes in the thirteenth century, had been converted and 'colonized', the only major population group in Central Europe still outside the Christian world, apart from the Lithuanians, were the Pruzzen tribes. In 1226 the Polish Duke Konrad of Masowia sought to bring about the defeat and conversion of the troublesome Pruzzens by inviting the Teutonic Order to enter his territory. The knights then embarked upon a long war with the Pruzzens which eventually ended with the total defeat of the latter. As the area was pacified, the knights began recruiting colonists from the German heartlands and established a powerful state. Unsurprisingly, the Order quickly emerged as a rival to both Christian Poland and pagan Lithuania. The presence of a common enemy brought Poland and Lithuania into alliance as symbolized by dynastic personal union, and the Lithuanians converted to Christianity. The armies of the new Polish-Lithuanian Commonwealth defeated the knights decisively at Tannenberg (Grunwald) in 1410. In Poland the memory of this defeat, and the perception of the knights as the brutal incarnation of the German *Drang nach Osten* was revived in the nineteenth century and lingers in the popular consciousness to this day. The knights never recovered from the defeat of 1410, and the end of the Order was not far off. In 1525 in the course of the Reformation Grand Master Albrecht von Hohenzollern secularized the Order and the state was transformed into a Protestant duchy in vassalage to the Polish king. When the descendants of Albrecht died out in 1618, the Brandenburg line of the Hohenzollern family, who had ruled Brandenburg since 1415, inherited the duchy of Prussia. This fusion of the two territorial units signaled the rise of the Hohenzollern family and state. After the Hohenzollerns adopted the title of Prussian kings in the eighteenth century, the name 'Prussia' later came to be used for the whole state.

Thus the foundations of the two German states which were to have a profound effect upon East Central Europe in the following centuries, namely Austria and Brandenburg-Prussia, were laid during the first phase of the formation of the *Germania Slavica*, and the German assimilation of the Alpine and Elbian Slavs, and of the pagan population of the Teutonic Order's state. The term *Germania Slavica* describes the German lands which had been inhabited by Slavs, and which had come under German rule by very different ways, varying from forceful conquest to peaceful assimilation. These territories, which may also be referred to as (historical) eastern Germany, emerged as a transitional zone in the western and northern fringes of Central Europe. We now come to a second important developmental phase, which enforced the German presence in the area and which simultaneously spread the *Germania Slavica* towards Silesia and Pomerania, as well as part towards Bohemia During this process additional common features were created which resulted in Central Europe gaining a common historic and regional character.

Economic development and 'German settlement of the East'

Once again we are faced with a phenomenon which with the rise of nationalism has been reinterpreted and misappropriated in order to serve the agendas of nineteenth and twentieth nationalists. From the German perspective, the German colonists were noble missionaries who brought civilization to the backward east. From Polish and Czech side the German immigrants were presented as the foot soldiers of the continued *Drang nach Osten*. Only in the decades after the Second World War were these interpretations replaced by more sober, non-nationalistic assessments of the facts. This process of 'German colonization' is increasingly regarded as being part of an attempt by indigenous rulers to improve agriculture and stimulate commerce through the importation of both colonists and new methods of agricultural production and commercial practices from Western Europe, mainly from the German lands. For their part, the settlers expected better living conditions than they were used to in their places of origin. The so-called 'German settlement in the East' was in fact part of an economic shift which took place in the whole of Europe.

The effort to upgrade agriculture and commerce centred around the foundation of new towns and villages. The settlers were not only attracted by relatively generous grants of land in sparsely populated areas, but also by an improved legal status. The new communities were founded under the so called 'German Law'. Often, existing settlements with non-German inhabitants were refounded under such new legal codes. Not only villages and small towns were founded, but often also cities, mainly under the Magdeburg variant of 'German Law'. In most cases, the legal status of a city under 'German Law' was conferred upon established towns or other settlements. Unlike other settlements which performed the functions of cities, theses newly founded and refounded cities laid the ground for the development in Central Europe of the what Max Weber called the 'occidental city', which possessed judicial autonomy and allowed self-government of the civic community. In effect, this whole process was one of what would now be called modernization, rather than colonization or expropriation.

This aforementioned process led to significant changes in the ethnic structure of Central Europe. More territories embraced the German language, including, for example, Silesia. Interestingly, in the more easterly regions a reverse process of assimilation occurred in the late Middle Ages. Here the German immigrants for the most part assimilated into their non-German environment. So although by around 1400 the proportion of German-speaking inhabitants of Central European cities was high, with in many cases German speakers constituting a majority, by 1600 there had been a clear reversal of this trend. For example, although Cracow was probably 90 per cent German-speaking in 1400, some 200 years later German-speakers constituted only 10 per cent of the population. On the other hand, medieval German linguistic islands were for centuries preserved in the Zips in Slovakia and in Transylvania until the latter part of the twentieth century.

In Bohemia at the time in question, the settlement of Germans took place primarily in sparsely settled border zones. Again it is interesting to note that just as the Bohemian kings were encouraging German migrants to settle these border areas, so did the rulers of rival adjacent duchies. They both sought to populate their border areas with Germans in order to ensure that such areas to be settled by their subjects (German immigrants) in order to secure these territories against the competing claims of their neighbors. Given what was later to occur in the area, it is interesting to note that such policies were stimulated by non-national concerns, and national identification had no significance here.

However, the migrations and the expansion of the areas of settlement not only resulted in increased contact between different ethnic groups, but also in many conflicts. The German immigrants to Central Europe often received legal status better than that which was enjoyed by the indigenous population. In addition they were often economically powerful and culturally influential. The fact that tension resulted should not surprise us. Such tensions came to the fore most strongly in the fifteenth-century Hussite movement in Bohemia, although the Hussite movement consistently embraced German adherents. This movement combined religious, and social aims as well as objectives which can be described as Czech-national. (Kaminsky, 1967)

A further factor which contributed towards the alteration of the ethnic composition of Central Europe was the inward migration of Jews. Jewish immigration was originally occasioned by pogroms and associated anti-Semitic atrocities which since the end of the eleventh century had been stimulated by the rise of the Crusader movement. It was, however, also connected to the development of trade and a money economy in the late Middle Ages, into which Central Europe was becoming integrated. Crucially, canonical law forbade Christians from employment in professions such as banking. In need of bankers and others with similar skills, medieval potentates turned to Jews, who, being forbidden to enter into a whole range of professions reserved for Christians, naturally gravitated towards those professions they could enter. Jewish migration became part and parcel of the same developmental process which drew Germans into the cities of Central Europe. A second wave of Jewish immigration commenced when the German movement eastwards came to a standstill in the middle of the fourteenth century. It was once again triggered by pogroms, this time in Germany, where Jews were blamed for the plague of 1347–48. Above all, Poland and Lithuania became the most important centres of Jewish life in the Late Middle Ages, and it is here that Yiddish, a language based on medieval German developed (Weinryb, 1973).

The understanding of the term nation in the pre-modern era was more manifold than in modern times. It predominantly incorporated groups of a common legal status. Its most transparent feature could be found in the estate-nations. Affiliation to the nation in these cases was identical with the right of political participation and was therefore bound to the membership of political personal associations. In this way the nobility of the Holy Roman Empire of the German Nation, of the Crown of Poland or the Kingdom of Hungary saw itself as respectively constituting the German, Polish or Hungarian nation. The remainder of society could not be addressed as nation. They were for the most part illiterate peasants whose loyalties extended to their immediate family and locality, and their church. In the absence of literacy, mass communication and transportation, it could not be any different. So the term nation in such a sense could be used for the Szeklers, Saxons and Magyars in Transylvania, who had political rights of participation, but it could not be used for the Romanian population of Transylvania, who had no political representation. Another use of the term nation could be found, for example, at church councils or at universities. Here the members were divided into 'nations' on the basis of language and geographical descent with the aim of creating bodies of more or less the same size, which often had also roles in decision making processes (Schulze, 1998). This predominately political-legal concept of nation must be differentiated from the idea of nation built upon the idea of shared ethnicity. Nevertheless, ethnicity was often very significant in pre-modern times. Language and culture were also factors on which people based the their view of themselves and of the 'Other', and therefore often was an important element in conflicts. What later became a feature in the modern concept of nation in Central Europe was that the criteria for establishing national provenance were largely ethnic, and that ethnically delimited borders were postulated as being 'natural'. With that an enormous potential for conflict was created.

Decline and differentiation

As a result of the processes described in the previous section, until the late Middle Ages the political and social structures of Western and

Central Europe grew increasingly closer. As we shall now discover, from the early sixteenth century the two parts of the continent once more began to drift apart. Immanuel Wallerstein has described this division of the continent, which led to the centres of trade becoming increasingly situated in North West Europe, whilst Eastern Europe was reduced to a periphery that sent food and raw materials to the centres and as such remained economically less developed. For Wallerstein this constitutes part of the transition to the 'modern world-system' (Wallerstein, 1974). Even though Wallerstein's theory has been disputed, the fact that the political and economic divergence of the continent took place cannot. The early modern period is marked by this emergent east–west economic dualism, the internal border of Europe being more or less delineated by the course of the Elbe. With regard to agriculture, to put it simply a proto-capitalist mode of production was beginning to emerge in Western Europe, especially in the Netherlands and England. Conversely, east of the Elbe, a 'second serfdom' arose. It was here that in the course of the sixteenth and seventeenth centuries, the feudal landowners extended their own estates, often at the expense of the peasants, and thereby increasingly deprived the peasants of their rights and increased the corvée. This tendency was especially pronounced in Poland and in the German populated areas east of the Elbe.

This contrasts with, for example, the situation in England, where the landlords achieved the same objective namely to increase their income within the context of an overall decline in production – by means of the enclosure movement. Here the peasants were expropriated, with the land later being leased to a tenant. The feudal rent was thereby transformed into a capitalistic ground rent, dependent on market conditions. As we have just remarked, in Central Europe, on the contrary, a refeudalization of the agrarian production took place, and the landlords increased their income by increasing the feudal rent (Kriedte, 1980).

The result in Central Europe was that the landowning nobility emerged stronger than ever with enhanced economic and political power. Powerful estate parliaments existed throughout the region. The agricultural economy and estate democracy centred on the nobility and mutually reinforced one another. The political position of the landowning nobility enabled them to strengthen their domains and to limit the rights of peasants and of city dwellers. This in turn enhanced their economic supremacy. Such a development could be seen most clearly in Poland. Here the nobility succeeded in gradually eroding the rights of the sovereign. Upon the extinction of the Jagiellonian dynasty in 1572 Poland was transformed into an elective monarchy chosen by the nobility, which accounted for a good 6–8 per cent of the population. A distinctive factor here was the legal equality enjoyed by all sections of the nobility regardless of rank. Thus major landowners, who frequently had estates the size of small principalities and their own armies, were for the purpose of governance the equals of small noble landowners, who like peasants in fact often worked on their farms.

Similar circumstances arose in Hungary. A great many of the Hungarian nobility, in fact about 5 per cent of the population, also achieved a politically influential position. In Bohemia on the other hand, unlike in either Poland and Hungary, where the cities had been more or less politically eliminated as well as experiencing large scale economic decline from the later part of the sixteenth century, the interests of the cities continued to counterbalance those of the landed gentry. Of decisive significance to both Bohemia and Hungary was their defeat by the Ottomans at the battle of Mohacs in 1526, when the Jagiellonian King Louis II of Hungary and Bohemia was killed. As Louis lacked an heir to either crown, of which the former included Silesia, they went to Ferdinand, a brother of the Habsburg emperor. This was in fact the beginning of the ascendancy of the Habsburg empire as a great multinational power in Central Europe. However, the Habsburgs were not yet able to repulse the Ottomans. As a result of the Ottoman victory at Mohacs Hungary was divided into three. Only the western and northern parts came under the rule of the Habsburgs, with Transylvania and the Hungarian central regions coming under Ottoman sway. It was only with the defeat of the Ottomans at the gates of Vienna in 1683, in which the Polish army under King Jan Sobieski played a decisive role, that the process of expelling the Turks from Hungary began; a process which was not completed until the peace of Belgrade in 1739. With the Ottomans firmly on the retreat, the Habsburgs strove to centralize the administration of the empire and curb the rights of the Hungarian nobility. The decisions of the Hungarian parliament in 1687 and 1722/23 resulted in a more inclusive integration of Hungary into the empire, although Hungary continued to enjoy a higher degree of autonomy than other parts of the Habsburg monarchy. In Hungary itself, a rebuilding programme was started in the areas most devastated by the anti-Ottoman campaigns. Between 1720 and 1790 at least 160,000 Germans migrated to the area. However, Germans only constituted a minority among those who were settled in the devastated regions as part of a rebuilding programme.

By way of contrast to Hungary, where the nobility maintained considerable rights, the Bohemian nobility, which was for the major part Protestant, had been severely weakened by the crushing defeat of the Protestant party early in the Thirty Years War by the imperial army at the battle of the White Mountain in 1620. Now the Habsburgs were able not only to consolidate their grip on Bohemia but also to commence the Counter-Reformation in a Protestant heartland where in 1618 Habsburg anti-Protestant policies had helped trigger the Thirty Years War. Through the initial victory of Habsburg absolutism and the Counter-Reformation in Bohemia and Moravia, the German language continued to gain in status over its Czech counterpart, which descended more and more into a mere vernacular. The reduction in power suffered by the Czech nobility, and the growing cultural dominance of the Germans was later to prove a rallying point for the Czech national movement.

The rise of Prussia

The rise of the second German great power in Central Europe, namely Brandenburg-Prussia under the Hohenzollerns, gathered pace in the eighteenth century. Above all at this time, it was conducted against, and at the expense of, Austria. Between 1740 and 1763 Prussia engaged Austria in three wars over Silesia, of which Vienna finally formally ceded all but a small fragment to Prussia in 1763. Yet the rise of Prussia in the eighteenth century was only possible through a precarious cooperation with Russia which held together because they shared a common interest in obtaining control of Poland. Once the Prussians had convinced Austria that alliance with Prussia on Prussian terms would bring benefits to both, a Central European concert of powers emerged comprising Prussia, Russia, and Austria. The dynamics of this system finally led to the division of Poland which, as we shall see, with the Third Partition of 1795, was divided between Russia, Prussia and Austria. Poland was not to re-emerge as a state until 1918, and as will become clear in the following chapter, when it did, it was to lay territorial claim to Silesia.

Returning to the matter in hand, we have already noted how in 1618 East Prussia went to the Brandenburg line of the Hohenzollerns. During the Polish–Swedish war of 1655–60 Friedrich Wilhelm, 'the Great Elector', succeeded in releasing East Prussia from its vassalage towards Poland. Another way in which Friedrich Wilhelm laid the foundations for the rise of Prussia to the status of a European great power was by curtailing the rights of the nobles and in strengthening his own position. In Brandenburg and East Prussia the political rights of the estates were strong. As in Poland, the influential position of the nobility was based on the economics of the 'second serfdom' and on the export of grain. However, in contrast to the Polish example, Friedrich Wilhelm succeeded in strengthening the position of the monarch. This made it possible for him and his successors to raise substantial funds for the creation of a comparatively large standing army and thereby increasing the weight of Brandenburg-Prussia in the regional competition for power. He met greatest opposition to the introduction of absolutist government in East Prussia, where Polish influence and the 'golden liberty' for the nobles was most influential. However, by the closing years of the eighteenth century only Poland retained the traditional Central European form of noble democracy, which as we have seen could not stand against the rising power of its absolutist neighbours (Carsten, 1954).

With the defeat of Sweden in the Great Northern War of 1700–21, Russia emerged as the definitive dominant power in the Baltic region. Poland, and in particular the Polish nobility, also found themselves on the losing side in this contest for supremacy. The Polish political class proved itself to be incapable of undertaking any reforms which might have been capable of saving the Commonwealth. In essence, the absolutist or autocratic regimes of Prussia and Russia were more successful in mobilizing the resources of their respective countries than was the Polish democracy of the nobility, which over a long period of time had proven itself to be incapable of reform. In fact, those who advocated change found themselves thwarted by the Machiavellian interventions of the neighboring powers, who of course had an interest in maintaining the powerlessness of the Polish Commonwealth. The institution of *Liberum Veto* in the Polish parliament, the *Sejm*, played a fateful role here. The Commonwealth increasingly found its room for both internal and external manoeuvre subject to foreign approval. For example, in 1721 Russia was granted the right to intervene in any attempts to change the Polish constitution.

Prussia had previously given its assent to Russia domination over (parts of) Poland. It now became Russia's partner in Poland, although the alliance was to break down temporarily during the Seven Years War, when Russia joined in with Austria in an attempt to curb the power of Prussia, and in particular to reverse Prussian control of Silesia, almost all of which it had seized from Vienna in 1742. Fortunately for Frederick the Great, at the moment of his incipient defeat the Russian

Czarina died, and her successor retreated from the war in Prussia. At the resulting peace of Hubertusburg in 1763, the acquisition of Silesia by Prussia was confirmed. Prussia was now a power to be reckoned with. Austria and its Saxon allies had been put in their place. Russia's interest in having Prussia as partner in its indirect rule of Poland had proven to be decisive (Zernack, 1991).

The first partition of Poland occurred in 1772. It was stimulated by the competition for power between the three hegemonic great powers in Central Europe. For Austria it provided some compensation for the Russian presence in most of Poland, which had already been further entrenched in 1768. It was also the price for further support from Russia in a war with the Ottoman empire Austria was engaged in. Prussia had much to gain from such a deal, because it enabled the Hohenzollern state to create a land bridge between its Brandenburg heartlands and East Prussia and in doing so to gain control over Poland's Baltic Sea trade. Therefore, Prussia took the lead in brokering the deal. In Poland itself, the shock of division at last stimulated efforts seriously to reform the structures of the state. The result was that on 3 May 1791 the *Sejm* passed the first modern codified constitution in Europe. Even if this attempt to fend of its enemies failed, the constitution did at least stimulate the process of Polish nation-building, precisely because it sought to enfranchise the wider population. These reformist endeavours, which of course were stimulated by the examples of France and America, met not only with internal resistance, but also aroused fears among Poland's enemies that the French example might be emulated on their very borders. Russian pressure, together with internal resistance, became so great that in fact the reforms of 3 May were to a large extent reversed. In the course of these events Russia and Prussia annexed another chunk of Polish territory in 1793. This time partition stimulated a full-scale rebellion led by Tadeusz Kosciuszko, whose defeat brought about the final division of Poland between Russia, Prussia and Austria in 1795 (Müller, 1984).

For Poland, the partition meant also the end of Central European estate-democracy, as Polish society entered into a phase of modernization and increased opportunities for social classes other than the nobility. The old conception of nation and of citizen, which was confined solely to the nobility, changed under the influence of the Enlightenment towards a concept of nationhood and citizenship which included all inhabitants of the country. In the late nineteenth century, the reform movement of the latter part of the eighteenth century became an important point of reference, as the Polish national movement strove to develop a concept of the Polish nation based on the idea of self-determination of the people.

With the division of Poland, so the division of the continent was complete. Central Europe was now ruled by the absolutist powers of Russia, Prussia and Austria, whilst liberal-civic national formations were being gradually realized in the west of the continent, principally in France, Britain and the Netherlands. In this respect Germany belonged to the eastern part of the continent. Also the two 'half-German' absolutist great powers Prussia and Austria, buttressed by their conservative alliance with Russia, the so-called 'Holy Alliance', stood against the formation of a democratic German nation-state. They made it impossible to embark upon German nation-building in a democratic manner, as was demonstrated by the failure of the revolution of 1848. Eventually the aim of the German national movement, i.e. the creation of a German nation-state, was realised by Prussia in the wars against Austria in 1866, which resulted in the exclusion of the latter power from Germany, and France in 1870–71. Through the realization of a German-nation state which in effect represented little more than the political and territorial expansion of Prussia, so the imperial Prussian role in Central Europe became incorporated within the new state. For Prussia the re-establishment of a Polish state was unacceptable, precisely because important parts of its territory would have reverted to Poland, and with that it would have lost weight within Germany as a whole. Such considerations formed the backdrop to the implementation of policies after 1871 which led to the intensification of the suppression of Poles in Prussia, and which simultaneously contributed to the radicalization of German nationalism in the *Kaiserreich*. In contrast to imperial German nationalism, the nationalism of the Central European national movements assumed a more emancipatory and democratic character. In this respect, Polish nationalism was closer to the French model than to the German. The denial of the right of self-determination to the Poles, an intensified policy of Germanization toward the end of the nineteenth century, combined with the processes of modernization, resulted in the fact that national identification became more important for a growing number of people. The competing and contradictory claims over territory and entire population groups from one hand the Polish and on the other the Prussian-German side were bound to lead to conflict.

The application of such abstract principles gave rise to competing and contradictory claims over territory and entire population groups. The territory of Silesia, which the Prussians had gained in 1742, and which in previous centuries had been the province of the Austrians, Poles and Bohemians, was to become an object of desire for both Polish and German nationalists. In Upper Silesia in particular, which in common with the whole of Silesia had not been a part of a Polish state since the Middle Ages, there emerged among the indigenous population toward the end of the nineteenth century, ever-stronger national identification with either Poland or Germany. Silesia became an arena within which the Prussian-German state and the Polish national movement pursued their respective aims, and as such was to be a theater in which these contradictions were thrown into the sharpest relief.

Bibliography

Carsten, F., *The Origins of Prussia*. Oxford, Clarendon Press, 1954.

Conze, W., *Ostmitteleuropa. Von der Spätantike bis zum 18. Jahrhundert*. Munich, Beck, 1992.

Evans, R., *The Making of the Habsburg Monarchy 1550–1700*. Oxford, Oxford University Press, 1979.

Fata, M., 'Einwanderung und Ansiedlung der Deutschen (1686–1790)', in G. Schödl (ed.), *Land an der Donau*. Berlin, Siedler, 1995.

Graus, F., *Die Nationenbildung der Westslaven im Mittelalter*. Sigmaringen, Thorbecke, 1980.

Hagen, W., *Germans, Poles, and Jews: The Nationality Conflict in the Prussian East 1772–1914*. Chicago, University of Chicago Press, 1980.

Kaminsky, H., *A History of the Hussite Revolution*. Berkeley, University of California Press, 1967.

Kann, R., *The Multinational Empire: Nationalism and National Reform in the Habsburg Monarchy 1848–1918*, 2 vols. New York, Octagon, 1964.

Kann, R. and David, Z., *The Peoples of the Eastern Habsburg Lands, 1526–1918*. Seattle, University of Washington Press, 1984.

Kriedte, P., *Spätfeudalismus und Handelskapital. Grundlinien der europäischen Wirtschaftsgeschichte vom 16. bis zum Ausgang des 18. Jahrhunderts*. Göttingen, Vandenhoeck u. Ruprecht, 1980.

Ludat, H., *An Elbe und Oder um das Jahr 1000: Skizzen zur Politik des Ottonenreiches und der slavischen Mächte in Mitteleuropa*. Weimar, Böhlau, 1995.

Maczak, A. et al. (eds), *East Central Europe in Transition from the Fourteenth to the Seventeenth Century*. Cambridge, Cambridge University Press, 1985.

Meyer, H. C., *Drang nach Osten: Fortunes of a Slogan in German-Slavic Relations: 1849–1990*. Bern, Lang, 1996.

Müller, M., 'Deutsche und polnische Nation im Vormärz', in K. Zernack (ed.), *Polen und die polnische Frage in der Geschichte der Hohenzollernmonarchie 1701–1871*. Berlin, Colloquium, 1982.

Müller, M., *Die Teilung Polens 1772–1793–1795*. Munich, Beck, 1984.

Naumann, F., *Mitteleuropa*. Berlin, Georg Reimer, 1915.

Schlesinger, W. (ed.), *Die deutsche Ostsiedlung des Mittelalters als Problem der europäischen Geschichte*. Sigmaringen, Thorbecke, 1975.

Schulze, H. *States, Nations and Nationalism: From the Middle Ages to the Present*. Oxford, Blackwell, 1998.

Seibt, F., *Deutschland und die Tschechen: Geschichte einer Nachbarschaft in der Mitte Europas*. Munich, Piper, 1997.

Subtelny, O., *Domination of East Central Europe: Native Nobilities and Foreign Absolutism 1500–1715*. Kingston, McGill-Queen's University Press, 1986.

Walicki, A., *Philosophy and Romantic Nationalism: The Case of Poland*. Oxford, Clarendon Press, 1982.

Waliicki, A., *The Enlightenment and the Birth of Modern Polish Nationhood*. Notre Dame, University of Notre Dame Press, 1989.

Wallerstein, I., *The Modern World-System: Capitalist Agriculture and the Origins of the European Economy in the Sixteenth Century*. London, Academic Press, 1974.

Wandycz, P., *The Price of Freedom: A Short History of East Central Europe to the Present*. London, Routledge, 1993.

Weinryb, D., *The Jews of Poland: A Social and Economic History of the Jewish Community in Poland from 1100 to 1800*. Philadelphia, Jewish Publication Society of America, 1973.

Wippermann, W., *Der Ordensstaat als Ideologie: Das Bild des Deutschen Ordens in der deutschen Geschichtsschreibung und Publizistik*. Berlin, Colloquium, 1979.

Wippermann, W., *Der 'deutsche Drang nach Osten': Ideologie und Wirklichkeit eines politischen Schlagwortes*. Darmstadt, Wissenschaftliche Buchgesellschaft, 1981.

Zernack, Z., *Osteuropa. Eine Einführung in seine Geschichte*. Munich, Beck, 1977.

Zernack, K., *Preußen-Polen-Deutschland. Aufsätze zur Geschichte der deutsch-polnischen Beziehungen*. Berlin, Duncker & Humblot, 1991.

Zernack, K., 'Polen in der Geschichte Preußens', in O. Büsch (ed.), *Handbuch der preußischen Geschichte, ii*. Berlin, de Gruyter, 1992.

Zernack, K., *Polen und Rußland: Zwei Wege in der europäischen Geschichte*. Berlin, Propyläen 1994.

4
Silesia and the Dawning of the Modern Era[1]

Some observations on the nature of Silesian identity

Most theorists of nationalism contend that in Europe prior to the end of the eighteenth century, what we now label as national consciousness did not exist (Gellner, 1983; Hobsbawm, 1983; Anderson, 1991; Hroch, 1968). Historians usually make the same observation with regard to Silesia. Conventional wisdom holds that during the course of the nineteenth century the inhabitants of Lower Silesia came to identify themselves with Germany, and in Upper Silesia identification with either Poland or Germany became the norm. Our study will show that in Silesia, from the beginning of the sixteenth until the early years of the nineteenth century, a Silesian consciousness dominated over allegiance to either a German or Polish identity. In order to demonstrate this hypothesis and to understand the nature of the society which the Prussians acquired when they annexed Silesia in 1740, we must first make some observations concerning the nature of identity in Silesia whilst it was still ruled by the Habsburgs.

The writings of Silesian historians such as Joachim Curaeus (1532–73), as well as those of the clergy and politicians, together with actions undertaken by individual Silesians as well as the Silesian estates, confirm the hypothesis that from the sixteenth century there existed a high level of civic patriotism. For example, Curaeus expressed his national consciousness through verse which extolled Silesia: 'How comes it I do not understand/that one has the Fatherland/So much and and so dearly kind/that it never leaves the mind?' (author's translation), and even demanded from his countrymen that they should honour the fatherland more than their own parents. In order to contextualize such sentiment within a broader European perspective, we can point to the fact that the nobility of the First Polish Republic, together with the estates of Bohemia and their Swiss and Dutch counterparts, also possessed a national consciousness during this period (*Nationsbewußtsein*) which can be compared to that of the Silesians. Various factors account for this state of affairs having come about in Silesia. They included the economic prosperity of the region, in particular the growth of mercantile capitalism which nurtured the growth of a literate and politicized urban bourgeoisie which came to articulate an economic and political agenda, and the opportunity to participate in the governance of Silesia via the Silesian estates (*Schlesischer Fürsten-und Ständetag*). The estates were a parliamentary body to which the bourgeoisie, the Silesian princes and other nobility, together with the clergy, sent elected representatives. From the end of the sixteenth century the bourgeoisie succeeded in extracting political concessions from the aristocracy, the Habsburg emperors, and importantly also began to 'think Silesian'. The work of Curaeus bears this out. He describes the specific characteristics of Silesia, the extent of its territory, the nature of its autonomy and privileges within the Habsburg empire, and even in classic primordialist fashion, traces the ancestors of the contemporary Silesians to the dawn of history itself (Curaeus, 1601: 1–23). In other words Curaeus affirmed the existence of a specific political nation of Silesians with its own indigenous rights based on history and autonomy. It was another Silesian historian, Jacob Schickfuß, who in 1625 used the term 'people' (*Volk*) to describe the Silesians (Schickfuß, 1625: 8).

Throughout the seventeenth and the first half of the eighteenth century, historians in Silesia, the most important of whom were Lichtstern, Thebesius and Köhler, utilized Curaeus' belief in a common Silesian ancestry to identify, chart and construct a specific Silesian national history. They chronicled how Silesia had broken with the Polish Crown in the 1330s, and described subsequent events in a way which not only emphasized the distinct nature of Silesian society, but as with Curaeus, reinforced the notion of Silesia's special status within the Habsburg empire. Of course different historians represented different constituencies. Some stressed the importance of the princes and the wider nobility, others the importance of the townsmen. What unites all these historians of the Habsburg period is that they developed a political programme combining freedom of conscience, and confirmed Silesia's right to autonomy and self-governance.

At times the bourgeoisie and the Silesian princes, to a lesser degree other sections of the nobility and peasantry, undertook actions aimed at achieving the political goals expressed by the above-mentioned writers. Throughout the entire Habsburg period the Silesian estates extracted major concessions from the Habsburgs. The estates obtained these concessions mostly by financial means. They paid taxes to the Habsburgs as well as making voluntary contributions to the imperial treasury, and in return received political concessions. During the Thirty Years War of 1618–48 a substantial number of Silesians took up arms in defence of their 'fatherland'. In 1622 several thousand peasants in the county of Glatz died defending their territory against imperial Catholic troops. Other examples of civic action during the Thirty Years war are verified by eyewitness reports. Such actions underline the contemporary viability of the Silesian political nation. Hence, the example of Silesia confirms the hypothesis of Benedikt Zientara 'that the difference between the formation of modern nations and earlier forms of national bondage before the eighteenth century lies in the quantity, but not in the quality' (Zientara, 1996: 21).

Silesia reached the zenith of its power on the eve of the Thirty Years War. After some hesitation, the Silesian estates sided with their rebellious Bohemian counterparts against Ferdinand II. They did so because they wished to preserve both their autonomy and tradition of religious freedom from a centralizing emperor who wished to destroy both secular and religious dissent. However, the victory of the imperial forces at the battle of White Mountain in 1620 signalled the waning of Silesian power and the total defeat of the Bohemian estates. With the benefit of hindsight we can also say that it signalled the end of any possibility that Silesia might ever emerge as a nation-state in the contemporary sense of the term and thus follow the path of the Swiss and the Dutch. Despite promises by the emperor that in return for financial indemnities he would honor Silesian privileges, after 1636 Ferdinand and his successors deprived the estates of most of their power.

The demographic and economic effects of the war were perhaps even greater than the political consequences. In some areas up to two thirds of the population was dead. In addition, the emperor's policy of Counter-Reformation and re-Catholicization drove the Silesian bourgeoisie into exile in their thousands (Jaeckel, 1982: 63). In the absence of an indigenous political competitor the aristocracy recovered both economic and political power. The cities declined not only because of the policies of the emperor but also because the Swedish invasions of Poland and the decline of the Polish Republic disrupted trade with the east. In addition, at this time the commercial center of Europe moved to the western part of the continent. As a result in terms of economic and political development, Silesia became more clearly a part of Central-Europe. In such circumstances the development of a Silesian nation under the auspices of political autonomy proved to be impossible. However, the memory of Silesia before 1620 remained and provided a point of orientation for Silesian scholars and political activists. They scored one last victory when they extracted major concessions from the emperor in the Convention of Altranstadt in 1707. Although the protagonists of the Silesian cause were primarily Protestant, Catholics such as Johann Peter Wahrendorff also rallied to the cause. This shows that the political nation of Silesia was attractive beyond denominational and linguistic boundaries. The fact that an individual might have spoken Polish, Czech or German as a first language did not exclude anybody from membership of this nation.

Despite the fact that Polish speakers were not discriminated against, the aforementioned historians were keen to counter the view of some Polish writers who held that Silesia was a historic Polish territory. The former insisted that the Silesian Piasts had voluntarily acceded to the sovereignty of the Bohemian Crown, and also pointed to variations in socio-economic and political structures which served to differentiate Poland from Silesia. In particular, the Polish nobility was criticized as being overly interested in the acquisition of money, titles and honour to the detriment of the country as a whole (Gdacjusz, 1969: 285–60).

In fact Gdacjusz, the most important early modern Silesian who wrote in Polish, did not describe Polish speaking Silesians as Poles, but referred to them as *Wasserpolowie,* or literally 'Water Poles'. He emphasized the differences between the Polish/Slavic Silesian dialect and standard Polish, and claimed that this dialect was frowned upon by Poles themselves as being 'un-Polish' (Gdacjusz, 1969: 146). It was during this time that the linguistic and cultural influence of other parts of the German-speaking world upon Silesia grew, as armies entered from Saxony, Bavaria and elsewhere. Indeed as a consequence of the Thirty Years War and its aftermath, the definition among the Silesians themselves as to who constituted the 'other' seems to have undergone a gradual shift. In the early stages of the war Protestant Swedes and others were welcomed as liberators from the oppressive rule of a Catholic despot. However as the war and Counter-Reformation continued, so identification with 'Germany' grew. This phenomenon came about for a number of reasons. First, as we have noted, both the Silesian princes and in particular the bourgeoisie had been weakened after the defeat at the White Mountain in 1620. Secondly, those representatives of Silesia who remained Protestant needed to cultivate links with German principalities in order to countervail pressure from the emperor (Weber, 1992: 99). Finally we might add that the conduct of the Swedish troops and other foreign invaders caused widespread revulsion and a solidarity of German speaking Silesians against invaders who did not speak German.

Closer contact with the various parts of Germany brought about a change in perception concerning the identity and the provenance of the Silesians. Whilst some continued to cling to the perceptions of Curaeus and Schickfuß, others such as Thebesius strove to prove the Germanic roots of the Silesians (Thebesius, 1733: 3–9). Despite growing links between Silesia and the rest of the German-speaking world, on the whole Silesian identity and consciousness remained unaffected by linguistic points of reference until the late eighteenth century. Rather, what counted was identification with the territory, social station and religious denomination, with the importance of the latter gradually decreasing as the aftershocks of the Thirty Years War gradually petered out. Although there was a general reluctance to assign Silesians to either the Polish or the German national group, Lichtstern and Köhler divided Silesia into a German and a Polish part, with the River Oder forming the border between the two (Lichtstern, 1685: 782; Köhler, 1710: 9). Having said that, both sought to avoid categorizing any part of the population with either putative nation, and for most Silesians Bohemia still remained their most important point of external reference. One can conclude that throughout the Habsburg period there was continuous identification with the Silesian political nation. Although possibilities to establish autonomy and to participate in self-governance decreased, the Silesians still held to a specifically Silesian idea of an imagined community as a point of collective and individual reference.

Enter Prussia

The course of the first Silesian War demonstrates the frail nature of the bonds between the Habsburgs and the Silesians. The population tended to avoid taking part in the defence of the province, with the Habsburg cause receiving wider support only in parts of Upper Silesia (Popiolek, 1956: 67–70). On the other hand, we should not equate apathy towards the Habsburgs with enthusiasm for Prussia and Frederick II.

During his long reign, in Silesia as elsewhere in his kingdom, Frederick II above all sought to modernize. The remaining political rights which resided with the Silesian estates were removed, and a modern civil service was introduced (Baumgart, 1993) Silesia also began to industrialize. Blast furnaces first appeared in Upper Silesia in the 1750s, and the promise of regular work attracted migrants from the villages in their thousands. Industrial growth was however limited, owing to Silesia now being cut off from its former trading partners to the east and the south and by structural problems enhanced by Prussian economic policy. It was also further restricted by the consequences of both Silesian Wars and the subsequent Seven Years War.

In the countryside, the peasants suffered as a result of the aristocracy's ability to reinforce its power. Although Frederick had originally said that he wanted to improve the lot of the peasantry, his wariness of the aristocracy meant that projects for social reform were placed on the back-burner (Baumgart, 1994: 458). Inevitably conflict occurred between the aristocracy and a peasantry which was impoverished and overburdened by taxation. In the south-eastern part of Upper Silesia this state of affairs was at its worst. Both land inheritance laws and exceptionally high tax burdens saw sections of the peasantry driven to perdition. This helps explain the later popularity of the Polish cause among the peasantry of this region. The peasantry had not received any benefits as a result of the transfer of power from Vienna to Berlin. Also it was in precisely these areas that resistance to the Prussians had been greatest in 1741, as the local Catholic population mobilized to defend their Catholic emperor against a foreign Protestant king. The overall situation in Upper Silesia and the attitude of the peasantry in particular, contributed to the growth of an increasingly negative attitude on Frederick's part toward all things Polish and Catholic. In Lower Silesia the situation was markedly different. Frederick turned to an early form of public relations campaign (Conrads, 1990: 223) and made frequent visits to enhance local identification with Prussia. Although he succeeded in becoming popular especially among the nobility and Protestant clerics, Frederick failed to fashion a Prussian consciousness among the wider populace. To the distaste of Prussian state servants, most Silesians still identified themselves exclusively with Silesia. As the Silesian historian Johannes Ziekursch pointed out in his study of the most important periodical in Silesia at the turn of the eighteenth and nineteenth centuries, the *Schlesische Provinzialblätter*: 'It constantly talks only about Silesia, as if it were an independent country on a lonely island in the middle of a vast ocean' (Zierkursch in Gerber, 1955: 92).

A marked change in the collective consciousness of the population of Silesia arrived with the Wars of Liberation in the wake of

Napoleon's lost war against Russia. This time Silesians did not simply passively stand by; rather they actively participated in the expulsion of the French (Bartsch, 1985: 203). With the final defeat of Napoleon in 1815, the German national movement had been invigorated. Silesian identity now had to compete with inclusive and all-embracing German identity. Whereas in 1814 Silesians were still mainly interested in commemorating Silesian war heroes and the liberation of Silesia, in 1815 they wanted to celebrate German heroes and the liberation of Germany (see the debates in the *Schlesische Provinzialblätter* of 1814/15, in Gerber, 1995: 353–5). Patriotic fervour grew among all sections of society, especially the bourgeoisie. More and more Silesians became aware of the fact that they were members of a political entity that was much greater than their home region, and that they shared a chapter of history and a common language with other inhabitants of this territory (Baumgart, 1994: 873). Although this outpouring of national pride enthused Catholics and Protestants alike, it did not mean that Silesians now primarily regarded themselves as Germans or Prussians, or indeed both. The national euphoria of 1815 faded as suddenly as it had begun.

During this time, national identification became increasingly dependent upon language. In the late 1820s there was a wave of public demands to give the German language general precedence over Polish. In common with all absolutist states of the period the Prussians had been pursuing linguistic harmonization within the public service, but the new demands emanating from the German bourgeoisie went well beyond that (Hahn, 1988: 24). The Prussian authorities began to persecute the Catholic Church, which functioned as a major pillar of Polish culture and language. In May 1833 an order was issued in which it was stated that if in the opinion of the secular authorities, a congregation had become too small, then Catholic churches must be closed. This applied much more to Polish/Slavic speaking communities than it did to German speakers. The Prussians had become convinced that the reasons for Upper Silesia's comparative backwardness were to be located within the national character of its inhabitants. The chosen solution was to 'civilize' the Upper Silesians by introducing the German language and culture and by breaking their bond with Catholicism. This policy met widespread resistance from an increasingly self-conscious Polish speaking populace, and was an inadvertent foretaste of the hard-fought struggle for hearts and minds which in the twentieth century was to blight the whole of Silesia and in Upper Silesia in particular.

The struggle for hearts and minds

By the 1840s a veritable 'language battle' had broken out (Gerber, 1995: 325). In 1846, the Silesian born historian Heinrich Wuttke released a book with the title 'Poles and Germans; Political Reflections', in which he demanded the 'Germanization of the entire population'. As far as he was concerned those who refused to cooperate should leave Prussia (Wuttke, 1846: 91). Wuttke sought to justify the continuing division of Poland and declared himself against the right of self-determination, precisely because the granting of such a right would be based upon the principles of democracy and majority rule, which he also opposed. This publication was in fact an early demonstration of what was later to prove to be a deadly combination of devotion to Prussia, German nationalism and hostility towards democracy and Catholicism. Several prominent Silesians attempted to defend both Polish Silesians and Poles in general against such antagonistic attitudes, but civil disturbances in Poznania in 1846 led to a further hardening of views on the Polish question on the part of German liberals and conservatives.

In Upper Silesia in particular the condition of the peasantry continued to worsen as the aristocracy consolidated more and more land. In addition as the industrial working-class grew in size so did its impoverishment (Pierenkemper, 1992). This was particularly so for the weavers of the mountain ranges situated in the south of Lower Silesia. Resultant social tensions increasingly manifested themselves in the shape of attempted rebellions. Silesia therefore came to be considered to be the 'restless province' (Herzig, 1994). In Upper Silesia, social barriers in part corresponded to the German–Polish linguistic border. The small upper class consisted of landowners, many of whom became industrial magnates in the nineteenth century, higher civil servants and army officers from Prussia. This strata of society was faced with first a rural and then also with an urban proletariat, which mainly comprised of Polish Silesians. After 1840 more and more Poznanian i.e. Polish literature found its way into Upper Silesia. However, the expectations of Polish nationalists that Upper Silesia would be fertile soil for their project were as yet a little too high. Upper Silesia's Polish or bilingual population mainly lived in the countryside, and as elsewhere in Central Europe the enthusiasm for national movements among the peasantry lagged behind that of urban dwellers (Hroch, 1968: 138 ff.). In fact many Upper Silesians were ashamed about the non-German elements of their culture, and attempted to submerge such features in the cause of 'social advancement'. Given that Poland did not actually exist as a state, Polish-oriented Upper Silesians also lacked a firm territorial frame of reference upon which they could pin their hopes. However, the German national movement was becoming ever more clearly defined in ethno-linguistic terms, and in Prussia especially once again in denominational terms. The result was that Polish/Slavic speakers were becoming increasingly alienated from the state in which they lived.

It is worth pausing at this point to take stock of the situation in Silesia on the eve of 1848. The consciousness of Silesians had undergone a radical shift since the sixteenth century. In the early modern period, national consciousness was political in nature and until the beginning of the nineteenth century oriented toward Silesia. Only from the beginning of the nineteenth century did German national consciousness play a major role, submerging and subordinating the Silesian consciousness of German speaking Silesians. By 1848, a new notion of national identity was beginning to emerge in the area. Previous notions of loyalty to a sovereign, and territorial and political identification with the territory of Silesia were under threat. As a new definition of nationhood arose, so many Silesians felt themselves to be excluded from the German nation as now defined. A discussion of how these issues were resolved is to be found later in the narrative. As we are about to see, external as well as internal forces were once again to play a major role in shaping the destiny of the region.

National awakening in Prussian Silesia

The origins of the modern nation-state are to be found in Tudor England, and were later given full philosophical and political expression during the American War of Independence and in revolutionary France prior to Napoleon's armies' bearing the message of nationalism throughout Europe. The momentum of France's eastward expansion brought about the final collapse of the of the moribund Holy Roman Empire. It also gave the inhabitants of the former empire their first glimpse of 'the other'. One of the most important consequences of the Napoleonic Wars was the gradual rise of German nationalism on the basis of Herderian thought. In fact, the first attempt to give substance to the German national movement came with the War of the Fourth Coalition (1813–14) against the French Empire, which in Germany soon became known as the as the War of Liberation.

The war commenced at the Silesian capital of Breslau. Whereas Silesia bore witness to one of the initial manifestations of German nationalism, nationalist ideology did not leave a lasting impression on what was then a Prussian province, it having been suppressed after the Congress of Vienna in 1806 which restored a semblance of the ancien regime. In fact, nationalism only re-entered Silesia in the wake of the revolutionary events of 1848. In the three decades between 1815 and the so-called 'Springtime of Nations', the idea of a German-nation state had been kept alive in western German provinces which bordered the newly established nation-states of France, Belgium and The Netherlands. Also during this period, in 1831–2 and 1846 the Polish *natio* (nobility) had failed in its attempts to restore the Commonwealth of Poland-Lithuania. Paradoxically, their failure set the scene for the emergence of modern Polish nationalism which sought to unite all putative Poles within a single nation-state. What is more, in the 1830s Prussia, drawing on the French example in conjunction with Herder's ideas on language as developed by von Humboldt, toyed with the possibility of homogenizing its population through the medium of the standard German language (Davies, 1981: 132). Industrialization and urbanization, together with the social and legal reforms of the Napoleonic period, facilitated the implementation of this project. The resultant mobility had drawn Prussia's inhabitants out from the rural periphery and into the urban centres, a phenomenon which in turn was bound to promote greater identification with the provinces and the Prussian state.

The springtime of nations

In 1848, the social unrest ignited by the February Revolution in Paris quickly spread westward, leading to the uprising in Berlin and the occurrence of disturbances throughout Silesia, especially in Upper Silesia. The urban poor demanded better living conditions whilst the peasantry demanded the final abolition of serfdom, which despite the rapidly increasing pace of industrialization remained strongly entrenched in Upper Silesia. Yet it should be made clear that talk of combining democratic representation with the establishment of a German nation-state was limited only to a narrow stratum of liberal-minded academics, civil-servants and intellectuals who earned 1848 the nickname of 'the revolution of professors'.

Hence the elections to the German National Assembly at Frankfurt aroused little interest among the workers and peasants of Silesia. In part this apathy was engendered by rudimentary political Catholicism, which viewed nationalism as being incompatible with the universal message of the Church. The Catholic clergy also viewed with suspicion any political movement which might result in the creation of a Protestant dominated *Kleindeutschland*.[2] The Catholic Church was also fully aware of the fact that the majority of its adherents in Silesia were Upper Silesian Slavs who had little command of *Hochdeutsch* and whose status in such a Germany would be uncertain. These people spoke various western Slavic dialects closely related to standard modern Polish and Czech.[3] Indeed, at the National Assembly in Frankfurt, by way of recognition of this linguistic reality, Fathers Jozef Szafranek and Cyprian Lelek respectively demanded limited official recognition of standard Polish and of the west Slavic dialects of the Moravecs in the Ratibor and Leobscütz counties of Upper Silesia. Indeed, in the second half of the 1840s a handful of Polish-language periodicals began to appear in Upper Silesia, and Lelek himself published a Moravian language textbook for Moravian speakers in the southern part of Prussian Upper Silesia.

The Catholic Church espoused such goals in order better to communicate with the faithful, and in order to satisfy their socio-political aspirations. At that time the Catholic and Protestant churches together controlled and staffed the educational system. In the Olmütz archdiocese of southern Upper Silesia, Lelek's endeavours resulted in the establishment of bi- and monolingual schools in which the Moravian dialect was employed as the medium of instruction. Similarly, standard Polish became the medium of instruction in bi- and monolingual Upper Silesian elementary schools in the other predominantly non-German-speaking areas. The system was completed with the establishment of Polish teacher training colleges and compulsory Polish language lessons at the Breslau diocesan seminary. This development was facilitated by the strong historical links between the Catholic Church in Silesia and the Polish archdiocese.

In what turned out to be a move of crucial importance for the Polish national movement, Father Bernhard Bogedein, who as school councillor of the Oppeln Regency, i.e. Upper Silesia, was charged with introducing these sweeping changes, could not find local teachers versed in standard Polish and so imported them from the Province of Posen (Swierc, 1990: 8). This decision was important because it contributed to the later forging of direct links between Upper Silesia and Posen which was the center of the Polish national movement in Prussia. Initially however, the genesis of Polish national sentiment in Upper Silesia was more apparent in Austrian East Silesia in the form of the Polish/west Slavic press.

Toward a German nation

The first attempt at forging 'clear-cut' national groups in Prussia came with the census of 1861 in which the 'nationality' of the respondent was determined according to linguistic self-assignment. The census disregarded cases of bilingualism, and in addition employed the arbitrary categories of 'German', 'Polish', 'Moravian' and 'Bohemian' which lumped together speakers of various dialects as speakers of standard languages. Thus having been constrained to answer this question in line with general assumptions on nationality, an arbitrary definition of national provenance was created. The census purported to show that Lower Silesia was overwhelmingly German, with an additional 50,000 Polish, 30,000 Sorbian and 10,000 Bohemian-speakers (Kokot, 1973: 20, 74–5). Upper Silesia was shown to be much more linguistically/ethnically diverse with a total of 420,000 German, 665,000 Polish and 51,000 Moravian-speakers (Triest, 1864: 33–4).

The census also showed that that Silesia had a non-Catholic majority, with only 47 per cent of the province claiming to be Catholic (Bahlcke, 1996: 94). Catholics were heavily concentrated in Upper Silesia and were overwhelmingly Slavic speakers, unlike Protestants, who overwhelmingly spoke German. Thus in the Bismarckian Reich created in 1871, Upper Silesia along with Bavaria became the natural stronghold of political Catholicism. In the wake of the establishment of the Second Reich, Bismarck attempted to forge national integration by various means. These included taking over the educational system as well as the registry of births, marriages and deaths from the Catholic Church, and attempting to limit its social and political role. In 1873, the so-called *Kulturkampf* was complemented in ethnically heterogeneous areas by the banning of languages other than German from the educational sector and all spheres of public life controlled by the state.

Subsequently, the Church and Slavic-speaking Catholics of Upper Silesia became close allies against a state which had turned against people who had previously identified themselves as Prussians. The Catholic Church was allowed to continue to use standard Polish and Moravian during sermons at masses, as well as during confession and in religious instruction whilst the faithful mobilized in favour of the *Zentrum*. Despite having abandoned the *Kulturkampf* in 1886–7, Bismarck's policies had turned the *Zentrum* into the largest single party in Silesia and into *the* party of the Oppeln Regency. They also contributed to making it the second strongest in the Reich as a whole. The *Kulturkampf* also inadvertently fostered the birth of the Polish and

Moravian-language press. The rise of the press and its lasting influence was of course also due to the almost total disappearance of illiteracy, but we should not underestimate the depth of alienation caused by the *Kulturkampf*.

Following the cessation of the *Kulturkampf*, the Church began to give tentative support to the nation and state-building endeavours of Berlin. As a result the *Zentrum* gradually ceased to represent the interests of Slavs in Upper Silesia and elsewhere. In so doing it created a political vacuum which came to be filled by the Polish and Czech national movements. The former proved to be especially significant due to numerous links established during the *Kulturkampf* between the Posen Catholic hierarchy and various Polish societies and national activists in Upper Silesia (Kulak, 1990: 64). From the 1890s the Polish national movement began to penetrate Upper Silesia and more especially the industrial cities of eastern Upper Silesia, where they established publishing houses, periodicals, libraries and various associations which strove to spread Polish national consciousness among Polish speakers.

The Polish national movement had gained further room for maneuver as a consequence of the relaxed attitude taken toward it by Caprivi's administration of 1890–94. In addition, in 1893 a rift appeared in the Upper Silesian *Zentrum* when the Polish-speaking *Katolik* faction emerged. Also at about this time, the few Upper Silesian Polish speakers studying subjects other than theology at Breslau university became influenced by Polish students from Posen who had established branches of two clandestine nationalist organizations in the Silesian capital. Albert (later Wojciech) Korfanty, who was subsequently to play a decisive role in Upper Silesian politics, belonged to the inner circles of both organizations, and in 1903 with their support won a mandate to the *Reichstag* from an Upper Silesian constituency voicing radical socialist and anti-*Zentrum* slogans.[4]

The entry of Poland

Korfanty´s victory marked the decisive arrival of Polish nationalism into Upper Silesia, despite the best efforts of the *Zentrum*. Polish activists continued with their endeavours to create Polish national consciousness in the industrial towns of Upper Silesia. By 1914 they had established almost 500 organizations with a claimed membership of nearly 45,000. They also had succeeded in establishing numerous Polish-language reading rooms/libraries, which attracted over 85,000 patrons between 1911–12 (Michalkiewicz, 1985: 331–40). Although hard-core activists numbered no more than 120 individuals (Molik, 1993: 77), in 1905 the German authorities reacted in a heavy-handed manner by banning the use of all languages other than German as the medium of religious instruction throughout Silesia. In 1908 they went even further and implemented a series of measures which among other things attempted to ban the use of Polish and Moravian at public meetings.

This hardline approach had been brought about by a number of factors, apart from sheer distaste for all things Slavic in general and Polish in particular on the part of sections of the imperial elite. First, the Reich was, in common with all other putative nation-states, seeking to homogenize the population. It was also seeking to stem the *Ostflucht* of primarily German-speakers to the industrial centres from the backward provinces of Pomerania and East Prussia which lay east of the rivers Elbe and Oder. Last but by no means least, Berlin was petrified lest Polish nationalists make common ground with the revolutionary movements in Czarist Russia. In short, the government hoped that by taking such measures, Polish nationalism would lose its appeal, and the eastern parts of the Reich would retain a German character.

Unsurprisingly, the ever-increasing tempo of industrialization in eastern Upper Silesia meant that the area did not suffer from the *Ostflucht*. On the contrary, between 1850 and 1910, the population soared from 106,389 to 833,676. In other parts of Upper Silesia a similar situation could be witnessed, and census data indicates that the region as a whole was attracting an increasing number of Germans from other parts of the Reich (Stüttgen, 1976: 327). Yet despite this phenomenon (Catholic) Slavs continued to predominate over German-speaking Protestants, a fact which was to prove a continued source of irritation for the authorities. Moreover, immigration was not simply limited to Germans. The promise of work in the Upper Silesian industrial basin prompted the migration of Polish speakers from the Province of Posen as well as Austrian and Russian Poland, and so helped to maintain the Slavic majority in the area.

The geopolitical context of Austrian Silesia

It is now appropriate to switch our focus to that small part of Silesia that remained with Austria after the Silesian wars, and the transfer of the remainder of the territory to Prussia. Our analysis begins with the year 1848 and ends with the outbreak of World War One. In terms of intellectual content, the most important point is this. During the period in question, a society was under transition. As feudal-aristocratic structures increasingly came to be challenged, so individual and collective criteria of identification were altered. As we shall see, in the case of what in 1918 became Czech Silesia, conflicting Polish, Czech and German identities came to the fore. Let us now return directly to the matter in hand.

The revolutionary events of 1848 affected the countryside of Austrian Silesia more than they did the urban areas. What rapidly became an uprising spread across the region, eventually also affecting urban areas (Gawrecki, 1992a: 59–60). On 31 August 1848, by way of recognition of the seriousness of the problem, the Imperial Diet adopted a law on the abolition of obligatory labor, which the Emperor Ferdinand signed on 7 September. However, this did not satisfy the peasantry, and unrest continued to grow. Eventually rural unrest was quelled for two reasons, first because Vienna acceded to their basic demands, and secondly because the peasants themselves had failed to present comprehensive demands for the wider democratization of society.

As for the towns, the revolutionary events were of varying intensity. The fall of absolutism and of the implementation of a new constitution were positively received, and townspeople temporarily immersed themselves in a flurry of revolutionary activity. German democrats and liberals who desired the absorption of the Habsburg Empire within a new German state were particularly prominent. In a foretaste of what was to follow over the next one hundred years, they found themselves in conflict with the demands of the nascent Czech national movement, which was agitating for self-determination of the Czech part of the empire. In the wake of these pressures, defenders of monarchical absolutism made a series of concessions, which resulted in among other things, an extension of the franchise to the bourgeoisie. In addition, the elections to the Frankfurt parliament in 1848 were met with marked enthusiasm on the part of the German population of Austrian Silesia, who returned seven deputies to said body.

During this period, members of the Czech national movement limited their activities to a campaign for solidarity among Slavs and to support for the emerging Polish national movement. The facts that Opavsko region of Austrian Silesia was not represented at the Slavic congress in Prague and that some Czechs came out against the Congress, indicate that at the time the Czech national movement was less developed than its German counterpart. In fact the Slavic population of Austrian Silesia was represented by Polish delegates at the congress, although Czechs were present as guests (Grobelny, 1958: 47–104).

On the ground, revolutionary guards were dispatched from Austrian Silesia to aid insurgents elsewhere in the empire, but imperial troops soon restored order. However conservative absolutism was never fully to recover. Moderate liberal politicians came to the fore, although the conditions for the overall growth of democratic political life as well as for the Polish and Czech national movements were somewhat restricted by the partially successful counter-revolution. Yet a discernible process of Czech and Polish nation building continued to proceed. Activists demanded the introduction of Czech and Polish languages to schools and that both languages be used in the conduct of official business. Tesin became the centre of the Polish national movement and looked to Cracow for guidance, whereas the Czech movement tended toward Opava.

In terms of representational reform, 1848 brought about changes to the Silesian *Landrat*. It was enlarged to include nine representatives of the nobility and nine from the towns and countryside. Later the number of deputies in each curia increased to sixteen. The assembly drafted a new constitution which was proclaimed on 30 December 1849. However, it was never implemented in full, and on 31 December 1851 the newly self-assured monarchy struck back and declared all such constitutions to be null and void (Grobelny, 1958: 61–109).

Instead Vienna appointed a governor to Austrian Silesia, who in turn in 1853 was transformed into a *Land* president. Territorial boundary changes then proceeded apace. In the period between 15 November 1860 and 29 March 1861, Silesia was again temporarily united with Moravia. After this date it once again became an autonomous *Land* within the Monarchy, although competencies and internal administrative boundaries continued to be tampered with almost at will. The introduction of universal male suffrage in 1907 guaranteed Silesian deputies fifteen mandates to the imperial parliament in Vienna. The demarcation of election districts constituted an act of deliberate discrimination, as a much higher number of votes were needed to elect a Czech or Polish deputy than to elect a German counterpart.

Ethnic identification and the growth of population

If we now turn to other matters, we find that the population of Austrian Silesia was developing fast, especially in industrial areas. In

1869 it had 438,585 inhabitants and by 1890 the population had grown to 605,649. The industrialization of Austrian Silesia manifested itself also in the professional and social composition of Silesia's population. As late as 1860, the agricultural component prevailed over its industrial counterpart. Yet by 1900 the situation had been reversed; 239,000 individuals were materially dependent on agriculture, 313,000 on industry, 52,000 on trade with almost 77,000 being employed in the public services and free professions (Gawrecki, 1992a: 61). With regard to the religious composition of the population, the percentage of Roman Catholics steadily grew as Polish migrants entered the area seeking work, as did the number of Jews. By 1910 84.4 per cent was reckoned to be Roman Catholics, 13.6 per cent Protestant and 1.8 per cent Jewish.

Although there had been a census question on national affiliation since 1880, once again the results are rather unreliable because the decisive bureaucratic criterion for determining nationality was the so-called language of general intercourse. Given that German was in fact the sole such language in the area, the number of registered Germans was inflated to include who spoke German alongside their mother tongue. This and other practices, the consequences of which were to promote the germanization of the entire population, led to confusion over how many Poles and Czechs lived in the area. According to an estimate of 1857, 51 per cent of the population of Austrian Silesia was Slavic, 48 per cent was German and 1 per cent Jewish. By 1910, 180,000 people (24.3 per cent) declared Czech to be their language of general intercourse, 235,000 (31.7 per cent) declared that they spoke Polish as their first language, and 326,000 (43.9 per cent) declared German to be their language of choice. Such results demonstrate that despite the best efforts of imperial officialdom, within the population itself identification with the Czech and Polish movements was growing. Unfortunately we do not know how much this was due to continuing migration, especially from Poland, any more than we have any clear idea of how census officials chose to classify ambiguous data.

Returning to matters more explicitly political, the 1860s saw arise in liberal influence, especially in town councils. Another characteristic feature of the period was that increasing numbers of people were involved in political life in general and in the workers' movement in particular. Various political currents and movements began to form, although traditional interests continued to be present. Other increasingly pervasive features of political life were attitudes to the monarchy and the growing strength of nationalism. The use of German as the language of public administration led to the Germanization of Slavic sections of society, a phenomenon which, as we have already noted, Czech and Polish activists strenuously opposed.

German liberals asserted themselves mainly in urban areas and created their own press. In smaller towns and mountain areas conservative and clerically oriented political streams prevailed and the Agrarians also began to gain influence. Unsurprisingly German politicians in Silesia mostly supported Prussia during war with France (1870–71), and remained indifferent to the defeat of Austria by Prussia in 1866. In the 1880s, a differentiation among German liberals became apparent. The position of the left can be characterized as being simultaneously both more radical and nationalistic. Modern hyper-nationalism and anti-Semitism made their debuts in the 1890s. Nationalistic groups around the weekly *Deutsche Wehr* and after 1907, those based around the journal *Neue Zeit,* split from the progressive liberals. Proto-German National Socialism was represented by the *Nordmark* society.

In the midst of this nationalist competition, ethno-national movements specific to the region also began to appear. Hlucinsko became a stronghold of Catholic clericals, who had some sympathy with demands for linguistic parity from the *Moraveci*. So-called *Slonzakovci* became active in Tesinsko from the 1860s. They demanded local autonomy, exhibited a pro-German orientation and a dislike for the Polish national movement, as was evidenced in a string of periodicals they published up until the early years of the twentieth century.

The Polish and Czech national movements

The 1850s saw the first real flowering of the Polish national movement. The publication of the first Polish textbook for Polish schools in 1854 and of a Polish hymnbook in 1857, became palpable symbols for the Polish national movement. In the 1870s and 1880s a number of Polish educational and economic associations were established. This active policy paid off by way of the securing of Polish national representation in the Silesian *Landrat*. However, neither Czech nor Polish deputies managed to gain any significant influence in that organ. In the late 1870s tensions began to appear in the Polish national movement. This was evidenced by the establishment of a rival Protestant association *Polityczne Towarzystwo Ludowe* (People's Political Association) in opposition to the *Towarzystwo katolicko-politiczne Ksiestawa Cieszynskiego* (Catholic-Political Association of Tesin) which had been founded in 1873. At the end of the nineteenth century, the town of Frystat became a centre of activity of radical Polish nationalists who evinced a marked anti-Czech bias. Yet disappointment for the Polish national movement followed the elections to the Imperial parliament of 1907. In Austrian Silesia, social democrats swept the board, with only one candidate from the Union of Silesian Catholics preventing them from gaining every seat on offer. This defeat prompted a rethink in the Polish camp and in 1911, the *Polskie Zjednocenie Narodowe* (Polish National Union) was born. This party formed a coalition with the Polish clericals in the elections to the Imperial Diet of 1911 and gained a single mandate, which in itself can hardly be claimed to have been any kind of triumph, and indicates just how weak notions of national identity still were among huge sections of the populace (Grobelny, 1992: 61–75).

The Czech national movement in Opava Silesia began to develop more purposefully from the 1860s largely thanks to the activities of the Opava-based professor Antonin Vasek. A clear surge in the activities of Czech nationalists can be perceived from the 1870s. In 1877 *the Matice opavska* (Opava Foundation) was established and it was not long before purely Czech educational, song, theatre, and even firefighters societies began to appear. In addition, various business societies and associations were formed. In 1881 Czech sermons were renewed in Church of St. George and one year later in Opava, the first Czech kindergarten was started. Perhaps most importantly, in 1883 in Opava, the first Czech High School in the whole of Austrian Silesia was founded by the aforementioned Opava Foundation (Pavelcik, 1983: 70–73).

By the turn of the century, a creeping polarization of the population became apparent, as ever more successful nationalist elites pressed forward with increasingly incompatible demands. In the latter half of the nineteenth century, the Czech national movement in Tesinsko concentrated its activities in Frydek, where the *Cesky ctenarsky spoke* (Czech Literary Society) was formed. In 1908 an independent weekly *Obrana Slezska* (Defense of Silesia) commenced publication in Orlova, and concerned itself with politics in Tesinsko. It also occasionally printed the *Vlastivedna priloha* (Regional History Supplement) which was designed to introduce its readers to the Czech version of the history of Tesinsko. Opava came to assume the mantle of the coordinating centre of the Czech national movement in Austrian Silesia by playing host to the Silesian branch of *Narodni rada ceska* (The National Czech Council), and the *Starostenske sbory slezske* (Silesian Mayoral Corps).

As in other parts of the empire, in the latter part of the nineteenth century, workers' societies, often led by priests, were formed. After a law on associations was adopted at the end of 1860s, a number of societies were created to promote the self-help theories of Schultz-Delitsch, which later came into conflict with newly formed societies of a socialist orientation. Due to the prevalence of the textile industry, workers' organizations were formed in places with a concentrated textile production. The town of Krnov thus became a centre of the socialist movement, and the Brantice municipality near Krnov became the organizational centre of all socialist societies in Silesia as well as in northern parts of Moravia. The years of economic crisis which followed, brought about the persecution of workers' movements as well as ideological conflicts within the socialist camp. In fact, the socialist movement did not become widespread until the late 1880s, and more especially after 1 May 1890. The growth of industrialization (steel works, mines) and the related social situation contributed to the fact that Ostravsko now became the centre of the workers' movement. The years 1894, 1895 and 1896 saw mass workers' demonstrations and in 1900 a general strike was organised. However, significant differences of opinion and personal conflicts were prevalent among the activists, and often they were not unrelated to questions of national identity. The fact that the Czech, German and Polish social democrats produced separate newspapers indicates that national solidarity overrode class considerations. The turn of the century saw the growing influence of party political organisations; workers' cooperatives and sport and education movements began to flourish. The increasing influence of social democracy is shown by the election in 1897 of two social democratic deputies to the Imperial diet. After the introduction of universal suffrage, social democrats dominated in Tesinsko, and they gained several mandates in Opavsko as well. The workers' movement in Silesia was strongly influenced in its development by a significant dispute between autonomists and centralists. The tension between autonomists and centralists gained in intensity. Czech trades unionists were accused by their Polish counterparts of attempting to promote the Czechization of Polish workers and suspended all contact with them. Most significantly for the future, nationally oriented socialist parties began to grow in strength and so reinforce the growing ethnic cleavage.

Cultural life and political change

During this time, the cultural maturity of the populace increased. Illiteracy was eliminated before the First World War. It had been especially high in Austrian Silesia as a consequence of mass migration from

Galicia during the nineteenth century. In 1880 only 73.6 per cent of adult population in Silesia was literate. By 1910 the figure was 94.2 per cent. This expansion in mass literacy was directly linked to the growth of mass education. In 1860, there were nine secondary schools with a total of 3,400 pupils, and 410 first-level schools with 61,300 pupils. By 1911 there were 562 primary schools with 109,305 pupils and 40 secondary schools with 6,399 pupils. In the latter category, six were Czech-language schools, one was Polish and 33 were German. Alongside this system of educational apartheid, the pressures to Germanize continued, as German was invariably the language of post-secondary education. It is also important to note, with reference to understanding what happened in the area between 1918–1948, that the population at large was actively participating in the creation of a situation that was in no way conducive to foundation a nation-state in the area built upon notions of civic consciousness (Gawrecki, 1992a: 63).

World War One paralysed normal political and social life. The militarization of industry was begun in the autumn of 1914. There were differing reactions to the outbreak of the war. Germans tended positively to accept war at the side of Wilhelmine Germany. Poles expected the restoration of Poland. The attitude of Czechs toward the war was negative. They sympathized with Russia and hoped for the defeat of the Central Powers. Many a Czech Silesian in fact volunteered for service against the armies of the Central Powers. Inevitably, as the war dragged on the supply situation worsened, the price of food and other goods rose and with them so did the dissatisfaction of the populace. In 1916 and 1917 protest demonstrations occurred throughout the region. The outbreak of revolution and the fall of Czarism in Russia fueled disaffection and anti-war demonstrations. From the second half of 1917, under the influence of the above-mentioned rallies, political life was renewed. The Silesian *Landtag* and various municipal authorities publicly declared their continuing support for the German character of Silesia. In August 1917, a joint Czech/Polish conference took place, in an effort to promote a joint anti-German strategy. However, the participants' ideas of Silesia's post-war destiny were diametrically opposed. The Poles promoted the fusion of Teschen with Galicia. Czechs were in favour of the integration of Austrian Silesia into the new hypothesized Czechoslovak state. The Bolshevik coup in Russia and the negotiations in Brest Litovsk led to further mass anti-war agitation. Ideas of national self-determination and social liberation inspired broad masses of people, and were reflected in the general strike of 15 October 1918 in Austrian Silesia and elsewhere in the rapidly disintegrating empire.

Ethnic identity in Upper Silesia on the eve of war

Having made these observations on the overall political, industrial and ethnographic character of Upper Silesia at this time, it is appropriate for us to make some more detailed observations on the identity of the people of this region. This is important for a number of reasons. First, it will enable us to increase our understanding of the nature of ethnogenesis, both in general terms and also as a phenomenon specific to the case. Secondly, it will help us to understand the contemporary nature of identity in Upper Silesia, and help explain why even today Central Europe as a whole is still something of an ethnic patchwork.

In contemporary Upper Silesia, a large majority of the population identifies with Poland. However, both the rate of migration to Germany since 1945, the presence of a large German population, together with the continued presence of smaller ethno-linguistic groups, reinforces the fact that, as a borderland, Upper Silesia has never been fully penetrated by any of the strategic ethnies and nation-states which have laid claim to it. By 1871 most of the indigenous inhabitants considered themselves to be Silesians and Prussians. In Lower Silesia especially, German-speaking Protestants had acquired a German national identity which coexisted together with the aforementioned regional identities.

The ethno-national border between the increasingly German section of the population and the Slavic-speakers of Upper Silesia was as in medieval times reinforced by the ecclesiastical boundaries. Those who adhered to the *Deutschtum* came to consider Slavic-speakers to be 'uncivilized', and both groups shared a stereotypical dislike of Poles and Galicians. Given that most Upper Silesians today see themselves as Poles, the change in perception further reinforces the notion that national identity is just as much a construct as is every other form of (collective) identification.

Moreover, prior to the birth of the Polish national movement, Poles from *Wielkopolsksa* did not regard Upper Silesia's Slavic speakers as Poles, referring to them simply as *Odraks*. As a result, prior to the emergence of modern nationalism, and in fact sometimes in parallel with it, Upper Silesian Slavs developed identities which were dependent more than anything else upon older ecclesiastical boundaries. Those who lived within the diocese of Breslau were dubbed *Wasserpolacken* by the Germans, although they referred to themselves as *Szlonzoks*. In the Upper Silesian section of the Olmütz diocese, on the other hand, *Moravecs* who spoke Moravian began to emerge.

Moravecs were also to be found across the border in Austrian Silesia, but the two groups were separated from one another by German-speaking settlements. What is more, the former group were peasants who until 1918 hardly ever ventured outside their immediate neighbourhoods, unlike the *Szlonzoks* who participated in the urbanization and industrialization of Upper Silesia, and who came to develop a specific west Slavic German creole. In turn the development of this creole served to separate this group from the *Slonzaks* of east Austrian Silesia, who despite their Protestantism, acquired a Polish orientation from the latter half of the nineteenth century.

With the promotion of German national identity members of all these groups came to identify with Germany, especially if they had received a further or a higher education. However, those who only completed elementary school and who also served in the German army, simultaneously came to identify themselves as Germans and *Szlonzoks*, or as Germans and *Moravecs*. This phenomenon was eventually to receive official recognition through the introduction of a bilingual/binational rubric on census forms.

In short, many Upper Silesians eventually came to consider themselves to be simultaneously German and Polish. However, such self-assignment should not be construed as having been a badge of national identity in the modern sense of the term. It was only from the 1880s with the arrival of the Polish national movement that contemporary notions of national identity began to appear in German-ruled Upper Silesia. Indeed, in areas of Upper Silesia which the Czechoslovak national movement laid claim to, no parallel movement occurred among the *Moravecs* until 1918.

Following the collapse of the Central European empires at the end of the first World War, one of the few things to unite Czechoslovak, German and Polish nationalists was the perceived hypocrisy of Upper Silesians who from the ethno-nationalist perspective seemed to change their identities according to whoever happened to be talking to them at the time. To students of nationalism as a phenomenon, this should come as no surprise. However, German, Polish and Czechoslovak nationalists were wedded to an idea of primordial national identity which implied national identity was somehow genetically predetermined. Thus when they were confronted with people whose collective consciousness was not monistic but multiple, and as such contradicted the shibboleths of primordial nationalism, small wonder that they failed to understand the situation, and came to regard Upper Silesians with a degree of hostility and suspicion. It is to the consequences of that fateful encounter that we now turn.

Bibliography

Anderson, B., *Imagined Communities: Reflections on the Origin and Spread of Nationalism*. London and New York, Verso, 1991.

Bahlcke, J., *Schlesien und die Schlesier*. Berlin, Langen Müller, 1996.

Bartsch, H., *Geschichte Schlesiens. Land unterm schwarzen Adler mit dem Silbermond. Seine Geschichte, sein Werden, Erblühen und Vergehen*. Würzburg, Weidlich, 1985.

Baumgart, P., 'Provinz Schlesien. Schlesien als preußische Provinz zwischen Annexion, Reform und Revolution (1741–1848)', in G. Heinrich et al. (eds), *Verwaltungsgeschichte Ostdeutschlands 1815–1945. Organisation-Aufgaben-Leistungen der Verwaltung*. Stuttgart: Kohlhammer, 1993.

Baumgart, P., 'Schlesien als eigenständige Provinz im altpreußischen Staat (1740–1806)', in N. Conrads (ed.), *Deutsche Geschichte im Osten Europas*, iii: *Schlesien*. Berlin, Siedler, 1994.

Borak, M., 'Tesinsko v letech 1938–1945', in Kol. autoru, *Nastin dejin Tesinska*. Ostrava, Advertis, 1992.

Chlebowczyk, J., *Nad Olza. Slask Cieszynski w wiekach XVIII, XIX i XX*. Katowice, Slask, 1971.

Conrads, N., *Die Durchführung der Altranstädter Konvention in Schlesien 1707–1709*. Cologne, Böhlau, 1971.

Conrads, N., 'Politischer Mentalitätswandel von oben. Friedrich II. Weg vom Gewinn Schlesiens zur Gewinnung der Schlesier', in P. Baumgart et al. (eds), *Kontinuität und Wandel. Schlesien zwischen Österreich und Preußen, Ergebnisse eines Symposiums in Würzburg vom 29. bis 31. Oktober 1987*. Sigmaringen, Thorbecke, 1990.

Conrads, N., 'Schlesiens frühe Neuzeit (1469–1740)', in Conrads (ed.), *Deutsche Geschichte im Osten Europas*, iii: *Schlesien*. Berlin, Siedler, 1994.

Curaeus, J., *Newe Cronica des Herzogthumbs Ober- und Nieder Schlesien: Warhaffte und grüntliche beschreibung von dem Namen, Ursprung ... Geschichten und Tadten der alten Schlesien*. Leipzig, Grosse, 1601.

Davies, N., *God's Playground: A History of Poland*, iii: *1795 to the Present*. Oxford, Clarendon Press, 1981.

Dietrich, R., 'Der preußische Staat und seine Landesteile in den politischen Testamenten der Hohenzollern', in P. Baumgart (ed.), *Expansion und Integration. Zur Eingliederung neugewonnener Gebiete in den preußischen Staat*. Cologne and Vienna Böhlau, 1984.

Gawrecki, D., 'Vyvoj Hlucinsaka do r. 1945', in *Ideologicka konference k 60. vyroi navraceni Hlueinska k ceskoslovensym zemim*. Opava, Profil, 1980.

Gawrecki, D., 'Slezsko po roce 1742 (1848–1918, 1918–1938)', in Kol. autoru, *Slezsko*. Opava, Matice slezska, 1992 (a).

Gawrecki, D., 'Tesinsko v obdobi mezi sviitovymi valkami (1918–1938)', in Kol. autoru, *Nastin dejin Tesinska*. Ostrava, Advertis, 1992 (b).

Gdacjusz, A., 'Wybor pism' in H. Borek and J. Zaremba (eds), *Warszawa*. Panstwowe Wydawnictwo Naukowe, 1969.

Gellner, E., *Nations and Nationalism*. Ithaca, Cornell University Press, 1983.

Gerber, M. R., *Die Schlesischen Provinzialblätter 1785–1849*. Sigmaringen, Thorbecke, 1995.

Grobelny, A., Cesi a Polaci ve Slezsku v letech 1848–1867. Ostrava, Krajske nakl., 1958.

Grobelny, A., 'Tesinsko od jara narodu k samostatnym statum (1848–1918)', in Kol. autoru, *Nastin dejin Tesinska*. Ostrava, Advertis, 1992.

Hahn, H., 'Die Gesellschaft im Verteidigungszustand. Zur Genese eines Grundmusters der politischen Mentalität in Polen', in Hahn (ed.), *Gesellschaft und Staat in Polen. Historische Aspekte der polnischen Krise*. Berlin, Spitz, 1988.

Hensel, J. A., *Johann Adam Hensels protestantische Kirchengeschichte der Gemeinen in Schlesien*. Leipzig, Siegert, 1768.

Herzig, A., 'Die unruhige Provinz. Schlesien zwischen 1806 and 1871', in N. Conrads (ed.), *Deutsche Geschichte im Osten Europas*, iii. Berlin, Siedler, 1994.

Hobsbawm, E. J., *Nations and Nationalism since 1780: Programme, Myth, Reality*. Cambridge, Cambridge University Press, 1983.

Hroch, M., *Die Vorkämpfer der nationalen Bewegung bei den kleinen Völkern Europas. Eine vergleichende Analyse zur gesellschaftlichen Schichtung der patriotischen Gruppen*. Praha, University of Karlova, 1968.

Jaeckel, G. (ed.), *Thebesius, Georg, Geschichte der Liegnitz-Brieger Piasten (1733)*. Lorch, Weber, 1982.

Kamusella, T., 'The Emergence of National and Ethnic Groups in Silesia 1848–1918'. Draft PhD, n.d.

Köhler, J. D., *Schlesische Kern-Chronicke oder kurtze jedoch gründliche geographisch-historisch- und politische Nachricht von dem Hertzogthum Schlesien*. Nuremberg, Hein, 1710.

Köhler, J. D., *Der Schlesischen Kern-Chronicke anderer Theil*. Frankfurt and Leipzig, Buggel, 1714.

Kokot, K., *Problemy narodowosciowe na Slasku od X do XX wieku*. Opole, Instytut Slaski, 1973.

Kulak, T. (ed.), *W strone Odry i Baltyku. Wybor zrodel (1795–1918)*, iii: *O ziemie Piastow i polski lud (1795–1918)*. Wroclaw, Volumen, 1990.

Lichtstern, F., *Schlesische Fürsten-Krone*. Frankfurt, Knoch, 1685.

Michalkiewicz, S. (ed.), *Historia Slaska*, iii: *1850–1918*, pt 2: *1890–1918*. Wroclaw, Ossolineum, 1985.

Molik, W., 'The Elites of the Polish National Movement in Prussian Poland in the Late 19th and Early 20th Centuries', *Polish Western Affairs* 2, 1993.

Pavelcik, J., 'Narodnostni boje na Opavsku', in Kol. autoru, *Poehled dejin Opavska*. Opava, Profil, 1983.

Pierenkemper, T. (ed.), *Industriegeschichte Oberschlesiens im 19. Jahrhundert. Rahmenbedingungen-Gestaltende Kräfte-Infrastrukturelle Voraussetzungen-regionale Diffusion*. Wiesbaden, Harrassowitz, 1992.

Popioek, S., 'Stosunek Ludnosci slaskiej do zaj cia Slaska przez Prusy w latach 1740–1763', *Kwartalnik Opolski* 1, 1956.

Schickfuß, J. (ed.), *Curaeus J, New vermehrete schlesische Chronica und Landes Beschreibung*. Leipzig, Schürer, 1625.

Schieder, T., *Friedrich der Große: Ein Königtum der Widersprüche: Frankfurt* a. m., Propyläen, 1983.

Stüttgen, D. et al., *Grundriß zur deutschen Verwaltungsgeschichte 1815–1945* Ser. A: *Preußen*, vol. 4: *Schlesien*. Marburg (Lahn), Johann-Gottfried-Herder-Institut, 1976.

Swierc, P., Ks., *Bernard Bogedain: 1810–1860*. Katowice, Muzeum Slaskie, 1990.

Thebesius, G. and Scharffen, B. G. (eds), *Liegnitzische Jahrbücher*. Jauer, Jungmannen, 1733.

Triest, F., *Topographisches Handbuch von Oberschlesien*. Breslau, Korn, 1864.
Wahrendorff, J. P., *Lignitzische Merckwürdigkeiten*. Budißin, Richter, 1724.
Weber, M., *Das Verhältnis Schlesiens zum Alten Reich in der Frühen Neuzeit*. Cologne, Böhlau, 1992.
Weczerka, H. (ed.), *Schlesien (Handbuch der historischen Stätten Deutschlands* xiv*)*: Stuttgart, Kröner, 1977.
Wuttke, H., *Polen und Deutsche: Politische Betrachtungen*. Schkeuditz, Blomberg, 1846.
Zientara, B., *Swit narodow europejskich*. Warsaw, Panstwowy Instytut Wydawniczy, 1996.

Notes

1. In this chapter Philipp Ther wrote on Silesia in the pre-national era. Tomasz Kamusella on German Silesia, and Petr Kacir on Austrian Silesia.
2. *Kleindeutschland* (Little Germany), was the German nation-state created in 1871, which deliberately excluded Austria, and as such was decisively Protestant in ethos.
3. In German Silesia up until 1918 the written language most commonly used in Moravia and Austrian Silesia, although being similar to Bohemian Czech was termed Slavic or Moravian. Contemporary Czech was itself only codified in the mid-nineteenth century.
4. Like so many others, Korfanty's father had migrated from Galicia to Silesia.

5
Upper Silesia 1918–45[1]

With the outbreak of the First World War, the German authorities interned a number of pro-Polish activists. Consequently as elsewhere in Germany, the activities of various political organizations, including those of Polish nationalists, came to a standstill, and regardless of ethnicity the population was mobilized for war. The attempt to unite the population was enhanced by conscription, and in Upper Silesia by military supervision of industry coupled with fear of a possible Russian incursion into Germany. This threat became more tangible when at the close of 1914 Russian troops entered East Prussia and almost broke into the Oppeln Regency. With plans for the mass evacuation of civilians and for the destruction of factories and mines in place, the situation was saved by Field Marshal Paul von Hindenburg's successful counteroffensive. In the wake of popular relief, and in order to demonstrate Upper Silesian loyalty to Germany, the Upper Silesian industrial town of Zabrze was renamed Hindenburg in 1915 (Bahlcke, 1996: 121–2).

When in early 1915 hopes for a swift conclusion to the conflict were dashed, and the war of attrition set in, Berlin and Vienna changed tack in an attempt to ensure the loyalty of their Polish-speaking subjects. On 5 November 1916 the 'Kingdom of Poland' was proclaimed. However, the kingdom was little more than a legal fiction. Polish nationalist activists refused to have anything to do with it on a number of grounds. First, neither its status, competencies nor territory were spelled out. Secondly, they gambled correctly that Austria-Hungary and Germany would lose the war, and that Russia would be exhausted by it. So they chose to bide their time in the hope of taking advantage of the situation when hostilities finally ceased. As the war dragged on Polish nationalist activity revived. This overall revival was also apparent in Upper Silesia, although it was not as marked as in other parts of Germany with a substantial Polish population.

The deteriorating state of the economy was made worse by the severe winter of 1916–17, which brought hunger and even starvation. The highly volatile social situation resulted in growing opposition to the continuation of the war and numerous strikes, which among other things forced the government to concede electoral reform and the relaxation of censorship. In Upper Silesia the wartime prohibition against conducting religious instruction in Polish was lifted in 1917. From the second half of that year, Polish deputies to the Reichstag began to voice the hitherto novel idea of self-determination for Poland (Kwiatek, 1991: 35–7). Help for the Polish cause then appeared from two different quarters

The outbreak of the October Revolution, preceded as it was by the radicalization of the situation in Russia following the February Revolution and abdication of the Czar, emboldened the revolutionary left in Germany. Then on 8 January 1918 US President Woodrow Wilson proclaimed the Fourteen Points which set the general conditions of the would-be peace, accepted the national principle as the basis of the political organization in Europe, and provided for re-establishment of the Polish state. Bolstered by growing international support for Polish-self determination, on 11 January during a session of the Prussian *Landtag*, Korfanty demanded stronger protection of national minorities throughout Germany. His hand was further strengthened on 6 June following his election to the *Reichstag* for an Upper Silesian constituency. From this elevated position he now began to demand that Prussian-German territory should form a constituent element of an independent Poland (Kwiatek, 1982: 241). Korfanty showed that he was a proponent of the so-called 'Piast concept' which the prominent Polish nationalist Roman Dmowski had popularized in the 1890s. It envisaged the creation of a Polish nation-state that would include substantial chunks of Germany. As such it clashed with the older 'Jagiellonian concept' supported by Jozef Pilsudski, which sought the re-establishment of a federal Poland roughly within its pre-partition borders.

The re-establishment of Poland

The short respite the Central Powers gained after the conclusion of the Treaty of Brest-Litovsk on 3 March 1918 was not sufficient to prevent the gradual collapse of Austria-Hungary. As the old empires entered their final days, the independence of Czechoslovakia was proclaimed. The new state incorporated the Czech national programme, which demanded the re-establishment of the union of Bohemia, Moravia and (Austrian) Silesia. The Catholic *Zentrum* began to demand autonomy for the region in the hope of limiting the lure of the social democrats, and found ready support among Upper Silesian Catholics. On 9 December 1918 the party (renamed in Upper Silesia as the *Katholische Volkspartei*, KVP, Popular Catholic Party), with the support of local industrialists, called for independence of Upper Silesia, causing the president of the Oppeln Regency to declare all such activity treasonable. The threat of execution did not stop the spread of the separatist movement but rather caused it to split into two branches. Hans Lukaschek with the further support of the KVP agitated for the autonomy of Upper Silesia within Germany, while the *Zwiazek Gornoslazakow/Bund der Oberschlesier* (ZG/BdO, Association of the Upper Silesians) demanded the creation of an independent bilingual state (Cimala, 1982: 23).

The ZG/BdO quickly gained a membership of around 150,000 (Wanatowicz, 1994: 25). Most of them were Catholic *Szlonzoks* who spoke a western Slavic dialect, and whose staggering support they gave to the organization showed that demands of the ZG/BdO reflected the wants and needs of the *Szlonzoks* in the postwar period. However, they lacked external support, and Berlin and Warsaw used them as mere pawns in an increasingly fraught situation. Politicians in both capitals were at least united in the belief that only Germans and Poles lived in Upper Silesia, and that *Szlonzoks*, if they existed at all, did so only as members of one of the wider national groupings. For good measure, the Allies were also at one on this score.

However, the Poles were not yet ready for a confrontation, as they were occupied in the east fighting the Ukrainians and the Soviets in order to consolidate the 'Jagiellonian concept' canvassed by Pilsudski. The situation had not gone unnoticed in Prague, and during a swift attack between 23–30 January 1919 the Czechoslovak army enlarged Prague's share of East Silesia at Poland's expense (see below). Above all they sought to ensure control over the whole Ostrau-Karwin industrial basin, which was the only supply of coal and steel for the Czechoslovak state.

Meanwhile at Versailles the Polish government, backed by France, sought to further as much as possible its claims against Germany. On 7 May 1919 the draft of the Peace Treaty was presented to a German delegation, which was appalled (among other things) at the proposed surrender of most of Upper Silesia principally to Poland, with southern areas designated to Czechoslovakia. They claimed that the area was inhabited by Germans, *Szlonzoks* and *Moravecs,* and that the latter two groups did not identify themselves as either Poles or Czechs as claimed by Warsaw and Prague. They also pointed that Upper Silesia had rarely been under any form of Polish rule, and that the transfer of Upper Silesia to Poland would make it even more difficult for Germany to cope with the burden of reparations. The United Kingdom agreed with this line of argument afraid that the European balance of power could tilt too much in favor of France and its Central European clients against a weak and unstable Germany. They also feared that the possible acquisition of the Dombrowa, Upper Silesian and Ostrau-Karwin industrial basins by Poland would unduly strengthen the former *vis-à-vis* Czechoslovakia and Germany. Thus, in 1920, the Allies decided to grant the whole of East Silesian Ostrau-Karwin basin to Prague, even though this left 70,000 Poles/Polish-speakers in Czechoslovakia (Gawrecki, 1992: 85). Fatefully, they also decided to conduct a consultative plebiscite in Upper Silesia in order to facilitate the final decision on its ultimate destiny.

When the Treaty of Versailles came into force on 10 January 1920, Germany lost about 70,000 square kilometres of its territory and over seven million inhabitants. In Silesia the losses were limited to 512 square kilometres of sparsely populated fragments drawn from four Lower Silesian counties, together with the 316 square kilometres of the southern part of the Hultschiner Ländchen which resulted in around 40,000 *Moravecs* being transferred to Czechoslovakia (Bahlcke, 1996: 126).

On the basis of Article 88 of the Treaty of Versailles, the plebiscite area was to include almost all of Upper Silesia minus several of its western counties which were not claimed by Warsaw, together with a fragment of one Lower Silesian county. The German administration was duly evacuated from this area, and on 11 February the Inter-Allied Commission headed by the French general Henri Le Rond took over the plebiscite area. By this time, inter-communal relations had plumbed new depths. The first (Polish) Silesian Uprising had already occurred between 17 and 26 August 1919. The poorly armed insurgents, who received no material help from Warsaw, which itself was engaged in a life or death struggle with Bolshevik Russia, were easily defeated by their better armed and more numerous opponents. It was within this context that Berlin decided to accede to some of the demands of the ZG/BdO. On 14 October 1919 the Oppeln Regency was detached from the (Lower) Silesian Province and included within a new Upper Silesian Province of *Land* Prussia. Not to be outdone, on 15 July 1920 the Polish *Sejm* passed the Organic Statute of the Silesian voivodeship which granted wide-ranging autonomy to any part of Upper Silesia ceded to Poland.

As the plebiscitary campaigns intensified, alongside verbal and pictorial vilification, violence and terrorism became rife. In addition, the Polish side precipitated the Second Upper Silesian uprising between 17 and 25 August 1920. Somehow, the plebiscite was held between 13–20 March 1921. Unsurprisingly, when the results were declared they also became a matter of dispute. They showed that 55.3 per cent of all electoral communes (*Gemeinde*) had voted for Germany and 44.7 per cent for Poland. Put another way, 59.4 per cent of eligible voters had opted for Germany and 40.3 per cent for Poland. The furious Poles then turned on the allies for having allowed migrants from Upper Silesia to have participated in the vote.

That the Polish side should do this was truly ironic, given that it was the Polish delegation at Versailles which had insisted on the inclusion of 'outvoters' on the assumption that they would overwhelmingly declare for Poland. The fact of the matter was that for most of such people, years of residence in the Ruhr and other western German industrial heartlands had further oriented them toward Germany. The Poles also put forward the wholly specious argument that as their votes covered a larger geographical area than had the votes for Germany, which were largely concentrated in urban areas, they had in fact 'won' the plebiscite. For good measure, Warsaw rightly claimed that widespread German intimidation had tilted the balance in favour of Germany in some areas, whilst failing to acknowledge that Poles had also used intimidatory tactics. Berlin took the results to be a clear victory and requested that the Allies transfer no further territory to Poland. However as we have noted, Article 88 deemed the plebiscite as to be advisory and not binding with regard to future decisions on the fate of Upper Silesia.

Understandably, the Allies could not make any clear decision on the basis of the plebiscite, and soon geopolitical factors came into play. France sided with Warsaw, with the United Kingdom and to a lesser extent Italy, tending toward Berlin. Afraid that the area would be left largely in German hands, Polish activists sought to force the situation by launching the Third Silesian Uprising on 2 May 1921. (Weczerka, 1977: lxxxvi). Despite initial successes, the Polish forces were unable to achieve all their military objectives, and were eventually defeated by hastily assembled *Freikorps* units at the hugely symbolic religious shrine of Sankt Annaberg in August of that year. The Allies eventually imposed a cease-fire, which left the Polish side in control of the bulk of Upper Silesia's industrial capacity. It is also worth noting that indigenous Upper Silesians fought on both sides (Körner, 1981). More often than not these, people rather than being either clearly German or Polish, may be identified as Szlonzoks who were engaged in, among other things, the process of gaining a national as opposed to a regional or local identity.

The consequent developing national divisions cut across towns, villages and families. The Conference of the Ambassadors of the Allies reinforced growing emotional division with a territorial one when on 20 October 1921 it sanctioned the division of Upper Silesia in accordance with the plans approved by the League of Nations. Poland gained 29 per cent of the plebiscite area with 46 per cent (996,000) of the population, and most of the industrial basin containing 75 per cent of the industry, 79 per cent of the coalmines and 85 per cent of the coalfield (Bahlcke, 1996: 133). To make the result 'workable' the League of the Nations then had to coax Germany and Poland into signing the Geneva Convention on 15 May 1922. The convention provided for the establishment of a minority rights regime, but in reality simply served to fan the flames of hypernationalism on both sides of the border for the fifteen years it was in force (Wanatowicz, 1994: 39).

Upper Silesia between Poland and Germany

Although according to the 1910 census the majority of Upper Silesia's populace were Polish-speakers, it seems that large numbers of them voted for Germany because they did not feel themselves to be Poles but rather Szlonzoks who above all were attached to their region and Prussia/Germany. It is also important to note that attachment to Germany seems to have been correlated to economic expectations. It was largely the young and the poor who gambled on Poland, as they had little to lose. The remainder, realizing that independence was impossible and banking on a general improvement in living standards after the foundation of the Weimar Republic, decided to entrust their future to Germany. As for the inhabitants of the Polish sections of Upper Silesia and East Silesia, they found themselves in the autonomous Silesian voivodeship with its own Sejm, regional constitution, and capital at Katowice. Finally, we can note that eventually the inhabitants of the Hlucinsko and the western part of East Silesia found themselves assigned to the Czechoslovak Province of Silesia.

Unsurprisingly, these arbitrary divisions triggered off considerable migratory movements. Between 1922 and 1925 up to 170,000 Germans left the voivodeship for Germany (Bahlcke, 1996: 149). By 1939, the figure had reached 190,000 (Serafin 1996: 88). In the 1920s up to 100,000 Poles made the reverse journey and 10,000 left Czechoslovak Silesia for Poland (Serafin, 1996: 80), with smaller movements taking place in the 1930s. In 1925 the population of the German Province of Upper Silesia amounted to 1,372,000 (Stüttgen, 1976: 325). Of this number 151,000 (11 per cent) were Polish speakers, and 385,000 (28 per cent) claimed to be bilingual (Masnyk, 1989: 15). The remaining 836,000 (61 per cent) were German speakers, a figure which included 10,000 (0.73 per cent) Jews (Jonca, 1995: 56). On the other hand, the population of the Silesian voivodeship amounted to 1,295,000 in 1931 (Serafin, 1996: 81). 91,000 (7 per cent) were German-speakers. In addition, due to the dire levels of poverty in Galicia, the number of Jews in the voivodeship continued to grow, until it reached an estimated 27,000 in 1939 (Greiner, 1996: 179–80).

However, we need to treat such figures with a degree of caution. For example, they give us no indication of how bilingual people viewed themselves in terms of national provenance. We do not know whether or not people simply declared themselves to be members of whatever nationality best suited the authorities. All we know is how the officials acting under political pressures chose to interpret them. Neither side was prepared to recognize any category of identity which fell outside predetermined rubrics. As a result, there was no acknowledgment of the existence of *Szlonzok*, *Slonzak*, and *Moravec* ethnicity.

Naturally Berlin put a favourable gloss upon these returns. It calculated the total number of Germans in the Province of Upper Silesia to be 1,221,000, or 89 per cent of the population. This was achieved by adding the numbers of German-speakers together with that of bilingual speakers and German-speaking Jews. Warsaw, on the basis of the same data, arrived at a total number of 633,000 (46 per cent) Poles by adding together the bilingual speakers together with those who claimed only to speak Polish (Masnyk, 1989: 15). In the voivodeship, the authorities estimated the number of Germans to be anything between 130,000 and 210,000, based upon votes for the German parties, whilst German estimates of the number of Germans on the Polish side of the border ranged from between 230,000 to 350,000 (Greiner, 1996: 179).

These differences can be easily explained by the fact that alongside declared Poles and Germans there still lived huge numbers of *Szlonzoks*, *Moravecs* and *Slonzaks*. Members of these three groups enjoyed multiple identities. Acutely aware of the difficult position they were in, and more often than not unaware of or disinterested in any apparent contradiction between Polish and German national identities, they easily moved between the two, whilst in fact their primary allegiance was to the region itself and to their religious denomination (Kamusella, 1997).

The indigenous groups, especially the numerically largest *Szlonzoks*, were assiduously courted by Berlin, whereas Warsaw pursued a straightforward policy of assimilation. The outflow of Polish activists and self-declared Poles from the province during the Great Depression, as well as the campaign of Germanization, weakened the Polish national movement in the province, as is indicated by the steady decrease in votes cast for Polish candidates in successive elections. Moreover, after the division of Upper Silesia, a new category of German, the *eigensprachiger Kulturdeutsche* (non-German-speaking cultural German), began to be promoted. It assumed that the cultural element of nationhood to be more significant than the linguistic one, and facilitated the inclusion of *Szlonzoks* and *Moravecs* into the *Deutschtum* (Pallas, 1970: 31). Unsurprisingly, and bolstered by such notions, the census of 1933 made no provision for Polish speakers. Accordingly, it showed that there were in fact only 99,000 speakers of the 'Upper Silesian-Polish language', i.e. the Upper Silesian West Slavic dialect and the Germanic/Slavic creole, and 266,000 individuals who claimed knowledge both of this language and of German. In total, the census identified a total of 1,118,000 German-speakers (Kokot, 1973: 71; Masnyk, 1989: 15).

Unsurprisingly, such data was utilized by the National Socialists in their attempts to create a 'racially pure' Aryan race. Thus, the Act on Reich Citizenship of 15 September 1935 introduced two kinds of German citizenship: *Reichsbürger* for ethnic Germans together with the lower category of *Staatsangehörige*, which was reserved for non-ethnic Germans (i.e. Jews and national minorities). The *Szlonzoks* and the *Moravecs* were automatically made *Reichsbürger*, unless they explicitly demanded to be treated as members of a national minority (Wanatowicz, 1994: 158–9).

If we turn to the policy of the Polish government in their part of Upper Silesia, we find that it played into the hands of both the German government and minority activists. The official census returns were not reflected in election results, and minority activists secured the votes of

Szlonzoks who came to the conclusion that life in Poland did not fulfil their expectations. German minority candidates were elected to Poland's Sejm and Senate, the Silesian *Sejm* as well as to local councils. Between 1922 and 1929 14 (29.2 per cent) deputies in the Silesian *Sejm* were from the German minority. With the elections of 1930, their representation increased to 15 (31.25 per cent), although subsequently German representation decreased sharply as liberal democracy was curtailed and the rate of migration to Germany increased. (Bahlcke, 1996: 149–50; Greiner, 1996: 185–6). At the local elections of 1926 in the Upper Silesian section of the voivodeship the German minority gained a staggering 40.9 per cent votes (plus 2.2 per cent cast for joint Polish-German lists), although once again this figure represented a never-to-be repeated peak.

The discrepancy between declared nationality and voting behaviour can be accounted for in a number of ways. First, people did not necessarily vote according to ethnic criteria. Secondly, people of indeterminate nationality had no specific *Szlonzokian* electoral voice. Finally, the new state was beset by a variety of problems, which made the reality of independence less attractive than had been the idea. In the Upper Silesian voivodeship the problems were particularly acute. Although Warsaw quite successfully implemented measures of administrative standardization and managed to curb the postwar hyperinflation, its efforts were frustrated by frequent changes of government and the constant disputes with Poland's national minorities, which constituted one third of the total population, and sought either to secure greater autonomy or to break completely with Warsaw (Tomaszewski, 1985: 50).

Eventually, Pilsudski stepped back into politics with the *coup d'etat* of May 1926, in the hope of correcting an increasingly chaotic situation. There was some (inter-ethnic) opposition in Polish Upper Silesia, but it was easily quelled. Korfanty, at the helm of the *Chrzescijanska Demokracja* (ChD, Christian Democratic Party), unsuccessfully organized opposition against the coup. But Pilsudski's camp, dubbed the *Sanacja* (revitalization), won, and subsequently put Korfanty on trial before interning him at the camp for oppositionists at Brzesc in 1930 and eventually sending him into Czechoslovakian exile in 1935.

The voivodeship's local pro-Polish population resented Pilsudski's treatment of Korfanty, as well as the subsequent political marginalization of participants of the Upper Silesian uprisings. They were also unhappy at the inward flow of Poles from outside the voivodeship who quickly acquired prominent positions in administration and industry.

Most of all they disagreed with the policy of the Polonization of place-names, the gradual introduction of Polish as the only official medium of communication, irregular attempts at Polonizing personal names, the illegal[2] limiting of the autonomy of the voivodeship in the April Constitution of 1935, and discrimination against their non-Polish fellow-Silesians (Greiner, 1994; Linek, 1997: 149–50).

On the other hand Pilsudski, probably quite rightly, perceived the appeals to the League of the Nations by the German minority, supported by Germany against discrimination of Germans in the voivodeship, as part of a campaign aimed at securing a revision of the border. The treaties of Rapallo and Locarno simply accentuated Poland's fears, as did the re-entry of German troops into the Rhineland in 1936. At one point, he even toyed with the idea of persuading France to join with Poland in conducting a defensive war against an increasingly belligerent Berlin.

All these events occurred at a time of deep economic recession. In Poland, German workers were the first to be laid off and the last to be employed (Komjathy, 1980: 83). Increasing numbers of German-oriented Upper Silesians sought work in the relatively more prosperous Germany, where the National Socialist's massive programmes of public works, rearmament and the imprisonment or expulsion of increasing numbers of 'undesirables' were creating gaps in the labour market. After the Geneva Convention expired in 1937, Berlin and Warsaw signed the Minority Declaration which acknowledged that both governments had a protective function with regard to co-nationals on either side of the border. Not that this halted the pressure against Germans living on the Polish side of the border. German passport holders were expelled, and the Evangelical Church of the Old Prussian Union was subordinated to the voivodeship's administration (Krzyzanowski, 1996: 124). Crucially by 1938 the rate of unemployment for Germans fluctuated between 60 and 80 per cent compared with an overall rate in the voivodeship of around 16 per cent (Komjathy, 1980: 88).

In German Upper Silesia, the Polish minority was organized within the *Zwiazek Polakow w Niemczech* (ZPwN, Union of the Poles in Germany). From 1923 to 1939 the membership of the Union oscillated between 5,000 and 7,000 (Masnyk, 1994: 43). The Polish community was severely weakened by the steady outflow of self-declared Poles (mainly to Poland) and the fact that the large majority of Polish and bilingual speakers actually considered themselves to be *Szlonzoks* and German. Also, the standard of living in the German province was consistently higher than in the voivodeship, and as such continued to prove an attraction to Upper Silesians on the Polish side of the border. Moreover, Berlin offered greater support to the German minority in Poland than Warsaw could for Poles living in Germany. In German Upper Silesia, opting for Poland became unviable as it often meant losing one's job or having to move to Poland. In addition, it is also important to note that nationality was also served as an index of social status. Thus by becoming a German a *Szlonzok* could achieve a level of social advancement which otherwise might be denied.

The National Socialist agenda

Self-evidently, the situation of the Polish community in Germany worsened after Hitler took power in 1933. The National Socialist's policy of constructing an ethnically and genetically pure *Herrenvolk* was predicated upon a programme of protracted ethnic cleansing and ultimately of genocide. These plans were to prove to be especially dangerous for Poles, because the envisaged *Großdeutsches Reich* was to be created at the expense of Polish territory and the Polish population, most of whom were to be classified as *Untermenschen*. Prior to 1937 National Socialist discrimination against Poles and Jews was curbed by the Geneva Convention. However, *Reichsbürger* citizenship was denied to members of the Polish minority and they were barred from entering the civil service. In fact, the Germanization of overtly Slavic place-names was begun as early as 1931, two years before Hitler's rise to power, and a similar process in respect of personal names commenced a year later. Inevitably, processes intensified after 1933, and in 1937–39 were supplemented with the removal of Polish shop signs and inscriptions (Linek, 1997: 148; Masnyk, 1989: 21–4).

As stated prior to the outbreak of war, Germany had the edge on Poland in terms not only of the economy but also by virtue of the fact it was the longer established state. Both points were of crucial importance in the competition for hearts and minds. Although Polish propaganda emphasized the point that the voivodeship was the most developed and modern region of Poland (Wanatowicz, 1994: 41–2), this fact had little relevance for resident *Szlonzoks* and Germans, who invariably compared their situation with that in German Upper Silesia. These factors were lost on many Poles, who believed that the Silesian uprisings had been a clear reflection of the will of a majority of Upper Silesians to unite with Poland. This attitude also ignored the fact that many of those who had fought on the Polish side had done so in the hope of securing a better future, and not through a deep-seated commitment to the cause of Poland.

Certainly instrumentalism was also a factor among many who had fought on the German side. By the early 1930s, it seemed that those who had bet on Germany had won. Given the general tensions, the post-1933 National Socialist dictatorship did little to dampen enthusiasm for Germany, and neither did the palpable lack of democracy in Poland after 1926 help matters. Polish and German propaganda continued to vilify the other, and the concept of a *Polnische Wirtschaft* in the voivodeship, as compared to the apparent wealth and order in the German province, had an effect on Upper Silesians irrespective of domicile.

These so-called *Zwischenschicht/warstwa posrednia* (in-between people), or those of uncertain national provenance, among the Upper Silesian population were in essence 'up for grabs' for both Polish and German nationalists. Because of discontent with Polish rule which had not fulfilled the hopes of the voivodeship's *Szlonzoks* and which in their eyes turned them into the second-class citizens in their own *Heimat*, only the Polish-educated younger generation identified with that state in any number. The older generation tended to look to Germany, if only because it offered better employment prospects and greater financial subventions. In sum, *Szlonzoks* tended to feel more affinity with (German) Upper Silesian province than with Poland. Hence, for Berlin it was easier to assimilate the province's *Szlonzoks* within the German nation and to curb any pro-Polish tendencies. Once again, economic factors and incentives, as well as the labour market, played a role.

By way of contrast, *Slonzaks* who found themselves living in the Polish voivodeship came to identify with Poland reasonably quickly, with those who remained in the Czechoslovak part of Silesia also assuming a Polish identity. Moreover, whereas Warsaw quickly suppressed the remnants of the *Slonzakian* ethnic movement, Prague actually encouraged it on its side of the border as a means of counteracting growing attachment to Poland (Kamusella, 1998).

What was to prove decisive in engineering the massive shift in identities and population which occurred from 1939, was first of all the *Anschluß* with Austria, and then the Munich Agreement of 1938, following which Germany annexed the Sudetenland from Czechoslovakia, much to the relief of the area's overwhelmingly German population. The process of constructing the *Volksgemeinschaft* to be contained within the borders of the *Großdeutsches Reich* had commenced.

As we shall see, Poland also annexed part of Czechoslovakia in the autumn of 1938, but did not long enjoy the fruits of its success. When Berlin and its Slovak allies liquidated Czechoslovakia in March 1939 the outbreak of the war became imminent. Further anti-Polish measures were introduced into German Upper Silesia. The use of Polish was banned in religious services, the Polish-language press was severely controlled and censored, and activists of Polish organizations were harassed and expelled. Warsaw responded in kind by meting out similar measures against the German minority in the voivodeship and elsewhere in Poland (Bahlcke, 1996).

The return of war

War broke out on 1 September 1939, preceded a day earlier by the German-staged 'Polish attack' on the radio station at the border city of Gleiwitz in German Upper Silesia. German troops overran the voivodeship in no time. The Polish armed forces collapsed almost everywhere, and in many areas of Poland vengeful mobs of civilians and leaderless defeated troops massacred German civilians, with around seven hundred being murdered in Upper Silesia alone (Pospieszalski, 1959: 39).

The German population of former Polish Upper Silesia together with numerous pro-German *Szlonzoks* welcomed the German troops hoping for a better economic and social future under the rule of Hitler (Bahlcke, 1996: 158). However, Hitler was more interested in making war and pursuing his fantastic schemes of racial purity than anything else. In September all Polish schools and organizations in the Oppeln Regency were dissolved; activists of such organizations along with Polish veterans of the Silesian uprisings were transported to the concentration camp at Buchenwald or simply arbitrarily executed (Masnyk, 1989: 24).

After having defeated Poland with the aid of the Soviet Union, which invaded Poland from the east on 17 September, the process of territorial division began anew. The western and northern areas of Poland were incorporated into Germany while other areas controlled by Berlin were turned into the *Generalgouvernement,* which in effect was little better than a huge reservation for Poles. The new Soviet–German border largely coincided with the eastern boundary of the post-1945 Polish state. The former Polish Silesian voivodeship was added to the Province of Silesia, together with the adjacent non-Upper Silesian counties (*powiaty*) of the Kielce and Cracow voivodeships. Most Upper

Silesian territory was the sub-divided between the regencies of Regency of Kattowitz to the east, and the Oppeln Regency to the west. The united Province of Silesia also regained those Lower Silesian areas which in 1920 had been lost to Poland (Stüttgen, 1976).

As the German war machine rolled on in 1940 and early 1942, so more 'Germanic' territory was incorporated within the *Großdeutches Reich*. The next task was fully to implement National Socialist theories of 'racial hygiene'. In the case of Silesia, the first step had been to gather all historically Silesian territories within the administrative borders of the Province of Silesia. The new Kattowitz Regency and the enlarged Oppeln Regency even included areas which had ceased to be part of Silesia in the fifteenth century. Yet, it soon became evident that the enlarged Province of Silesia with the whole Upper Silesian industrial basin was to be too big a strain on the Breslau provincial administration. In 1941 the province was divided once again into the Provinces of Lower and Upper Silesia. The latter consisting of the two regencies of Oppeln and Kattowitz (Stüttgen, 1976).

Mass expulsions were also set into train. In the years 1939–42, 81,000 Poles, mainly those who had arrived in the Silesian voivodeship after 1922, were expelled from the Kattowitz Regency. They in turn were replaced with 37,000 ethnic Germans from the territories seized by the Soviet Union, who were resettled in Silesia as part of the *Heim-ins-Reich* policy. Eventually the German authorities hoped to settle almost 400,000 Germans in the area. Such resettlements would of course have taken place at the expense of the Polish population, which was to be forcibly expelled (Dlugoborski, 1983: xlvii-xlviii).

In the realm of linguistic politics, even before the introduction of the official prohibition on the use of Polish in public, people were afraid to speak the language. After the stabilization of the situation, numerous persons began to speak in Polish again, which in turn prompted administrative measures to suppress the phenomenon and strengthen the position of German as the only official medium of communication. Such measures did not simply apply to standard Polish. All forms of local West Slavic dialect and Slavic-Germanic creole considered to be insufficiently German were ruthlessly suppressed.

Polish inscriptions, shop signs and monuments were removed, and the policy of Germanizing place and personal names was extended throughout the whole of Silesia. Of course not only did the usual bureaucratic agencies implement such measures. The Gestapo was also active in repressing manifestations of Polish language and culture, thus giving such policies a frightening new twist (Serwanski, 1963: 86–150).

However, the German authorities did tread relatively carefully with regard *Szlonzoks* and *Szlonzokian* traditions. They realized that too radical measures against the Slavic elements of *Szlonzokian* identity would have distanced this population from Germany. Given that this group was viewed as *Kulturdeutsch* and that Berlin needed soldiers and a qualified workforce, too stern measures against this group could have proved counter-productive. What is more, if the *Szlonzoks* could be properly Germanized there would be less need to resettle *Volksdeutsche* in Upper Silesia after the war.

Before the final plans for the 'Aryanization' of Upper Silesia could be drawn up and implemented in Upper Silesia, the ethnic make-up of the population had to be somehow established. The police carried out the task at the turn of 1939 and 1940 in the form of the *Einwohnererfassung* (registration of residents). In the survey residents were required to declare their nationality and language used at home (*Haussprache*). *Szlonzoks* and the *Slonzaks* were explicitly distinguished in this survey by the creation of a 'Silesian language' category. However, while *Slonzaks* were also permitted the category of 'Silesian nationality', *Szlonzoks* had to chose between German or Polish nationality.

According to the figures, in the Upper Silesian section of the former voivodeship, 106,000 (10 per cent) declared the Silesian language to be their *Haussprache*. 818,000 (77.8 per cent) claimed to be German-speaking: 125,000 (11.9 per cent) gave Polish as their mother-tongue; with 2,500 inhabitants declaring other languages, mainly Ukrainian[3], Yiddish and Czech, to be their normal mode of communication. Amazingly, 999,000 (95 per cent) declared themselves to be of German nationality, as opposed to 50,000 (4.2 per cent) who chose the Polish option and 2,800 who chose other nationalities.

From the data it is clear that in the Upper Silesian section of the voivodeship bilingual speakers of German and Polish only declared their knowledge of the latter, and those *Szlonzoks* with a poor command of German declared themselves either to be Silesian or Polish speakers. However, most of the population (even those who did not speak German) declared German nationality. The statistics also reveal that language was not necessarily coterminous with national self-designation. It should also be born in mind that these statistics were requested by the police force of an increasingly ruthless dictatorship, which was rendering manifest ever more clearly its hatred for Poles, Jews and other *Untermenschen*. To declare for Poland was therefore either an act of bravery, ignorance or stupidity, particularly if an individual had a knowledge of another language, be it German, Czech or a local dialect. Given these factors, coupled with a lack of first-hand knowledge of how the raw data were interpreted, but armed with the knowledge that people were well aware that a declaration for Poland meant drastically reduced social status, these figures cannot be taken as being wholly reliable of anything other than the National Socialist obsession with race. Finally, we should note that in those border counties incorporated into Silesia only in 1939, few individuals declared themselves to be German. Indeed, the distinctly un-German (i.e. Polish and Jewish) character of these area was only slightly altered by the subsequent expulsions of Poles and extermination of Jews.

We have already noted the pitfalls of taking figures at face value. However, the data presented earlier in the section, can be used as rough basis for estimating the numerical size of the *Szlonzokian* and *Slonzakian* ethnic groups, for illustrating the multiple character of their ethnic identities, as well as for indicating the relative strength of Polish identity severely tested though it was. It is also fairly clear that Polish national consciousness was shallow in the Upper Silesian section of the former voivodeship, and was probably strongest among Poles who had migrated there after the division of Upper Silesia (Bahlcke, 1996: 159).

Prior to commencing with the second stage of 'doing away with the Polish facade' which covered the 'true and dominant German core' of Upper Silesia, the extermination of the Upper Silesian Jews had commenced as early as October 1939, when 1,000 were deported to forced labor camps. Most of the Jews living in the enlarged wartime Upper Silesia were exterminated by 1943. The most notorious extermination camp was of course the Auschwitz complex of the enlarged wartime Upper Silesian province, the location of which accounts for the speedy extermination of the local Jewish population. In addition, many Jews, especially from the east Silesian section of the province, lost their lives in Theresienstadt camp (Borak, 1992: 110; Maser, 1992: 60–2). Numerous Soviet as well as many Polish and some Allied POWs lost their lives either at the forced labour camp located in the Upper Silesian village of Lamsdorf[4] and its subcamps, or at other forced labour camps within the province of Upper Silesia (Evans, 1995; Urban, 1994: 74).

The first hints at how Aryanization of the *Großdeutsches Reich* was to proceed, came in the autumn of 1939 in the province of *Wartheland* established on the territory of former *Wielkopolska*. The *Wartheland* National Socialist leadership proposed to segregate the population according to so-called racial criteria. Germans, the *eigensprachige-*

Kulturdeutsche, and other segments of populace suitable for Aryanization were to remain in the Wartheland while the rest were to be expelled.

This overall concept crystallized in the form of the *Deutsche Volksliste* (DVL, German National List). The DVL's four groups were:

1. persons who had actively reaffirmed their German national identity in the interwar period, mainly by having belonged to German associations;
2. persons who did not actively demonstrate their German national identity but retained this identity in full;
3. persons of Germanic origin, those with German spouses, or of unclear national identity;
4. Polonized persons with 'Germanic characteristics', who by virtue of such characteristics were presumed to have 'Germanic blood'.

Persons belonging to Groups 1 and 2 were entitled to *Reichsbürgerschaft*, whereas those belonging to Group 3 were only entitled to become only *Staatsgehörige*. Those from Group 4 obtained *Staatsangehörigkeit* only through individual conferment, which could be withdrawn within ten years. A decree of 4 March 1941 signalled the beginning of the exercise to establish the DVL. In Upper Silesia this process took off in the middle of the year. Obviously the implementation of such a scheme created a huge array of problems. In particular, attempting to work out who was entitled to enter into Group Three proved to be a bureaucratic nightmare. In response a further decree was issued on 31 January 1942 which simplified registration procedures but made the conferment of *Staatsangehörigkeit* revocable within the period of ten years (Boda-Krezel, 1978: 13–20). Of all former Polish areas now incorporated to the Reich, Upper Silesia contained the greatest number of Third Class Germans (Jastrzebski, 1995). Above all it included the indigenous *Slonzaks* and the *Szlonzoks* (Boda-Krezel, 1978: 14). Thus as far as the National Socialists were concerned there were few pure Aryans in the area, and the local people had become 'infected' with 'inferior' Slavic/Polish blood. This relegation of status experienced at the hands of the National Socialists by a majority of German and German-oriented Upper Silesians is something which they rarely mention today. Neither is the fact that entry to the *Volksliste* was easier in the *Wartheland* than in Silesia.

The DVL established a racial pecking-order within the putative Aryan race. In effect the groups considered to be eligible for *Reichsbürgerschaft* were:

- *Reichsdeutsche* (Reich Germans), persons who had held German citizenship before 1 September 1939;

- *Umsiedler* (resettlers), i.e. ethnic Germans evacuated from areas seized by the Soviet Union;
- *Volksdeutsche*, former citizens of pre-war Poland of proven German descent, by virtue of their inclusion on the *Volksliste*.

DVL Group 3 was in effect a *Zwischengruppe* (in-between group), clearly indicating that the authorities considered them to be capable of Aryanization only once they had been 'disinfected' of alien Slav influences. To a lesser extent, members of DVL 2 were also viewed in such a way, but crucially they enjoyed the *Reichsbürgerschaft*, and with it both better rations and a higher social status.

In Upper Silesia, both members of Group 4 and those denied entry to the DVL were considered to be Poles. In the Lodz area of *Wielkopolska*, Group 4 was rather disparagingly referred to as the *Lebensmittel Liste* (foodstuffs list), which indicates that some at least viewed its members as Poles who were (understandably) passing themselves off as Germans.[5] To complicate matters yet further, DVL 4 was itself subdivided into various categories, but crucially members of Group 4 enjoyed the revocable *Staatsangehörigkeit*, which spared them the fate of Poles who remained outside the DVL.

Although members of the latter two groups were considered to be less than fully German, there were important differences between the two. Members of Group 3 could proceed to secondary and tertiary education, whereas only elementary and basic vocational education was available to members of Group 4. On the other hand, members of both groups were barred from holding any positions of authority within the state and party machines and were denied membership of the National Socialist party (Boda-Krezel, 1978: 24–5).

It is important to note that this action was carried out only in those areas of the Reich which had not belonged to Germany at the onset of war. In other words, in Silesia it was implemented in the majority of the counties of the Kattowitz Regency and in three counties of the Oppeln Regency. Everybody residing within the borders of the former Silesian voivodeship had to fill in the DVL questionnaire,[6] but in the counties of the former Kielce and Cracow voivodeships such questionnaires were issued only on demand. The assumption being that these areas were overwhelmingly Polish in character, thus obviating the need for such a comprehensive exercise.

Analysis of the returns shows that in the Upper Silesian section of the former Polish voivodeship, 'only' 54,000 out of the total population of 1,119,000 were deemed to be incapable of Aryanization. Then again, comparatively few of the inhabitants were regarded as true

Aryans. In the east Silesian section of the former voivodeship the figure of 282,000 showed just how 'un-German' the area was, as did the figures from the former Kielce and Cracow voivodeships now included in the enlarged Silesian province.

Apart from further illustrating the National Socialists' obsession with race, and their attachment to bureaucracy, these statistics also serve as a rough basis for estimating the number of the *Szlonzoks* and the Slonzaks in Upper Silesia. However, we must bear in mind that as the DVL exercise was not carried out on the territory of the interwar Oppeln Regency a large caveat must be added. Most of the *Szlonzoks* were placed on DVL Group 3, although the more enthusiastic often managed to gain entry into Group 2, with those who were pro-Polish sometimes actually being included on Group 4. Bearing these qualifications in mind, the number of the *Szlonzoks* may be gauged at the combined memberships of the DVL Groups 3 and 4 together with half the membership of the DVL Group 2, which equals 848,000. If we then assume that 800,000 out of the total population in 1939 of 1,582,000 in the interwar Oppeln Regency considered themselves to be *Szlonzaks* – and what data there is bears this assumption out (Stüttgen, 1976: 325) – it seems that the total number of Upper Silesians whose ethnic identity did not correspond to perceived notions of national identity was approximately 1,650,000, to which figure a further 244,000 must be added from east Silesia.

The figures are to a large degree confirmed by the results of the Polish policies of homogenization and ethnic cleansing which were applied in Upper Silesia (as elsewhere in Poland) after the Second World War, and which emulated the DVL in attempting to discern who was or was not a Pole. The number of persons from the territory of the interwar Oppeln Regency, who were verified as Poles stood at 852,000 in 1949 (Misztal, 1984: 159–60).

It is worthwhile remembering that as should be clear by now, *Szlonzoks* and *Slonzaks* had multiple ethnic identities, which enabled them should the need arise, to 'pass themselves' as Poles/Germans/ Silesians according to circumstance. Moreover, both the German and Polish authorities before, during and after the war were determined to include them as members of their own national communities, regardless of the wishes of the people effected. To make matters worse, the possession of such multiple identities, and the seeming ease with which such people could transfer national allegiance, only served to create hostility toward them from people who were more clearly either German or Polish nationals.

The postwar aftermath

Although the postwar fate of Upper Silesians of uncertain national identification is dealt with in more detail in the next chapter, it is worthwhile at this point to make some observations with regard to postwar events. First, prior to the first allied air raids of June 1944, those who had not suffered either from political-racial persecution, or who had not lost close friends and family at the Front, had somehow remained oblivious both of the nature of the concentration camp system and of the wider war itself. Secondly, lurid and largely truthful accounts of atrocities committed by the Red Army in the East Prussian village of Nemmersdorf (Mayakovskoye) in October that year, together with other similar reports, began to engender an atmosphere of panic among the civilian population. The ground war arrived as late as January 1945, with the Soviet offensive which engulfed most of Upper Silesia east of the River Oder by March. For various reasons only a small part of the civilian population was evacuated in the face of the Soviet onslaught, which resulted in the Soviets and then the Poles being able to employ much the same labour force previously used by the Germans.

Moreover, the population at large fared badly. The front line troops pillaged, raped and committed arson. The Soviet army took control over government, industry, infrastructure, archives, and most importantly, over the repressive network of forced labour and concentration camps, which now were put into use against National Socialist party members, known and presumed anti-communist Poles, and tens of thousands of 'German' civilians. Many of these people quickly found themselves dispatched to slave labour camps alongside industrial equipment and plant which was being seized as reparations.

The excesses perpetrated on the civilian population worsened after the Oder was crossed in March 1945, and the Soviet troops crossed the prewar border of Germany. By the end of the war, almost all of the province of Upper Silesia was overrun by Soviet troops with the exception of its south-western corner and the East Silesian section west of Teschen (Fuchs, 1994: 684). The transfer of Upper Silesia to the Polish communist administration commenced as early as March 1945. This administration also took over the German concentration camp system, which was enlarged by the NKVD. The Poles used it in a manner similar to that of the Germans: first, for ensuring industrial production, second, for liquidating political opposition, and third, for homogenizing the population, i.e. for expelling Germans and Polonizing the remaining verified/rehabilitated populace. In their place came increasing numbers of refugees from central Poland, together with expellees from former eastern Poland (Kamusella, 1998a). So far in this chapter we have explored the fate of areas of Silesia disputed between Poland and Germany. As with the previous chapter, we shall conclude our study with an examination of (former) Austrian Silesia

Czech nationalism ascendant

Interwar Czechoslovakia provides us with a textbook example of how not to run a multi-ethnic country. Czechs, Germans, Slovaks, Hungarians, Ruthenes and Poles were lumped together by the Western allies, who were hostile in particular toward German claims for self determination, and who sought to create a strong Czechoslovakia in the image of leading Czech politicians. If consociational mechanisms had been established and adhered to, the state might have stood a chance. Having said that, it is apparent that few politicians, rhetoric aside, were interested in reaching outside of their titular national community. Instead, they sought either to fashion Czechoslovakia in their own image or simply to destroy it. If the world recession of the late 1920s onwards had not been as severe as it was, again it is possible to argue that Czechoslovakia might have survived. However, as with all speculation, it is useless to mull the point over. The fact is that Czechoslovakia was destroyed by a group of short-sighted politicians who deliberately activated ethnicity in order to pursue their own ends. The tragedy is that all to often the population at large was all too willing to play its part. As we shall see, what was true of Czechoslovakia as a whole was also true of what in 1918 became Czech Silesia.

The creation of new states after the collapse of Austria-Hungary was accompanied by many political, national, economic and, last but not least, territorial problems. The main arguments of the ideologists of these newly forming states was the right of national self-determination. Economic or strategic arguments, and of course 'historical' claims, were also paramount. Not infrequently, the question of territorial boundaries became so acute that while diplomats were negotiating violence erupted on the disputed territory. The former territory of Austrian Silesia was to prove no exception to this rule.

The proclamation of the Czechoslovak Republic on 28 October 1918 was of course instrumental in leading to the final collapse of Austria-Hungary. In Czech Silesia, German politicians took the lead through the proclamation of the creation of the Sudetenland Province on 30

October 1918. In so doing claim was laid to the larger part of Czech Silesia, German-populated parts of northern Moravia and adjoining German-inhabited territory in Bohemia. In the affected areas, diplomatic representatives of the Czechoslovak Republic were relegated to a passive role. Vienna expressed its formal support for the German activists in Silesia but to little effect. In turn, the Czechoslovak government decided to solve the situation by a military occupation of the Sudetenland. By the end of January 1919, the army had taken control of the northernmost edges of Silesia.

Conditions in the Tesin part of Czech Silesia proved to be especially complicated. On 19 October, Polish activists established the *Rada Narodowa Ksiestwa Cieszynskiego* (the National Council of Tesin) on behalf of the embryonic Polish state. One day after the declaration of the independent Czechoslovak Republic, the *Zemsky narodni vybor pro Slezsko* (Land National Committee in Silesia) was established in Polska Ostrava and announced that it was taking control of the whole of the area on behalf of the Czechoslovak state. In an effort to counter this move, the *Rada Narodowa* issued a statement on 31 October 1918 that in fact it was taking control over government in the whole of the region on behalf of the Polish state. A problematic situation arose in mines and steel works. Mines with a majority of Polish workers backed the Polish state and fighting between Czech and Polish miners broke out in the pits. Food supplies broke down, and strikes on both sides threatened both the mining and supply of the badly needed coal. On 2 November representatives of the two sides met for talks in Orlova, and an agreement was signed which provisionally divided the administration of the disputed territory pending the consent of the Czech, and (as yet non-existent) Polish governments. Violent demonstrations against the agreement broke out in Ostrava on 5 November, which prompted a further round of negotiations. These resulted in the conclusion of a supplementary agreement that complemented and defined more precisely a number of the provisions of the agreement of 2 November. The town of Frydek and six municipalities of Frystat district with a majority of Czechs on municipal councils came under the administration of the *Zemsky narodni vybor*. The districts Bilsko and Tesin were assigned to the *Rada Narodowa*.

Both sides saw this agreement as merely a temporary solution to a situation which was characterized by increasing social and national radicalism and inner-communal polarization. On the Polish side of the new border the *Rada Narodowa* extracted an oath of loyalty to the Polish state from public servants. Their Czech counterparts did likewise. The inevitable consequence of such policies was an increase in the number of complaints with regard to discrimination against people who found themselves living outside of their titular nation state. In Poland at the end of November 1918, elections to a constitutional assembly were announced. They were due to be held on 26 January 1919 and were scheduled to include Tesinsko, as well as the Slovak areas of Orava, Liptov and Spis. For the Czechs, this constituted a fundamental breach of the agreement of 5 November 1918, as Polish state authority was to be executed on the disputed territory. The Czechoslovak government protested but Warsaw refuted the objections. The Czechoslovak government then turned to the French for support and requested that they occupy the disputed territory. For their part German parties in Tesinsko and Ostravsko demanded the creation of a neutral state to be carved out from the industrial part of the region (Kacir, 1995: 7–17).

The forthcoming elections to the Polish *Sejm* probably speeded up the realization of a military operation in Tesinsko. On 23 January 1919 the Czechoslovak army commenced occupation of those areas of Silesia which fell under the administration of the *Rada Narodowa*. Given the inequality of the forces the progress of the Czechoslovak troops was rapid, and Tesin and Karvina were occupied within seven days. The front line stabilized at Upper Vistula, and on 30 January 1919 a truce was signed under entente pressure (Kacir, 1995: 16–17). As a result of the Czechoslovak victory, a vital coal basin had come under the control of Prague.

Following the cessation of hostilities complex and dramatic negotiations were conducted in Paris about the future of the disputed territory. The Polish side insisted that the agreements of 5 November 1918 be upheld. Czechoslovak representatives led by Edvard Benes, foreign minister and later President of Czechoslovakia, attempted to legitimize their demands by reference to historic, legal and economic arguments. The level of mutual estrangement was by this time so great that the inter-allied commission could find no common ground between the two parties. In the end the commission submitted its own compromise proposal, which was written into the so-called Paris protocol of 1919. This protocol affirmed the administrative arrangements of the agreement of 5 November 1918 and delineated a new demarcation line. The Poles signed the protocol on 1 February 1919, but Benes delayed until 2 March with a comment that the protocol neither prejudiced the definitive delineation of the border, nor the overall position of the Czechoslovak government. In accordance with the Paris protocol, an inter-allied commission arrived in Tesinsko on 12th December 1919; its task being to make recommendations to the coming peace conference. The commission with representatives from France, the United Kingdom, Italy and the USA had no executive or administrative powers.

The inter-allied commission was in a difficult position. Both the Czechoslovak and the Polish sides overwhelmed it with complaints. As soon as one side submitted an argument, the other replied in kind. It became ever more clear that the parties were not capable of achieving a mutually acceptable compromise. The final attempt to reach a bilateral agreement was made between 22 and 28 July 1919 in Crakow. The Poles made a proposal that the Bilsko district be included within Poland and that the Frydek district go to Czechoslovakia. They further suggested that plebiscites be held in the Tesin and Frystat districts. For its part the Czechoslovak delegation was fundamentally opposed to these overtures, on the basis that they ignored Czechoslovakia's 'historical right' to the area. The inter-allied commission faced with these attitudes began to draw the conclusion that the main obstacle to agreement was the attitude of the Czechoslovak delegation (Peroutka, 1991: 805–6).

By September 1919, Benes had come to believe that the French were coming round to his point of view, and on 27 September he took the decision to reverse previous Czechoslovak policy and accept Polish requests for a plebiscite (Kacir, 1995: 40). However, the plebiscite was to be of an advisory character only. The ballot was to take place within by the end of the year among persons of the age of 20 and over, and who were officially resident in Tesinsko before 1 August 1914.

The plebiscite was extensively debated in both the Czech and the Polish press, and campaigning began on both sides of the demarcation line. However, in January 1920 the commission decided to postpone the vote. The conflict became immediately more violent, and outright war loomed. Eventually the International Plebiscite Commission, this time including Czech and Polish representatives, came to Tesin on 30 October 1920. A contingent of French and Italian troops arrived together with the commission, with a brief to secure the withdrawal of Polish and Czechoslovak soldiers. The continuing tension and an increase in terrorism caused the postponement of the plebiscite from May to June 1920. In April Polish activists in Tesinsko appear to have become less sure that the plebiscite would go their way. Several factors were decisive in bringing about this change in attitudes. First, they were worried that the atmosphere of violence would deter many people from voting. Secondly, the Poles realized that a majority of Germans would either abstain or side with the Czechs. From that it was possible to deduce that the likely vote for Czechoslovakia in the eastern part of the disputed territory and elsewhere would balance the votes for Poland in the mining areas. The Polish plebiscite commission in turn forbade mayors to prepare registers of voters without which the vote could not take place. In September, representatives of the *Rada Narodowa* successfully lobbied the government in Warsaw to declare that under the circumstances no plebiscite could be held. The two sides were once again deadlocked. Although the Czech side was by now confident of victory, Benes agreed with a Polish proposal that the dispute be settled by means of internationally supervised arbitration, and quickly secured the consent of President Masaryk to this new alternative. (Gawrecki, 1992b: 84).

Inside the disputed territory the security situation continued to deteriorate. Bombings became commonplace, and armed groups operated at will. Eventually on 19 May 1920, the International Plebiscite Commission proclaimed martial law. The response of the paramilitary groups and their supporters was simply to ignore this latest decision of the Commission. Continued diplomatic efforts came to naught, and the Czechoslovak parliament further complicated the issue by reinstating the original demand for a plebiscite. By June, some measure of normality had been restored, but a new wave of strikes, which especially hurt the Polish economy served further to cripple industry. After a Polish attack on a police station on 1 July 1920, which left three policemen dead, the International Commission gave the allied armies full authority to restore order (Kacír, 1995: 58–64). On 10 July 1920 a further conference of leading Entente statesmen took place in Belgium. Both sides took part in the negotiations, and under pressure from the allies they declared that they would abide by the decisions of the allies. Eventually, on 28 July 1920 a decision was reached on the demarcation of the Czechoslovak–Polish border. The Poles were not happy with the decision, which was influenced by Czechoslovak economic and strategic-communication arguments, but given the Russian advance there was little they could do about it. Neither was there any great satisfaction on the other side of the border, especially among those who had sought to claim the whole territory (Gawrecki, 1992b: 85). This solution was by no means optimal and, as we shall see, it could be argued that it actually contributed to determining Poland on the course of action it took against Czechoslovakia in 1938.

The situation in the western part of Czech Silesia was also extremely complex. During the war, groups of *Moravci* had sought to ensure that Moravian enclaves be included in the hypothesized Czechoslovak state. As elsewhere in the region, the cessation of war invigorated such nationalist activities. However, the majority of inhabitants seemingly did not agree with the Czechoslovak option. At the Paris peace conferences the Hlucinsko area was joined to Czechoslovakia. According to census returns, by 1921, it had 48,005 inhabitants. They comprised 39,400 Czechs and *Moravci*, 8,035 Germans, and 501 Poles (Gawrecki, 1980: 34–35). It should be mentioned that in census returns, the authorities often over-stamped entries which gave German as the mother tongue with the word *Moravska* (Moravian), thus further complicating the issue, or, to be more accurate, helping to create a new one. Such practices once again illustrate the point that national allegiance was being determined from above just as much as it was spontaneously manifesting itself.

In Opava the Silesian *Land* administration was renewed in 1919. The introduction of universal franchise in elections to municipal councils was, as we shall see, to inadvertently have wide-ranging consequences for the country as a whole. In terms of public administration, in the first months after the creation of the Czechoslovak Republic, national committees with jurisdictions at the *Land*, district, and commune levels operated in Silesia, as was the case in the rest of the country. There were specific administrative arrangements for the part of Tesin Silesia that was under the Polish administration. As a sop to the Poles and Germans living on the Czechoslovak side of the border, so-called minority national committees became temporary advisory bodies of the Silesian Land government.

In an effort to solve inter-communal tensions, Prague later embarked upon what turned out to be an ultimately suicidal policy of centralization, which among other things resulted, on 1 December 1928, in the Silesian *Land* being merged with Moravia to form the Moravian–Silesian *Land*. In Czech Silesia itself, the regional press decried this development and advocated that residents symbolize their dissatisfaction, by displaying black flags. Indeed, in an uncharacteristic show of unity all Silesian political parties took a negative stand toward the merger of the two areas.

A peculiar coalition of autonomists, communists and German parties came formed the backbone of opposition to the new law. The affected population perceived the law as an attack on their ancient rights. Opponents of the merger frequently pointed out to the historical traditions of Silesia as an autonomous *Land*, and warned against encroaching on the rights of the Polish and German minorities. (Kacirova, 1995: 73–4).

Population growth and political life

In 1921, official figures showed that 672,268 people lived in Czech Silesia, including 49,530 foreign nationals. Of the Czechoslovak citizens in Silesia, 296,194 (47.6 per cent) were Czechs, 69,967 (11.2 per cent) Poles, and 252,365 (40.4 per cent) Germans. In Tesinsko, it was also decided to ascertain the number of *Slonzaci*, who in turn were subdivided into Czechoslovak, Polish and German *Slonzaci*. In 1921, 47,314 *Slonzaci* were found in Tesinsko, out of which 24,299 were Czechoslovak, 1,408 German, and 21,607 Polish. At the census of 1930, all 47,314 declared *Slonzaci* were registered as Czechoslovak nationals, of whom 30,828 indicated Czech nationality, three Slovak nationality, 10,106 Czechoslovak nationality, 191 German, 2150 Polish; 4,036 *Slonzaci* indicated no nationality. After Polish protests that the question asked did not properly address the issue of ethnic identity, another census was taken among the *Slonzaci*. In this census 4,486 Czechoslovak *Slonzaci* declared themselves to be Poles and 5,602 opted for a Czech identity (Gawrecki, 1992a: 66–67). Such manoeuvring once again demonstrates just how problematic it is take such statistics as a reliable starting-point for conducting empirical research on how people really perceived themselves.

Whatever the case, the first years of the Republic were marked by the reconstruction of political parties. From among Czech Silesian politicians there were, for example, members of the *Ceskoslovenska strana narodne socialisticka* (Czechoslovak Socialist Party). Others were affiliated to the Agrarian and Christian Democratic parties. The numerous German parties underwent a fundamental reorganization during this time. Most importantly, established parties such as the *Bund der Landwirte* (Farmers' League), *the Deutsche Christlich-Soziale Volkspartei* (German Christian–Social People's Party) and the *Deutsche Sozial Demokratische Arbeiterpartei* (German Social Democratic Workers' Party) found themselves competing against prototype National Socialist parties such as the *National-Sozialistische Deutsche Arbeiterpartei* (National Socialist German Workers' Party, DNSAP) (Gawrecki, 1992a: 67–8).

The division of Tesinsko contributed to a certain stabilization of relations between Poland and Czechoslovakia. Under the terms of a treaty concluded on 7 November 1921, both parties recognized the new border and pledged to suppress hostile propaganda. However, the treaty was never ratified. Despite this obvious lacuna, in April 1925, the Czechoslovak–Polish agreement on national minorities was signed, and during this period interethnic tension declined. Polish political parties with as self-evident Catholic orientation such as the *Zwiazek Polskich Katolikow* (Union of Polish Catholics), were formed. Others particularly the intelligentsia and Protestants gathered around the *Stronnictwo Ludowe* (People's Movement) which was founded in the autumn of 1922. On the left from 1921 the *Polska Socjalistyczna Partia Robotnicza* (Polish Socialist Workers' Party) attempted to combine principles of Polish nationalism with those of international solidarity. Indeed just about the only party which was genuinely multi-ethnic, rhetorical claims aside, was the communist party (KSC), although its support was mainly confined to Czechs and Germans (Gawrecki, 1992a: 96).

The parliamentary elections of 1920 were an early and immediate test of strength, although given the ongoing dispute with Poland they were postponed in both Tesinsko and Hlucinsko. Czechs gave most votes to social democrats and candidates of the People's Party; the Agrarians and the Czechoslovak National Socialist Party followed some way behind. In the German districts, joint lists of the *Deutsche Nationalpartei* (German National Party) and the *Deutsche National-Sozialistische Arbeiterpartei* gained most votes, although there was also a strong showing by the German social democrats. The elections of 1925 were on the whole unremarkable. The communists did well in some areas, the social democrats in others. In Polish-oriented areas Polish parties did well, and a variety of German parties captured the German vote. A curious situation arose in Hlucinsko, where the apparently predominantly Czech population returned more than half of its vote to the German Christian Social Party, thereby indicating that Slavs could transform themselves into Germans, despite the theories of primordialist nationalists.

The impact of inter-state relations

Throughout the inter-war period, inter-ethnic relations in Czech Silesia were of course influenced by the triangular Czechoslovak, Polish and German relationship. During the 1920s a degree of stabilization was achieved. The years 1925–33 were marked by cooperation between Czech and Polish political representatives in political, social and cultural areas, although the Poles were much more willing to cooperate with the Czechs than were the Germans. Polish and Czechoslovak socialists in particular worked closely with one another. An economic upswing contributed to a drop in the wave of strikes, which became increasingly local in nature. In the educational sphere, a number of schools of all types and levels were established to cater for the needs of the different linguistic communities, and cultural life flourished. However, it is also important to note that few of these associations made any attempt to reach out to people from outside the titular ethnic group with which a given association established its base. Or to put it another way, ethnic ghettoization was the norm.

In Silesia the parliamentary elections of 1929 brought no fundamental changes to representation of either Czech or Polish districts. Among the German inhabitants those parties which were inclined to cooperate in the state-building process made marked headway, the social democrats being the main beneficiaries, although the *Deutsche Christlich-Soziale Volkspartei* remained the most popular German party in the area. However, the deepening recession of the early 1930s led to renewed growth in ethno-social conflict. The increase in national antagonisms was especially reflected during layoffs of workers, which led to mutual recrimination and allegations that Germans and Poles were more likely to lose their jobs than were Czechs. In this situation nationally oriented trade unions asserted themselves. The recession saw a marked increase in Czech–German tensions, especially under the influence of the ever more popular National Socialist movement in Germany, whereas Czech–Polish relations remained relatively calm. In Silesia, the courts were increasingly brought into play in dealing with German irredentists. On 11 November 1933, ten months after the coming of Hitler to power, the Czechoslovak government issued a decree banning the *Deutsche Nationalpartei* and DNSAP. Unsurprisingly, the bulk of the leadership of these parties simply fled to Germany, from where they continued to campaign against Czechoslovakia. Crucially, German Silesian politicians on both sides of the border began to form closer links with the *Sudetendeutscher Heimatbund*. German language education was also increasingly being financed from Germany, and that led to the National Socialists gaining ever greater influence among the ethnic Germans of Czech Silesia, as elsewhere in the country. In order to get around the ban on German irredentist parties, the leading Czechoslovak-German politician Konrad Henlein, announced the establishment of a new political formation, the *Sudetendeutsche Heimatfront*, which in the 1935 elections, campaigned as the *Sudetendeutsche Partei* (SdP).

Perhaps the most decisive event of this time, in terms of defining the future of Czech Silesia, was the German–Polish non-aggression pact of 1934, which had the effect of fundamentally changing Czechoslovak-

Polish relations at both the international and regional levels. Thinking its western borders were now secure, the Polish government began a strident anti-Czechoslovak campaign. On the fifteenth anniversary of the occupation of Tesinsko by the Czechoslovak army, anti-Czechoslovak demonstrations were organized at the initiative of the Warsaw foreign ministry. In the Polish press, large numbers of articles reaffirmed Polish claims to the Czechoslovak part of Tesinsko. Such articles also claimed that the Polish minority in Czech Silesia was subject to discrimination and suppression, called for greater Polish–Hungarian cooperation, and accused Czechoslovakia of being little more than Moscow's puppet. In some parts of Czech Silesia, symbols of state were torn down and replaced with their Polish equivalents. In a number of villages the local Poles, allegedly with the knowledge and approval of Warsaw and local Polish diplomatic representatives, destroyed Czech language schools (Kolektiv autoru, 1997: 66–7).

On a more positive note, in the parliamentary elections in 1935 Polish socialists continued to lend their support to their Czechoslovak counterparts. The most important point to note is that with one exception, the pattern of voting was little different to that of the previous election. The exception was that in an ominous portent of what was to follow, the *Sudetendeutsche Partei* swept the board in virtually all German-speaking areas (Gawrecki, 1992a: 71).

Following the *Anschluß* with Austria in March 1938, demands for a revision of the Czechoslovak border reached fever pitch among supporters of this party. In a vain effort to forestall the capture of Czech Silesia by the National Socialists, the communist intellectual Ondra Lysohorsky together with anti-fascist Germans attempted to revive Silesian separatism. In order to lend this idea some kind of intellectual credence, they developed the theory of the *Lassky* nation and language. Lysohorsky claimed that prior to the collapse of the German and Austro-Hungarian empires, two million people had spoken *lascina* in north east Moravia and Silesia and that these people had unjustly been denied the right of self-determination after 1918. Unfortunately for him, Lysohorsky found sympathy only among a narrow circle of leftist intellectuals.

The road to nowhere

By 1938 there was once again crisis in the Tesin region. This was due not only to the activities of German National Socialists but also to the steadily worsening situation between Prague and Warsaw. Only the communist parties of both countries continued to advocate inter-ethnic cooperation. The non-socialist Polish parties created the *Zwiazek Polakow w Czechoslowacji* (Union of Poles in Czechoslovakia). They demanded that Tesinsko be declared Polish. In German-speaking areas, apart from the *Sudetendeutsche Partei* only the communists and the social democrats continued to function at a meaningful level. All others had either disintegrated, or become little more than paper organizations. Despite concessions made by Prague in July 1938 on the use of local languages, the representatives of the Polish and German minorities continued to press for a revision of the borders. The local elections of May and June 1938 were marked by a crushing victory of Henlein's *Sudetendeutsche Partei* among German speakers.

The crisis reached a new intensity in the summer of 1938. On the German side of the border, volunteer units were created in the Reich from among refugees from western Silesia and Hlucinsko. These units increasingly engaged in acts of terrorism on the Czech side of the border, primarily directed against Czech minority schools and government offices. The Czechoslovak government's decree on mobilization of 23 September 1938 temporarily restored a degree of order. However, after a short hiatus, German paramilitary units stepped up their assaults on the Czechoslovak state.

In the critical days of autumn 1938, the Polish national minority united with the German minority in its demand for autonomy. The Czechoslovak government promised concessions in an attempt to secure Poland's neutrality in the expected conflict with Germany. Polish foreign policy in some ways now mimicked the German approach. Warsaw was now counting on the break up of Czechoslovakia and satisfying its own territorial demands. Preparations for an incursion by the Polish military begun, and an army group with the aim of occupying Tesinsko was organized. On 21 September 1938, the Polish government sent a diplomatic note to Prague demanding 'clarification' of its attitude toward the Polish populace in Czech Silesia. To complicate matters even further, German and *Slonzaci* representatives began to campaign against the incorporation of Tesinsko in Poland, demanded a plebiscite, and began to lobby both Hitler and Chamberlain for support. On the same day, the Czechoslovak army was ordered to take control of specified posts at the Polish border. That same night clashes broke out with Polish paramilitaries. In order to create the impression that a popular rising was taking place, Polish insurgents spread their activities over as wide an area as possible. On 27 September the Czechoslovak government offered negotiations on disputed issues, and in a letter to his Polish counterpart, President Benes suggested that any change to the borders in Tesinsko should be based on mutual agreement. By way of response, the Polish government demanded the unconditional surrender of the Czechoslovak part of Tesinsko to Poland. The Czechoslovak government rejected this, but reaffirmed its willingness to discuss the situation and agree to international arbitration on the matter. Scenting victory, the emboldened Polish government once again rejected these overtures (Gawrecki, 1992b: 98–100).

The Munich Diktat of 29 September 1938, signed by Hitler, Mussolini, Chamberlain and Daladier without the consent of Prague, signalled the failure of the Czechoslovak state. Prague quickly accepted this *fait accompli*. The Czechoslovak army began to withdraw from the border areas on 1 October, to be replaced by the Wehrmacht. The territory of Opava Silesia was incorporated within the *Sudeten Gau Regierungsbezirk Troppau* (Sudeten Region administrative district Opava). Hlucinsko was joined to the *Altreich*, as part of the *Provinz Schlesien*. Alongside the evacuation of the Czechoslovak army, transfers of Czech families and German anti-fascists were organized (Orlik, 1961: 18–19).

After Munich, the Sudetenland province was established and Opava Silesia was later assigned to this province. According to the census of May 1939, 81 per cent of the inhabitants of this part of Silesia declared German nationality with the remainder declaring Czech nationality. As elsewhere, the German administration introduced an explicitly anti-Czech policy. This was manifested in the confiscation of Czech property, the distribution of land from Czechs to Germans, the closing of Czech schools, the abolition of Czech political and cultural associations, and random and arbitrary arrest. On 20 November 1938, Germany concluded a minority rights agreement with the rump and renamed Czecho-Slovakia. This agreement enabled Czech citizens from the ceded territory either to apply for German citizenship or to opt for Czecho-Slovakia. Czechs applying for German passports had to prove that they and/or their parents had lived in the *Sudetenland* on or before 1 October 1910, although furnishing such proof brought no guarantee of acceptance. Those who had their applications rejected were told to leave. The unequal nature of both this treaty and of bilateral Czecho-Slovak–German relations in general was illustrated by the fact no such regulation applied for Germans settled in what was left of former Czechoslovakia.

If we now turn to the position of the Polish government, we find that they were now ready to strike. On 30 September 1938 the Polish ambassador in Prague handed over an ultimatum to the Czechoslovak Foreign Ministry. The note included the demand for an immediate withdrawal of the Czechoslovak army and police from most of the Tesinsko territory, to be completed no later than 10 October. The Poles made it clear in the ultimatum that in case of rejection or no answer, complete responsibility for the consequences would lie with the Czechoslovak government. Czechoslovakia capitulated close to the expiration of the ultimatum. Given the situation, Prague felt that no other solution was available.

On 2 October the Polish army began its occupation of Tesinsko. On the same day, German activists in the area sent telegrams to Berlin demanding that Germany annex the area. However, for the moment Hitler had other fish to fry. The Germans of that part of Czech Silesia would have to wait their turn. The Poles united the newly occupied districts with the Polish district of Cieszyn. Both Czechs and Germans found themselves to be discriminated against. They were often thrown out of work and sometimes expelled from the area. Some 30,000 Czechs and about 5,000 Germans either voluntarily migrated or were thrown out. Czech education provision was liquidated and German educational provision was severely restricted. Czech associations and organizations were banned without any exceptions, and their property was confiscated. The discriminatory policies of the Polish state in turn provoked active resistance on the Czech side, but by early 1939, the Poles had all but crushed this oppositional activity. Later, after 15 March 1939, when the National Socialists occupied of the rest of Bohemia and Moravia, and Hitler's overall scheme became ever more apparent, a measure of Polish–Czech cooperation was achieved, but by that time even the rump Czecho-Slovak state had ceased to exist. The territories occupied by Germany on this date formed the Protectorate of Bohemia and Moravia. As for Slovakia, it was declared independent under the clerical-fascist leadership of a Catholic priest, Dr Josef Tiso.

The onset of war

On 1 September, as part of its all-round offensive against Poland, the German military occupied villages in the border areas of Tesinsko (Kolektiv autoru, 1997: 68–9). Under the terms of a decree issued on 26 October 1939, Tesinsko was formally incorporated within the territory of the Reich, as part of *Provinz Schlesien*. The Germans introduced a strict occupation regime, and immediately introduced a policy of

Aryanization. Poles were stripped of all property rights, such property in turn being redistributed among Germans. However, expulsions were limited by the need to use skilled Polish labour. The National Socialist tactics of 'carrot and stick' were extremely successful in promoting the Aryanization of the populace. At first many Poles and more especially Czechs could register themselves as Silesians. In addition with the introduction of the *Volksliste*, people of Silesian nationality were allowed to apply for inclusion onto the one of its four categories, usually the third. Better treatment, status and more rations, almost literally formed the 'carrot' part of the policy. Those who refused quickly discovered that their fate would be reduction to the status of *Untermenschen*, deportation, imprisonment or death. The result was that almost 70 per cent inhabitants of Tesinsko applied for the inclusion in the Volksliste. As the National Socialists tightened their grip, so the Poles especially became subjected to more vicious policies of discrimination. In addition to loss of property rights, they had to pay a 15 per cent income tax surcharge and in return suffered a cut in welfare provisions. A special and severe criminal code was introduced for Poles. Czechs, on the other hand, were not subject to such severe repressive measures, although they were denied the right of collective national identification and free association (Boric, 1992: 102–10).

After the aforementioned annexation of Hlucinsko to the Reich, a 'mid-term' census was conducted in January 1939 in order to determine the racial composition of the area, and of course to provide the authorities with a rough guide on how they might proceed with the Aryanization of the population. In the returns, 95 per cent of the inhabitants declared German nationality, and indeed German passports were available to anyone who applied, designated Jews, Roma and Poles being an obvious exception. Both the use of Czech and the local dialect were punishable by a fine of five *Reichsmark*, with the threat of imprisonment hanging over the heads of recidivists. During this period, the Gestapo arrested several thousand non-co-operative local inhabitants who were either put through National Socialist courts or, increasingly, simply dispatched to the ever-expanding network of concentration camps. Although, as we have noted the large majority of the population considered it self to be German, most of the people showed little interest in joining the National Socialist party, or its host of ancillary organizations. When they did, it was often for opportunistic reasons, for which most were later to pay a high price. Either way, around 12,000 people joined either the party itself or one of its fronts.

From 1942 onwards the National Socialists *Heim ins Reich* policy came to the Sudetenland. Germans from South Tyrol, Poland, Bukovina and elsewhere were to resettled in this area of the supposedly Thousand-Year Reich, whether they liked it or not. The Sudetenland in general, and the Opava administrative district in particular, simultaneously became the centre of the most extensive confiscation of Czech land and a sought-after area of German colonization. As for the Czech population, it was simply treated as an object, the existence of which had to dealt with and solved in a manner which suited the ideologists of National Socialism. The various proposals toyed with included mass expulsion to the East, assimilation with the local German population, or assimilation through dispersal throughout the Reich. Reality, however, this time in the shape of the Soviet army, intervened before any of these ideas could be put into practice (Grobelny, 1989: 158–170).

Not only that, as more and more German men went to the Eastern Front to die, so the need to use both local Slav and imported forced labour became ever greater. Although all such labour was subject to both discriminatory treatment and arbitrary violence and death, Poles and Russians received the worst treatment. They had to wear special identifying insignia, were excluded from all forms of German social and cultural events, were generally excluded from working alongside Germans and were kept under strict supervision (Grobelny, 1989: 158–65).

However, as is well known, the National Socialists did not succeed in permanently destroying Czechoslovakia, any more than they succeeded in any of their other aims. Inevitably, the defeat of National Socialist Germany meant that once again inter-state borders would once again change. The pre-Munich status quo was restored. Disputes between Czechoslovakia and Poland over the disputed areas of Czech Silesia lingered for years, and further 'population transfers' occurred. The biggest change occurred with regard to the German population of both Czech Silesia and Czechoslovakia as a whole. Under the terms of the Benes decrees of 1945, virtually the entire German population was forcibly expelled to Germany on the grounds of collective treason and collaboration. This expulsion is one of the issues which continues to sour Czech–German relations to this day, and is a point to which we shall return later. Let us now continue our analysis by surveying the situation in Silesia in the aftermath of the destruction of the Third Reich.

Bibliography

Allgemeines Verzeichnis der Ortsgemeinden und Ortschaften Österreichs nach den Ergebnissen der Volkszählung vom 31. Dezember 1910. Nebst vollständigem alphabetischem Namensverzeichnis. Vienna, 1915.

Apostolischer Visitator der Priester und Gläubigen aus dem Erzbistum Breslau, 1997.

Bahlcke, J., *Schlesien und die Schlesier*. Munich, Langen Müller, 1996.

Bakala, J., 'Z politickeho vyvoje na Opavsku v 19. a na zacatku 20. stoleti', in Kol. autoru, *Poehled dejin Opavska*. Opava, Profil, 1983.

Boda-Krezel, Z, *Sprawa Volkslisty na Gornym Slasku*. Opole, Instytut Slaski, 1978.

Borak, M., 'Slask Cieszynski w latach 1938–1945', in J. Valenta (ed.), *Zarys dziejow Slaska Cieszynskiego*. Ostrava and Prague, Komitet Czeskiej Administracji Terenowej i Narodowosci Rady Narodowej, 1992.

Borak, M., 'Tesinsko v letech 1938–1945', in Kol. autoru, *Nastin dejin Tesinska*. Ostrava, Advertis, 1992.

Cimala, B., 'Autonomisci gornoslascy', in F. Hawranek et al. (eds), *Encyklopedia powstan slaskich*. Opole, Instytut Slaski, 1982.

Cimala, B., 'Zwiazek Gornoslazakow/Bund der Oberschlesier', in F. Hawranek et al. (eds), *Encyklopedia powstan slaskich*. Opole, Instytut Slaski, 1982a.

Dlugoborski, W., et al. (eds), *Polozenie ludnosci w rejencji katowickiej w latach 1939–1945* (Documenta Occupationis, vol. xi). Poznan, Instytut Zachodni, 1983.

Dobrzycki, W., *Powstania Polskie*. Warsaw, PZWS, 1971.

Evans, A., *Sojourn in Silesia 1940–1945*. Ashford, Ashford Writers Press, 1995.

Fuchs, K., 'Vom deutschen Krieg zur deutschen Katastrophe (1866–1945)', in N. Conrads (ed.), *Schlesien*. Berlin, Siedler, 1994.

Gawrecki, D., 'Slask Cieszynski w okresie miedzywojennym (1918–1938)', in J. Valenta (ed.), *Zarys dziejow Slaska Cieszynskiego*. Ostrava and Prague, Komitet Czeskiej Administracji Terenowej i Narodowosci Rady Narodowej, 1992.

Gawrecki, D., 'Slezsko po roce 1742 (1848–1918, 1918–1938)', in Kol. autoru, *Slezsko*. Opava, Matice slezska, 1992.

Gawrecki, D., 'Tesinsko v obdobi mezi sviitovymi valkami (1918–1938)'. in Kol. autoru, *Nastin dejin Tesinska*. Ostrava, Advertis, 1992.

Gawrecki, D., 'Vyvoj Hlucinsaka do r. 1945', in *Ideologicka konference k 60. vyroei navraceni Hlueinska k ceskoslovensym zemim*. Opava, Profil, 1980.

Greiner, P. and Kaczmarek, R., 'Mniejszosci narodowe', in F. Serafin (ed.), *Wojewodztwo slaskie (1922–1939)*. Katowice, Wydawnictwo Uniwersytetu Slaskieg, 1996.

Grobelny, A., *Narodnosti politika nacistu a cesky prumysl 1938–1945*. Ostrava, Profil, 1989.

Grobelny, A., 'Tesinsko od jara narodu k samostatnym statum (1848–1918)', in Kol. autoru, *Nastin dejin Tesinska*. Ostrava, Advertis, 1992.

Hauser, P., *Slask miedzy Polska, Czechoslowacja a separatyzmem*. Poznan, Uniwersytet Adama Mickiewicza, 1991.

Iwanicki, M., *Ukraincy, Bialorusini, Litwini i Niemcy w Polsce w latach 1918–1990*. Siedlce, Wyzsza Szkola Rolniczo-pedagogizna, 1994.

Januszewska-Jurkiewicz, J., and Nowak, K., 'Zaolzie w granicach wojewodztwa slaskiego', in F. Serafin (ed.), *Wojewodztwo slaskie (1922–1939)*. Katowice, Wydawnictwo Uniwersytetu Slaskiego, 1996.

Jastrzebski, W. (ed.), *Ludnosc niemiecka i rzekomo niemiecka na ziemiach polskich wlaczonych do Rzeszy Niemieckiej (1939–1945)*. Bydgoszcz, Wyzsza Szkola Pedagogiczna, 1995.

Jonca, K., 'Schlesiens Juden unter nationalsozialistischer Herrschaft 1933–1945', in F.-C. Schultze-Rhonhof (ed.), *Geschichte der Juden in Schlesien im 19. und 20. Jahrhundert*. Hanover, Stiftung Schlesien, 1995.

Kacir, P., 'Problematyka narodowosciowa na Slasku Cieszynskim w drugej polowie XIX i na poczatku XXI na poczatku XX w. w ocenie czeskiej historiografii', in B. Linek et al., *Fenomen nowoczesnego nacionalizmu w Europie Wrodkowej*. Opole, Institut Slaski, 1997.

Kacirova, S., 'Zanik Zemi Slezske'. MA thesis, University of Opava, 1994.

Kamusella, T., 'Niemcy i Polacy w oczach Gorno Slazakow', *Kultura i Spoleczenstwo* 41 (1), 1997.

Kamusella, T., 'Wylanianie sie grup narodowych i etnicznych na Slasku 1848–1918', *Sprawy Narodowosciowe*, forthcoming.

Kamusella, T. and Sullivan, T., 'The Origins and Anatomy of the Ethnic Cleansing in Upper Silesia 1944–1951', in (ed.), K. Cordell *Ethnicity and Democracy in the New Europe*. London, Routledge, 1998a.

Kano, O. and Pavelka, R., *Tesinsko v polsko-ceskoslovenskych vztazich 1918–1939*. Ostrava, Profil, 1970.

Kocich, M., 'Opavsko v obdobi bur burzoazini CSR v. 1 1918–1938', in Kol. autoru, *Poehled dejin Opavska*. Opava, Profil, 1983.

Kokot, J., *Problemy narodowosciowe na Slasku od X do XX wieku*. Opole, Instytut Slaski, 1973.

Kolektiv autoru, *Tesinsko. Senov u Ostravy*. Ostrava, Advertis, 1997.

Komjathy, A. and Stockwell, R., *German Minorities and the Third Reich: Ethnic Germans of East Central Europe between the Wars*. New York and London, Holmes & Meier, 1980.

Kopiec, J., *Biskupowi Jozefowi Nathanowi w holdzie*. Opole, Sw. Krzyz, 1997.

Körner, G., *Einsatz des Selbstschutzes in Oberschlesien 1921*. Dülmen/Westfalen, Laumann, 1981.

Kozlowski, J., 'Niemcy w poznanskiem do 1918 roku', in A. Sakson (ed.), *Polska – Niemcy – mniejszosc niemiecka w Wielkopolsce*. Poznan, Instytut Zachodni, 1994.

Krzyzanowski, L., 'Kosciol katolicki i inne zwiazki wyznaniowe', in F. Serafin (ed.), *Wojewodztwo slaskie, 1922–1939*. Katowice, Wydawnictwo Uniwersytetu Slaskiego, 1996.

Kwiatek, A., *Spor o kierunek dzialan narodowych na Gornym Slasku (1918–1921)*. Opole, Instytut Slaski, 1991.

Linek, B., 'Polonizacja imion i nazwisk w wojewodztwie slaskim (1945–1949)', in W. Wrzesinski (ed.), *Wroclawskie Studia z Historii Najnowszej*, iv. Wroclaw, Instytut Historyczny Uniwersytetu Wroclawskiego, Wroclawskie Towarzystwo Milosnikow Historii, 1997.

Maser, P. and Weiser, A., *Juden in Oberschlesien*. Berlin, Mann, 1992.

Masnyk, M., *Ruch polski na Slasku Opolskim w latach 1922–1939*. Opole, Instytut Slaski, 1989.

Mende, E., *Der Annaberg und das deutsch-polnische Verhältnis*. Bonn, Bund der Vertriebenen, 1991.

Misztal, J., *Weryfikacja narodowosciowa na Slasku Opolskim 1945–1950*. Opole, Instytut Slaski, 1984.

Orlik, J., *Opavsko a severni Morava za okupace. Z tajnych zprav okupacnich uradu z let 1940–1943*. Ostrava, 1961.

Pallas, L., *Jazykova otazka a podminky vytvareni narodniho vedomi ve Slezsku*. Ostrava, Profil, 1970.

Pavelcik, J., 'Narodnostni boje na Opavsku', in Kol. autoru, *Poehled dejin Opavska*. Opava, 1983.

Peroutka, F., *Budovani statu I-III*. Praha, Lidove noviny, 1991.

Pollok, E., *Legendy, manipulacje, kramstwa prof. F. A. Marka w 'Tragedii gornoslaskiej', a prawdy o Slasku i powojennej dyskryminacji jego mieszkancow*. Przedborz, Wydawnictwo Zyrowa, 1998.

Pospieszalski, K., *Sprawa 58 000 'Volksdeutschow'*. Poznan, Instytut Zachodni, 1959.

Rothschild, J., *East Central Europe between the Two World Wars*. London, University of Washington Press, 1977.

Serafin, F. (ed.), *Wojewodztwo slaskie (1922–1939)*. Katowice, Wydawnictwo Uniwersytetu Slaskiego, 1996.

Serwanski, E., *Hitlerowska polityka narodowosciowa na Gornym Slasku*. Warsaw, Pax, 1963.

Stüttgen, D., et al., *Schlesien Grundriß zur deutschen Verwaltungsgeschichte 1815–1945*, Series A: *Preußen, vol 4*. Marburg (Lahn), Johann-Gottfried-Herder-Institut, 1976

Tomaszewski, J., *Ojczyzna nie tylko Polakow*. Warsaw, Modziezowa Agencja Wydawnieza, 1985.

Urban, T., *Deutsche in Polen. Geschichte und Gegenwart einer Minderheit*. Munich, Beck, 1994.

Valenta, J., 'Rozdileni Tesinska pred sedmdesati lety', in *Tesinsko*, 5 (4), Slesky Tesin, 1960.

Wambaugh, S., *Plebiscites since the World War: With a Collection of Official Documents*, 2 vols. Washington, Carnegie Endowment for International Peace, 1993.

Wanatowicz, M., *Historia spoleczno-polityczna Gornego Slaska i Slaska Cieszynskiego w latach 1918–1945*. Katowice, Wydawnictwo Uniwersytetu Slaskiego, 1994.

Weczerka, H., *Schlesien* (Handbuch der historischen Stätten Deutschlands vol. xiv). Stuttgart, Kröner, 1977.

Notes

1. Tomasz Kamusella wrote the sections on German and Polish Silesia. Petr Kacir wrote on Czech Silesia.
2. The curtailment of the voivodeship's autononmy was illegal because it was not approved by the Silesian *Sejm* as required by law.
3. In the years before 1914, several thousand Ukrainian/Ruthenian workers were encouraged to emigrate to the Upper Silesian industrial basin in an attempt to limit the growing influence of migrant Polish workers from Galicia and western Russia.
4. This camp had originally been constructed to house French POWs during the Franco-Prussian war of 1870–71. It was also used as a POW camp in World War I, and after the Germans vacated it in 1945 the Poles took it over as a concentration camp for Germans.

5. This information was supplied by the editor's mother, who was herself placed on the *Volksliste*. Her inabilty to speak German caused innumerable problems when she was transferred to a German school.
6. At the end of 1944 refusal to complete the questionnaire was declared a capital offence.

6
Polish and Czech Silesia under Communist Rule: A Comparison[1]

The intellectual context and historical legacies

Researching into postwar problems connected to the national question in Polish Upper Silesia is difficult. The difficulty lies mainly in the very topicality of the issue and the moral and legal implications of what occurred in the aftermath of National Socialist rule. Research in this area must also be undertaken with an eye to Polish-German inter-state relations, and all who engage in this work are dependent on historiographies which have frequently been written from a nationalist point of view.

Two opposing parties who approached the field from different perspectives, emerged in relation to the question of what has occurred in Upper Silesia since 1945 and why. Polish researchers have always had access to archival records, but until the late 1980s could rarely write on the past objectively due to ideological constraints. On the other hand, German researchers had access to Polish monographs, but often appended them with frequently one-sided accounts by the *Vertriebene* (expellees) and postwar migrants to Germany.[2]

Research still tends to concentrate upon the most controversial period, i.e. the period of expulsions, which commenced immediately after the war and continued until 1950. Subsequent research, especially on the Polish side, has tended to concentrate on analysis of the Action Link family reunification/repatriation programme. A few exceptions to one side, German scholars following the precepts of the *Grundgesetz* (Basic Law), tended to be oblivious to the transformations in identity which had been triggered off by the Polonizing policies of the Polish government. In a rather legalistic and purblind manner, they continued to presume that the indigenous population of Upper Silesia was unambiguously German. Both parties persisted in their mutually exclusive approaches until 1989, when with the final collapse of Polish communism came the reappearance of Poland's German minority, especially in Upper Silesia. Unfortunately, whereas German and Polish scholars are increasingly in agreement on post-1989 developments in this field, the aforementioned constraints continue to effect research into the period 1945–89. In addition after 1945, research concentrated mainly on Opole, i.e. western Upper Silesia. This legacy dictates that our observations will largely deal with the experiences of western Upper Silesia, but we will make reference to the eastern part of Upper Silesia, as well as Lower Silesia where possible and appropriate. Indeed, because the Polish government failed in its policies of assimilation throughout the whole of Silesia, this task is essential. Before dealing with what occurred in Upper Silesia, let us first mention events in Lower Silesia. Given that the population of Lower Silesia was almost exclusively German, the task that the incoming Polish administration set itself was in some ways more simple than that which confronted it in Upper Silesia.

Immediately after the war Lower Silesia along with other former *Deutsche Ostgebiete* incorporated into Poland, became somewhat multicultural. Alongside Poles lived the so-called 'indubitable Germans' who were not expelled as they were needed to man Lower Silesian factories and mines especially in the Walbrzych-Nowa Ruda industrial basin. The town of Walbrzych was especially mixed, as it contained both German and Jewish populations of some size, together with migrant Polish miners from France and Belgium, who sometimes spoke more French than Polish and returning servicemen who had fought for the Polish Government-in-Exile. After the thaw of 1956, the 'indubitable Germans' were allowed to organize themselves in German cultural societies, a privilege which remained forbidden to German-oriented Upper Silesians. In 1946 the German population of Lower Silesia amounted to 1,234,00, but by 1950 this had been reduced to perhaps as few as 200,000. After the implementation of the Action Link family reunification program in 1956, most Germans in Lower Silesia left for Germany and by 1961 only a few thousand remained.

The new inhabitants of the former *Deutsche Ostgebiete* were afraid that the Germans would one day return, recover their land and property, and once again leave the new inhabitants homeless and destitute. Within this context it is important to remember that the incoming Poles especially those from the *kresy*, were not only destitute, they were often barely literate and had also suffered extreme deprivation at the hands of more often than not, both the German and the Soviet armed forces and civilian authorities. For its part, the government reinforced the anti-German psychosis with a virulent propaganda campaign, and by the fact that no final binding agreement on the Polish western border had been concluded. As we shall see with regard to Upper Silesia, such a psychosis was a country-wide phenomenon.

For the sake of simplicity, the remainder of the narrative, which in essence deals with Upper Silesia, is broken down into the three broadly distinct chronological sections. The first deals with the years 1945–50, the second considers the years 1950–58, and the third covers the period 1959–89. It should be borne in mind that the initial national strategy of the postwar communist authorities was essentially primordialist. They sought to rid Poland of all remaining foreign elements. Alongside this endeavour, the party/state sought to assimilate those who considered themselves to be foreign, but whom the authorities considered to be inherently Polish despite their 'alien veneer'.

With regard to Upper Silesia this objective was to be fulfilled through the implementation of two basic and closely interrelated policies. The first was de-Germanization, which sought physically to remove all Germans from the region as well as physically to destroy all traces of German culture. The region was also to be subjected to re-Polonization, which in some areas in effect meant Polonization, which aimed at replacing deported Germans with Polish resettlers and changing the identity of those former Germans who remained after having been reclassified as Poles. The goal was to be the creation of a society which would be homogeneous with respect to its collective memory, its assessment of sociopolitical reality, and which would identify with the program of the communist party.

The all-embracing characteristic of this project dovetailed neatly within the one-party system established in Poland after 1947, and one should not be too surprised that nationalism and anti-German sentiment were continuously invoked with varying degrees of intensity by the party until its final defeat in 1989. Poland's geopolitical situation, memories of the circumstances of its westward shift in 1945, elements of the secular opposition and the Roman Catholic Church combined to lend legitimacy to the doctrine of integral Polish nationalism. Nowhere was this more true than in Upper Silesia, where the continuous wave of migration to Germany indicated that, as usual, political dogma and political reality had little in common with one another. Indeed, so abstruse was the dogma, that Polish officialdom refused to refer to Upper Silesian Germans as such and instead referred to the autochthonous and native population. Partly because of a wish to break with the legacy of the past, and partly because these terms are almost devoid of any real substance, they are not employed in this narrative.

It should be borne in mind that after the second World War, in addition to the incorporation of almost the whole of Silesia into Poland, equally significant territorial transformations of internal administrative boundaries took place. Initially, until 1950, all of Upper Silesia was included in the postwar Silesian voivodeship. In that year the voivodeship was divided between the new Katowice voivodeship, comprising the industrialized east of Upper Silesia, and the Opole voivodeship which comprised the western part of Upper Silesia and to which two Lower Silesian counties were transferred from the Wroclaw voivodeship. In 1975 a further redrawing of administrative boundaries resulted in the transfer of the Raciborz and Olesno counties from the Opole voivodeship to the Katowice and Czestochowa voivodeships respectively.

Vertreibung and re-Polonization: 1945–50

For the postwar inhabitants of Poland the acquisition of Silesia and other German territories was legitimized as an 'act of historical justice' and the 'return' of the eternally Polish Piast lands.[3] In this ideologized version of history the German population were characterized as 'colonizers,' and 'bandits' who should be 'repatriated' to their fatherland (Linek, 1998: 82–112). For the Germans subjected to expulsion, it was an act of unprecedented barbarity to which in the absence of active National Socialists and members of the armed forces, most of whom had fled, civilians, especially women, children, and the old, had to submit.

Unsurprisingly, there is no common agreement between German and Polish scholars, let alone the population at large on how best to describe and account for what happened to the German population after the war. The difficulties are already rooted in the very terminology employed. When Poles speak about repatriation or transfer of Germans, the latter conceptualize the phenomenon as expulsion (Madajczyk, 1996: 8–12; Ther, 1995: 267–75). Without wishing to become bogged down in this interminable and sterile debate, the first five years of the Polish assimilationist policies will be presented in accordance with the aforementioned de-Germanization/re-Polonization model. In the framework of de-Germanization policies, the following issues will be discussed: expulsion of the population recognized as indubitably German, repression of and discrimination against the remaining German population, combating pro-German attitudes among those Upper Silesians recognized as Poles, changes to place and personal names, as well as the removal of all physical traces of German culture. The policies of re-Polonization will be represented by the following issues: the 'verification' and 'rehabilitation' of the Upper Silesian population, the resettlement of ethnic Poles from Central Poland and the formerly Polish eastern *kresy* in Upper Silesia, and the process of cultural assimilation.

For most Polish researchers, as well as the population at large, the expulsion of the German population from the 'recovered territories' was the straightforward realization of the decisions taken at the Potsdam conference. In this context the pre-Potsdam expulsions were dubbed as 'wild'. However, whereas there may well be a difference between the two in international law, and although the second wave was more organized, they can scarcely be distinguished in terms of misery. It should be noted that the decision to expel Germans from within the borders of the new Poland was made at the absolute latest on 24 May 1945 at the meeting of the Central Committee of the governing *Polska Partia Robotnicza*/Polish Workers' Party (PPR) (Jaworski, 1973: 275), by which date several hundred thousand Germans had already been 'unofficially' expelled or interned into the very concentration camps so recently vacated by the German authorities. Two days later the leading communist Edward Ochab, then in charge of the *Ministerstwo Administracji Publicznej*/Ministry of Public Administration (MPA), presented a plan for the expulsion of the German population, whose short-term number in the new Poland was to be reduced to no more than 2,250,000. The German population was to be divided into three categories: the largest 'economically useless' group was to be deported as quickly as possible. The second group of specialists, mostly employed in industry, and largely in the industrial centres of Lower Silesia, were to remain for a certain period of time, and those whom it would not be possible to remove at once were to be moved to the countryside (Marczak, 1991: 19). However, as we shall see, a fourth category was employed, specifically for those who thought of themselves as German but whom the Polish authorities claimed as Poles.

It should be emphasized that communists were not isolated in their views. On the contrary, the various Polish resistance groupings accepted that expulsions would be necessary in order to render nation and state coterminous. It may also be noted that far-reaching changes had been introduced to communist ideology during Stalin's rule. Together with the building of socialism in one country, as elsewhere in Europe, the doctrine of (hyper-)nationalism had undergone something of a revival, especially during the Great Patriotic War. Indeed, both during and immediately after the war Stalin's chief ideologue, Andrzej Zhdanov, railed against cosmopolitanism, and the ideology of pan-Slavism re-emerged within which Polish communism found a comfortable niche (Walicki, 1996: 421–2; Wrzesinski, 1992).

As for the expulsions, they began in the Silesian voivodeship as early as February 1945, only days after Polish rule was re-established in prewar Polish Upper Silesia. The first postwar Silesian voivode (provincial governor) general Jerzy Zietek commented that Germans should be allowed five minutes to pack 20 kilograms of baggage before their expulsion. A month later another general, voivode Aleksander Zawadzki, reiterated Zietek's words in his directive to the *starosts* (senior county level officials), who were about to commence duties in counties on the territory of the prewar Oppeln Regency (Linek, 1997: 29).

In May 1945 the expulsions of the designated German population commenced in earnest. The methodology of expulsion consisted of several interlinked elements. The first step was to announce the date from which it would be prohibited for German population to reside in and visit certain areas. The authorities must have considered the early results of these actions to have been successful, because in October another decree was issued barring the German population from residing in Opole Silesia (Ruszczewski, 1993: 10–12). The methods used to achieve this goal were dual. First, *sztaby kierownicze* (directing staffs) were established. In addition to representatives of the administration they comprised members of the security apparatus and 'patriotic' civilian organizations such as the *Polski Zwiazek Zachodni*/Polish Western Association (PZZ) and the *Zwiazek Polakow w Niemczech*/Association of the Poles in Germany (ZPwN). The role of these bodies was to supervise the expulsion of the indubitably German population. The expellees were concentrated at *punkty etapowe* (transfer points), from which columns of expellees were headed toward the general direction of Germany, by whatever means of transport if any, was available. Those who were deemed unfit for work were generally expelled earlier than the general population and were allowed to leave for Germany under their own steam, which itself was an extremely risky business.

All Germans not subjected to immediate expulsion were to be gathered in isolation points. These were either forced labor camps, which role transfer points also filled, or German ghettos in urban areas. The organizational chaos which prevailed in 1945, combined with the lack of any systematic records, preclude any detailed comparative analysis of these ghettos and camps. Piotr Madajczyk found information on over 100 different isolation points (1996: 255–86). The list appears to be incomplete. Apart from anything else, he does not deal with the separately run camps which the Soviet authorities established in Poland. The camps, whether they were Polish or Soviet run, served a dual purpose. On the one hand, they served as places where Germans could be put to work prior to be being expelled. On the other, they often served as centres where revenge for the crimes of the National Socialist authorities could be exacted upon anyone unfortunate to have been interred. Such camps were often more than centres of toil and transit. Camps such as those established at Lambinowice and Swietochlowice-Zgoda have passed into German and Upper Silesian folklore by virtue of their reputation for ill treatment and death.

It is difficult to determine the number of people expelled from the region during this time. Polish estimates vacillate from about 100,000 to close to 200,000 (Nitschke, 1997a: 356). Given the lack of data on how many were deported to the Soviet Union, mostly never to return, the latter number seems to be nearer the truth. Although Madajczyk enumerates many examples of brutality and dehumanization which accompanied the expulsions, at least the first element of the Potsdam decision, which stipulated that the expulsions be conducted in an 'orderly and humane' manner, gradually came to be adhered to. According to Zdzislaw Lempinski in 1946, close to 160,000 people were expelled from Upper Silesia. He estimates the number in 1947 as being less than 15,000 and in 1950 as being not much more than 12,000 (Lempinski, 1979: 221–2). In sum, during this period as many as 400,000 people were either deported to the Soviet Union or expelled to Germany. It must also be remembered that many more were either killed toward the end of the war, or fled westward with the German armed forces never to return. Neither should it be forgotten that most of those who, after initially having fled, did return to their homes either were subsequently expelled or found themselves destitute and homeless, their properties having been acquired by incoming Poles.

The aforementioned camps were the most drastic form of repression, whose inmates especially between 1945 and 1946 had scant, if any, legal protection. The voivodeship authorities encouraged people to report any Germans they knew to be in hiding, and generally sought to maintain the anti-German climate. Those Germans who remained (legally) outside the camps in addition found themselves the subject of all sorts of official sanctions. They were forced to work for longer hours than Poles, and to give up of a quarter of their wages to the special *Fundusz Ofiar Terroru Hitlerowskiego* (Fund for the Victims of the Hitlerian Terror). They also found themselves excluded from Poland's health care and social security system, such as it was, and until September 1946 found it difficult even to obtain marriage licences (Linek, 1997: 27–8; Nitschke, 1997b: 75–80).

As we have mentioned, elements of the German population were in fact also claimed as Polish by the Poles. For this group of people there was, at least in theory, although often not in reality, an alternative to the ghettos or camps, aside from flight to Germany. Such people were eligible to receive documentation confirming that an individual was not in fact German, but Polish. In order to be so reclassified, applicants had to undergo the process of so-called 'rehabilitation' or 'verification'. The former action was applied to prewar citizens of Poland of German extraction, including residents of the Silesian voivodeship who had been included in one of the four categories of the DVL. To a large degree, the Polish authorities accepted the categories of German established by the National Socialists, although the official attitude toward members of the different categories of the DVL evolved with time. Initially, members of Groups 1 and 2 were recognized as indubitable Germans and as such were designated for expulsion. Members of Groups 3 and 4, after having signed the declaration of loyalty to the Polish nation and to the Polish state, were granted full civil rights. From 1947 members of Group 2 were usually granted Polish citizenship on application. However, given that the majority of such people were in concentration camps when this offer was made, and as a result of their experiences were hardly sympathetic to the authorities, the large majority elected to migrate to Germany. Although rehabilitation of those who had joined Groups 3 and 4 (70 per cent of all the cases) was conducted in the summer of 1945, in the intervening period they remained second class citizens. As such they were subject to all kinds of discrimination and had often lost the majority of both their goods and property, which they later found it difficult to get back, if only because it now belonged to a resettled Pole (Boda-Krezel, 1978).

An even worse fate was faced by the inhabitants of the prewar Oppeln Regency, who underwent an analogous process of 'national verification' in order to obtain Polish citizenship. Polish settlers and expellees arriving in this region treated the entire population as German, including even those who, before and during the war, had considered themselves to be Polish. In both parts of the region the all-round destitution of the incoming Poles, and their understandable ignorance of the ethnographic complexity of Upper Silesia, exacerbated the situation. Anyone in western Upper Silesia who obtained Polish citizenship had also to swear an oath of allegiance to the Polish nation. For those western Upper Silesians who had maintained their allegiance to Poland, even at the price of being sent to a German concentration camp; this was both insulting and humiliating (Misztal, 1984; Stoll, 1968).

As for the new arrivals into Upper Silesia, we can distinguish three sub-groups. The first consisted of arrivals from the *kresy* and former inhabitants of the *kresy* who had survived deportation to the Soviet Union in 1939 and 1940. They found themselves in Upper Silesia due to decisions taken without their knowledge let alone consent, or because they had fled from the *Ukrainska Armia Powstancza*/Ukrainian Insurgent Army (UPA). These people began to arrive on railway transports as early as March 1945. The second group of incomers came from the devastated areas of central Poland, attracted by stories of abandoned farms, homes and jobs for all. The third and much smaller subgroup of newcomers was constituted by a few thousand emigrants from western Europe, and members of the Polish armed forces who had served under Generals Anders and Sikorski, and who often faced official hostility upon their return, for having fought for the restoration of 'bourgeois Poland'.

Although each of the three basic groups (former German citizens, inhabitants of the prewar Silesian voivodeship and Polish settlers and expellees) each constituted around one third of the total population of the area (in 1946 it was 2.8 million), it was the incomers from central Poland who formed the bulk of the new administrative and political elite. This was due among other things to their higher level of education compared with the predominantly barely literate Poles from the *kresy*. The fact that they were anti-German was also much to their advantage. However, most importantly, the communist leadership was assiduous in its cultivation of this group. Voivode Zawadzki, who came from the Dabrowa basin adjacent to Upper Silesia, consciously built such a structure of administration which privileged this group of settlers.

The situation of the Upper Silesians, already made precarious by legally sanctioned inequality, was worsened by the habitual distrust of them expressed by civil servants. The latter suspected them of clandestine support for Germany, as their use of the German language seemed to indicate. Such tension was especially visible in Opole Silesia, where even Polish-oriented Upper Silesians tended to speak the Upper Silesian West Slavic dialect which was interlaced with a plethora of German (ic) linguistic loans, and not standard Polish.

To the bureaucratic mind, this situation could be rectified by cultural re-Polonization. The immediate target was those who were of school age. The educational system sought to belittle significance of family ties and to emphasize the integrity of the Polish nation and the eternal hostility of Germany toward Poland. In the years 1945–1948, the older generation was forced to participate in special 're-Polonization courses'. Besides learning the Polish language, the adults had also to learn about Polish history and literature. Outside of the classroom, the nationalist context was present during all kinds of festivals, celebrations of various anniversaries, youth meetings, and excursions to other parts of the new Poland, as well as in a whole host of other cultural events (Osekowski, 1994: 195–210; Strauchold, 1995).

It was a surprise for the authorities that course participants and schoolchildren spoke in German so often. The reappearance of the language in the streets made this realization even more acute. Initially, this phenomenon was explained by the presence of the not yet expelled Germans and as the continuation of linguistic habits instilled in the population during German rule. However, when the Polish state took control over whole Upper Silesia, that part of the population redesignated as Polish had in fact been instructed to start speaking Polish. The persistence of German provided a gauge to assess the size of 'pro-German sympathies'. After having searched for the legal basis which would allow the suppression of such attitudes, administrative instruments were eventually employed to punish persons expressing 'antipathy and disrespect for the Polish state', i.e. speaking German. These included fines, all kinds of economical pressure (deprivation one of one's job, business, etc.), and finally, for hardcore cases, the special forced labour camp established in Gliwice.

In a mirror-image of previous National Socialist practices, the linguistic battle was complemented by activities aimed at eradicating German personal names and erasing 'remnants of German culture'. At the personal level, this consisted of official pressure to Polonize names and surnames, and as such was resented as an unnecessary intrusion on the part of the authorities in the personal lives of the Upper Silesians. Polonization of surnames also aimed at doing away with all regional specificities. In the case of Christian names, people were forced to adopt Slavic ones and to ensure that newly born children did not receive Germanic names. In total, 280,000 people had to change/Polonize their Christian names and/or surnames due to this action (Linek, 1997).

Another action which directly infringed the privacy of the Upper Silesian population was the attempt physically to erase all traces of German culture from the area. For example, people were made to remove German inscriptions from the tombstones of deceased relatives, churches and roadside crosses. This element of the policy gained such momentum that German inscriptions were even removed from dishes, kitchen equipment, transportation tickets and grocery products. However, following the end of the mass expulsions at the end of 1947, anti-German activities were gradually toned down and civic rights were granted to the remaining German population, which did not, officially at least, include German-oriented Upper Silesians.

It is important to note that, for the Polish authorities, the verified and rehabilitated Upper Silesians did not enjoy the right to choose their own nationality. From the official perspective, these people were Poles, and were expected to act as such. However, as early as 1946 a trend appeared which the communist authorities could not and later did not want to deal with. Postal family contacts were resumed in that year, and as all forms of contact between families which had been divided by the war and its aftermath increased, so more and more of the 'verified' and 'rehabilitated' population sought to migrate to Germany where members of their families already resided.

The clandestine minority: 1950–58

The first half of the 1950s is frequently presented as the period of Stalinization of the sociopolitical life and the mechanical transposition of the Soviet model throughout Eastern Europe. This is true in terms of policies pursued in the socio-economic sphere. With regard to Poland's nation-building policies, there was on the other hand, a perceptible, albeit minor relaxation in the drive to homogenize the population. Apart from anything else, the overwhelming majority of unwanted Germans had been expelled, Ukrainian nationalist resistance had been broken, and for various reasons including officially sanctioned discrimination and pogroms, Poland's Jewish community continued to shrink.

Poland, like all other countries of the Soviet bloc, was deeply affected by the death of Stalin in 1953. In Poland the old dictator's death signalled the fall of his allies, and the return of Wladyslaw Gomulka to power in 1956. Initially Gomulka gained broad social support precisely because his patriotic credentials were not in doubt. Indeed, in the immediate postwar period he had held overall responsibility for the deportation of Germans from the 'recovered territories', and the resettlement of ethnic Poles in their stead (Ther, 1997: 124).

Gomulka, now keen to build bridges to the West and to establish relations with the Federal Republic, effectively abandoned the attempt to create an ethnically homogeneous Poland. Following the Act of Polish Citizenship of January 1951 'indubitable Germans' remaining in Poland were allowed to obtain German passports. The right to be educated in German had also been extended, as had the opportunities for greater cultural self-expression. With the coming to power of Gomulka, the last restrictions upon 'indubitable Germans' in Lower Silesia and elsewhere were removed. Those who wished to emigrate (probably over 90 per cent) were allowed to, and those who wished to stay in Poland were allowed to establish their own sociocultural societies. However, the post 1956 wave of migration from Lower Silesia was so great that in Wroclaw in 1963 the last German minority school in Lower Silesia was closed. Unsurprisingly, as the German minority there grew smaller, so the financial subventions from Poland and the German Democratic Republic (GDR) were reduced. In the end virtually all that was left was the German sociocultural society in Walbrzych, which incidentally is still in existence today.

These provisions applied to a relatively small group of the former German citizens. In Upper Silesia the 'verified' and 'rehabilitated' population was still denied the right to choose between German or Polish nationality. There is, however, little doubt that most of them, especially the verified ones, considered themselves to be Germans. Also many who had previously identified themselves as Upper Silesian, gradually began to express a pro-German attitude. This was hardly surprising, given that the incomers could barely distinguish between the two groups, and that life in Poland was especially uncomfortable for them both in political and economic terms. In Opole Silesia this phenomenon was so widespread that an outsider could have been forgiven for thinking that parts of region were inhabited exclusively by Germans (Tyrmand, 1989: 183). According to the estimates of Leszek Belzyt, out of the 1,300,000 former German citizens remaining within the borders of the new Poland, between 500,000 and 600,000 had a clear German identity, with the remainder of this total comprising Upper Silesians, *Szlonzoks*, Kashubes and Mazurs, of whom he considers only 200,000 could really be considered to be Polish (Belzyt, 1996: 58–9).

Pro-German attitudes may be also numerically assessed in another manner. Czeslaw Osekowski estimates that in 1952 about 200,000 people in Poland, of whom 130,000 were to be found in the Opole voivodeship, possessed temporary documents reaffirming their German nationality. These documents had been issued by various institutions, including embassies of the UK and the US, or the authorities of either German state. In effect this group had dual Polish and German citizenship. Also in a questionnaire that year preceding the issuance of internal passports in Upper Silesia, despite years of pressure, 80,000 adults declared their nationality to be German (Osekowski, 1994: 118–20).

The reaction of the authorities to such recalcitrance was similar to that in the 1940s. Persons considered to be pro-German 'ringleaders' and activists were arrested or laid off from their jobs, while the administration and security forces pressed the remainder to change their nationality declarations. At one point the government considered deporting these incorrigibles to the Rzeszow and Lublin voivodeships in eastern Poland, where they would be dispersed. Parts of these voivodeships were underpopulated due the war and the subsequent deportation of local Ukrainians and *Lehmke*. It was reasoned that such a resettlement programme would not only solve the identity problem in Upper Silesia, it would help economic recovery in south-eastern Poland. Eventually, the planned resettlement of Germans was not implemented for fear of further damaging the productive capacity of industry in Upper Silesia (Sakson, 1998: 209–13).

On the whole, this was a period when repression directed against Upper Silesians abated. For instance, they were not as pressed as their Polish neighbours to collectivize their farms. The use of German at home went largely unpunished, and greater leniency was shown to offenders who used German in public. Although Upper Silesians were still discriminated against and closely observed by the security forces, similar restrictions applied to numerous other segments of the non-Upper Silesian populace. The authorities were also suspicious of former members of the *Armia Krajowa*/Homeland Army (AK), the *Polskie Stronnictwo Ludowe*/Polish Peasant Party (PSL) and the *Polska Partia Socjalistyczna*/Polish Socialist Party (PPS), as well as toward former officials of the prewar regime. Crucially, however, Upper Silesian Germans had an alternative unavailable to theses groups, namely departure for the FRG.

The structure of social stratification shaped immediately after the war remained unchanged. Within its framework, indigenous Upper Silesians formed the unskilled and semi-skilled work force, whereas newcomers from the Dabrowa industrial basin predominated in top positions in industrial, party and governmental administration. This situation led to deepening of the class-cum-ethnic chasm which had first appeared during the interwar period. This division persisted despite communist rhetoric of proletarian solidarity, which demonstrates that national loyalties were deemed more important than notions of international fraternity. For example, of all former German citizens retained in Poland, only 380 attended universities in 1951/52. At the same time only 8 per cent of the youth of verified families attended secondary schools (Blasiak, 1990; Osekowski, 1994: 124).

The figures were so tiny not only because of the activities of the state but also due to self-imposed separation of the Upper Silesian populace from the outer world. This inward retreat was an answer to discrimination, and an instrument through which a modicum of security could be gained. Upper Silesians effected this separation through endogamy and by sticking to their own model of everyday life. Any changes in the group ethos emanated above all as a result of contact with the FRG, either through contact with friends and family or through the media, primarily radio. Naturally, such developments further served to estrange the German-oriented population from Poland and the Poles (Görlich, 1990: 362).

The authorities could not find any effective methods of curbing these tendencies. In the course of discussions commenced by the thaw of 1956, the Opole voivodeship authorities came to the conclusion that the simplest solution would be to recognize the existence of a German minority in Upper Silesia and to grant them the right to use the German language and to establish their own organizations. Pro-Polish rehabilitated Upper Silesian *Szlonzoks* immediately and decisively opposed this suggestion. The regional and national authorities in turn quickly realized that recognizing this group as German could easily create more problems than it solved. Such an act would have contradicted over a century of Polish nationalist dogma, and undermined Poland's case for retaining 'the recovered territories'.

For their part, pro-Polish Upper Silesians, mainly former ZPwN members, veterans of the Silesian uprisings, together with the Opole branch of the PSL, demanded permission to establish their own regional organization the *Zrzeszenie Opolan* (Association of the Opolanians). They also demanded that the area be granted regional autonomy as well as greater access to positions of authority in the state and party administrations. Given that these ideas also sat uncomfortably with the centre, they were also rejected (Linek, 1993).

Such schemes were in part designed to reverse or at least halt the tendency toward ever greater identification with Germany. Discussion of the subject conducted in the years 1955–57 in the regional and national press had little influence on the decisions of those Upper Silesians who were determined to leave their Heimat as quickly as possible. In fact emigration increased after the Red Cross organizations of the FRG and Poland concluded an agreement on this matter in December 1955. The fact that the Polish government was prepared to cooperate on this matter indicates two things. The first is that they wished to improve their virtually non-existent relations with Bonn, and secondly that they had failed to 're-Polonize' substantial sections of the Upper Silesian population.

The outflow of the Upper Silesian population from the region to both German states had never really stopped anyway. In the years 1950–51 between 40,000 (Polish sources) and 56,000 (German sources) people left Poland for Germany. However, it has not been established how many of them originated from Upper Silesia (Osekowski, 1994: 133–4). Between 1952 and 1955, within the framework of Action Link program, 12,000 more left Poland, mainly for the GDR. The turning-point for Upper Silesia took place between 1956 and 1958. During that period, out of 211,000 who left for the FRG, 111,000 were Upper Silesians (Korbel, 1995: 26, 28). Unsurprisingly, this wave of emigration had a negative effect upon Polish industry. As if this were not bad enough, relations with the Federal Republic barely improved. Therefore Warsaw called a halt to the programme in 1958 – not because the problem was solved, but because it had no idea of why the problem even existed. The fact that these people considered themselves to be German contradicted fundamental ideas on the nature of the Polish nation, and as such left the authorities both baffled and frustrated.

Emigration to Germany: 1959–89[5]

This section deals with two main themes. The first is the continued pattern of migration to Germany. The second is the emergence of German minority organizations in Upper Silesia in the mid-1980s. Despite the effective discontinuation of the Action Link programme, people still continued to leave for Germany. Between 1959 and 1970 out of 132,000 migrants to Germany over 82,000 came from Upper Silesia. That so many were allowed to leave Poland was thanks to the activities of West German and Polish diplomats who maintained unofficial contacts in third countries. From the perspective of both governments, and especially as the 1960s wore on, such communications were an effective supplement to more public demonstrations of the spirit of détente. From the point of view of domestic politics, Bonn could show it was doing something for those stuck behind the Iron Curtain, and Warsaw managed to get rid of a number of people who were in various ways a drain on resources and morale.

Of decisive importance was the Ostpolitik of Willy Brandt's SPD-led administration during the years 1969 and 1974. Having decided to jettison the shibboleths of the Adenauer era in order to improve interstate and interpersonal contacts in Europe, Bonn was now prepared to recognize Poland's western border in accordance with the norms of international law. It did so in December 1970, arguing that full recognition would have to await the conclusion of a general peace treaty or some analogous step. Warsaw reciprocated by presenting Bonn with a document which among other things dealt with the issue of Poland's German minority. It stated that: 'In Poland ... there has remained a certain group of people of indubitable German nationality, as well as people from mixed families among whom this nationality has prevailed'. Such persons were to be allowed to emigrate. The terms governing was to be allowed to emigrate, as spelled out in a secret codicil, were quite generous. They included descendants and spouses of former German citizens/ethnic Germans and siblings having relatives in the Federal Republic (Barcz, 1989: 9; Bielski, 1986: 222).

On the basis of these decisions, over 62,000 people left Poland by 1975 including 28,000 from Upper Silesia. 1975 was of course the year of the Helsinki Conference on Security and Cooperation in Europe. Edward Gierek, First Secretary of the Central Committee of the PZPR (*Polska Zjednoczona Partia Robotnicza*), and Chancellor Helmut Schmidt met there and decided that on the basis of the aforementioned documents, a further 125,000 would be allowed to leave Poland by 1979. These discussions were particularly arduous, as the Polish government claimed quite rightly that it had no idea of whether 125,000 was an appropriate figure, as it had only hazy estimates of how many Germans remained in Poland, and absolutely no idea of how many wanted to leave. In his typically brusque fashion Schmidt informed the Polish delegation that the DM2 billion credit on offer to Poland was dependent on him obtaining 125,000 exit visas. Otherwise the opposition controlled Bundesrat would veto the loan. In addition, a further loan of DM1 billion was agreed in principle, as was an agreement to allow reciprocal pension rights for war veterans who resided in the other's country, which Poland only started to pay in 1995 after having extracted further financial subvention from the German government from which these pensions are paid. In the event Poland got the loans, and between 1975 and 1979 as part of the package, 87,306 people left Upper Silesia for the FRG. It should come as no surprise that even pro-Polish activists from the interwar period now opted for Germany. It was not that they now felt themselves to be German. Rather, they were disgusted by the attitude of the PZPR toward them, and also by the existing sociopolitical situation, which was becoming increasingly chaotic with ever more people being condemned to a life of penury.

It was in the 1980s, as power slowly ebbed away from the PZPR, that the German minority took a leaf out of Solidarity's book and began to organize themselves. In 1984, and with the quasi-covert support of the *Landsmannschaft Schlesien,* 20 inhabitants of the Katowice voivodeship sought to register a German cultural society, but to no avail. The next year in Raciborz, without bothering to seek official permission, Blasisus Hanczuch established the first *Deutscher Freundschaftskreis*/German Friendship Circle (DFK). According to the organizers, by 1987 a number of DFKs had sprung up with a total membership of around 5,000. As they were illegal they were closely observed by the security forces and regularly harassed. However the party/state did not bar DFK members from meeting German journalists and diplomats. In January 1988 representatives of the DFKs succeeded in meeting German Foreign Minister Hans-Dietrich Genscher at the Federal Republic's embassy in Warsaw (Urban, 1994: 97–8).

Communist rule in Polish Upper Silesia: a balance sheet

Interestingly enough, the front-line activists were all older people who had at least received part of their education in German schools before 1945. That few younger people were prepared to become involved was perhaps a consequence of the long-term policy of re-Polonization. Of special significance in this respect was the total prohibition until the 1970s of teaching German at any level of education in Upper Silesia. Not that the younger generation took readily to standard Polish. Paradoxically, as the years went by, the Upper Silesian dialect, though looked down upon by outsiders and sophisticates gradually began to function as the unambiguous marker of Germanness, especially in Opole Silesia.

The dearth of any direct experience of Germany on the part of those born after 1945 may also have played a role. Having said that, the mediated image of the Federal Republic as a land of milk and honey, in opposition to the continuous economic and political chaos in Poland, was attractive. It was only on arrival that the migrants discovered that as far as the average (West) German was concerned, the newcomers were Poles in search of German jobs.

In relation to this trend it is worth posing the question recently repeated many times by Madajczyk (1996: 295): was there any alternative to the unfolding of the situation as described above? Madajczyk answers the question in the traditional vein, stating that if Polish policy had been more sensitive, the Polonization of Upper Silesia would have been much more effective. He also claims that had the communist state been more decentralized, the situation would not have deteriorated in the way that it did. However, it is not necessarily the case that a democratic system and the acceptance of regionalism would have ensured the assimilation of all Upper Silesians within the Polish nation. Neither would more freedom for such institutions as the Roman Catholic Church have had to led to wider Polonization, because many Upper Silesian priests in effect functioned as German national leaders in their parishes.

With regard to the events in postwar Upper Silesia, it must be emphasized that most of the Upper Silesian population had a deep-seated attachment to the *Deutschtum* prior to 1945. Many of them felt themselves to be part of the German nation, others felt themselves to be, if not German nationals, then loyal citizens of the German state, and almost every Upper Silesian had strong links with everyday German culture. Even if the relationship had been weaker, the postwar situation produced by expulsions which split numerous families would have eventually resulted in further migration, just as happened anyway.

The overall result of the activities of the political and administrative elites in Upper Silesia was the segregation of the postwar population into Upper Silesians and the rest who, in the eyes of the authorities, were the 'true Poles'. The stereotypes which emerged immediately after the war persisted until 1989. The policies of forced assimilation were mistaken, and no attempt at regional integration was made because centralization was the ultimate goal. Hence discussion on the new identity of Upper Silesia was recommenced only after the fall of the Polish People's Republic in 1989. Having completed our survey of Polish Silesia during this period, let us now turn to the Czech fragment.

Czech Silesia under communist rule

Czech Silesia was occupied by Soviet forces towards the end of the Second World War. In order to understand the postwar development of

Czech Silesia it is necessary to take three different factors into consideration: the results of the Potsdam Conference, the forcible expulsion of the overwhelming majority of Germans from Czechoslovakia as a whole, and communist attitudes towards ethnicity and nation-building.

The Potsdam Conference affected Czech Silesia in three different ways: the shifting westward of Poland's border with Germany, the restitution of the pre-1938 Czechoslovak–German border, and the 'transfer' of the ethnic German population under Article XIII of the treaty. As we have already seen, Poland's westward shift resulted in its acquiring the overwhelming majority of former German Silesia. It also resulted in the *Hultschiner Ländchen*, which at Versailles in 1919 had been awarded to Czechoslovakia and in 1920 was occupied by the Czechoslovak army, prior to being absorbed into Germany in 1939, once again becoming a territory adjacent to the Polish border. Ironically, the restitution of the pre-1938 Czechoslovak–German border confirmed the results of the 1742 Berlin Treaty between King Friedrich II of Prussia and the Habsburg Empress Maria Theresa, and the post-First World War division of this part of Silesia between Czechoslovakia and Poland. More important with regard to the future ethnic composition of Czech Silesia was the declaration under Article XIII of the Potsdam Conference. In order to 'solve' for once and for all the nationalities question, it was determined that Czechoslovakia, including Czech Silesia, was to be ethnically homogenized. The idea of settling such conflicts by migration, whether forcibly or by peaceful means, was of course hardly original. What is sometimes forgotten is the fact that with regard to postwar Czechoslovakia, the idea of applying such a solution, by means of force if necessary, originated during the war with the London-based Czechoslovak government-in-exile, and in particular its leader, Dr Edvard Benes. During his exile in London he lobbied the British government to support such proposals, firmly convinced that the very diversity of the original Czechoslovak state had been responsible for its downfall (Burcher, 1996: 5).

The postwar expulsions

Immediately after the cessation of hostilities, the Benes government re-established itself in Prague with Soviet approval. On 2 August 1945 Presidential Decree No. 33 was issued. This decree stated that all Germans and Hungarians who had not actively resisted the National Socialist occupation forces to be *persona non grata*.[6] They were stripped of their Czechoslovak citizenship, civil liberties and possessions. As in

Poland, separating the population according to bureaucratic criteria proved to be somewhat problematic. It may be concluded that this process of separating 'good' Germans from the remainder did not accord with the rules of natural justice (Brügel, 1974: 149). Such an observation is reinforced by the fact that, although the presidential decrees stated that persons who had been persecuted or sent to concentration camps by the National Socialists should have their citizenship reconfirmed, such a process took the ethno-religious provenance of the victims into account. In a staggering display of chauvinism, many Jews, despite the obvious suffering inflicted upon them by the National Socialists, were marked down for expulsion on the grounds that they had considered themselves to be German before the National Socialists began their campaign of extermination (Brügel, 1974: 165). In Czech Silesia the expulsion orders also embraced Poles, and sometimes those who simply designated themselves as Silesians. As in Poland the expulsions, especially those of the Germans, can be divided into 'wild' and 'organized' phases, with the expulsions becoming more organized but barely less brutal after Potsdam. The implementation of these policies in Czechoslovakia resulted in the expulsion of roughly three million Germans from the entire country, with an additional 30,000 Poles being expelled from Czech Silesia (Wiskemann, 1967: 235).

Benes' strategy was made clear in a statement in October 1945: 'we must get rid of our Germans, and they will go in any case' (Ryback, 199: 170). Rhodes is right to say that 'euphemistically speaking, the war and its aftermath "simplified" Czechoslovakia's ethnic composition through the Holocaust, the Soviet annexation of Ruthenia to the Ukraine, and the forcible expulsion of ethnic Germans after 1945' (Rhodes, 1995: 349). As the ratio of Czechoslovaks to non-Czechoslovaks dropped from 3:1 in 1930 for the whole of Czechoslovakia to 17:1 in 1991 for the Czech Republic (European Commission, 1997: 12; Hoskova, 1994: 91), from the late 1940s questions of ethnicity came to revolve almost exclusively around Czech–Slovak relations (Morison, 1995: 78).

Communist ideology and the nationalities question

Until 1948/49 all political forces in Czechoslovakia were united in the desire to solve minority issues by expelling unwanted minorities from the territory of the state. With the communist takeover in February 1948 the principles of international communism had to be implemented. In September 1945 the Sudeten German communist Karl

Kreilich summarized communist views on German ethnicity and nationalism in post-war Czechoslovakia: 'There must not exist any organized, nationalistic group in Czechoslovakia that would form a German minority. There must not be a special German character, no matter whether economic, political or cultural, in Czechoslovak life ... there must not be a German status or a German education' (Roucek, 1990: 200). The specifics of the case aside, Kreilich was reaffirming traditional communist ideology, which saw consciousness based on class position as opposed to national or ethnic identity as being the wave of the future. Nationalistic movements, and demands for status recognition on the part of ethnic minorities, were interpreted as counterrevolutionary bourgeois movements which needed to be destroyed. The political revolution set in train was paralleled by a social revolution aimed at creating a socialist society, which among other things would be free of national/ethnic antagonisms. Any territorial disputes between the new socialist states, such as the latent Polish–Czechoslovak dispute over Czech Silesia, were simply suppressed by the Soviet Union (Gilbert, 1980: 187).

In the reconstituted Czechoslovakia this Soviet veto on all territorial changes between the socialist states, except of course those which increased Soviet territory, greatly affected the Poles of Czech Silesia, above all in the still-disputed region around the Ostrava. The occupation of the Czech part of Tecisnsko in 1938 by Poland and the ensuing Polonization on this region left many Poles on the wrong side of the border after the return of the pre-1938 territorial status quo. Poles living in this part of Czech Silesia were torn between growing nationalism in Poland proper and appeals for international solidarity put forward by the communists, who, to confuse matters, were by no means adverse to stoking up nationalist emotions when it suited them. The estimated 60–80,000 Poles (Rhodes, 1995: 351; Wiskemann, 1967: 236) were not forcibly expelled in the same manner as the Germans, but the establishment of rule from Prague, and the accompanying attempt to impose a uniform Czech consciousness and culture in the area, made their position difficult. This process was itself exacerbated by Czech memories of Polish participation in the dismemberment of the prewar state, and the fact that many local Poles had supported Polish annexation of the region. It should therefore come as no surprise to learn that many Poles living in post-war Czech Silesia opted to emigrate to Poland.

As for the fate of the Germans of Czech Silesia, their fate was inextricably linked to that of the overall German population in the country, and must be viewed within that wider context. However, as we have already noted, given that national consciousness was not fixed to the same degree as it was elsewhere in Czechoslovakia, as in Polish Upper Silesia, Germans or German-oriented Silesians could slip through the net. Moreover once the 'wild' expulsions had been completed, decisions on who to expel were taken at the local level, which led to a variety of approaches on how best to proceed. Thus many much-needed German specialists were forbidden to leave, like their counterparts in Polish Lower Silesia, and those Germans who were married to Czechs or could prove their anti-fascist credentials were allowed to stay (Böse and Eibicht, 1989: 138).[7] According to official Czechoslovak statistics as of 1950 the process of expulsion was all but complete, with there being only 165,000 Germans still in the country, mostly in diaspora with small concentrations in some Bohemian and Moravian cities (Roucek, 1996: 214).

The fate of the ethnic Germans: inter-party politics and international relations

Czechoslovak state policy towards the German minority until 1989 can be divided into various phases, all of which were to some extent influenced by a mix of national and international considerations (Roucek, 1990: 200 ff.). The first of these phases occurred during the period 1945–48, and as we have already noted was a period during which a policy of ethnic homogenization was pursued. Large sections of the Hungarian and especially German population were expelled, and those who remained were placed under pressure to assume Czechoslovak identity. Given the general climate of hostility which existed, and that the Benes Decrees had declared such people stateless, such an objective was more difficult to obtain than it might have been.

In fact, it was not until Stalin had tired of Benes, and the subsequent communist takeover in 1948, that these despised and marginalized groups were offered the return of their citizenship on condition that before and during the war 'they did not fail in the duties of any Czech citizen or take any other citizenship' (Roucek, 1990: 201). The situation was further eased by Government Decree No. 252 of 29 November 1949 which sought to facilitate integration of Germans and Hungarians by simplifying the criteria through which citizenship might be restored. The need to conserve scarce skilled labour resources seems to have played a role here.

With the death of Stalin, we witness a new phase of postwar policy toward the German minority. Thus on 24 April 1953 all remaining

Germans were granted Czechoslovak citizenship, whether they wanted it or not. The communists justified this step in their usual fashion, citing it as reward for 'The excellent work of many German workers in our Republic serving the interests of peace and rebuilding, strengthened the trust of the Czechoslovak working class toward the remaining Germans so much that the leading Communist Party and the government thought it suitable and right to reinstate their citizenship' (Roucek, 1990: 203). These and other measures allowing for the greater expression of German identity seem to have had little effect. Whenever possible Germans still continued to emigrate, and a significant number of German workers participated in the 1953 strikes. Yet instead of returning to Stalinist methods, the government reacted with further efforts to promote the integration of Germans within wider society. The nomination of ethnic German candidates for local, regional and national elections began. From 1955 Germans were granted the right to learn their ancestral language. German-language news broadcasts were permitted on the radio from 1957, and the German-language journal *Aufbau und Frieden* (Reconstruction and Peace) began to appear three times a week. In promoting such policies the party hoping to achieve the eventual integration of the remaining German population within Czechoslovak society on the basis of class solidarity. That this policy was not successful was because Germans in Czechoslovakia kept themselves very much to themselves. Many also appear to have hoped either for the peaceful restitution of the old state or that eventually they would be allowed to emigrate.

In July 1960 a new constitution was promulgated, an event which once again marked a radical change in Prague's minority policy. Although Hungarians, Ukrainians and Poles were officially recognized as constituting ethnic minorities, no similar status was accorded to the remaining German population, in Silesia or elsewhere. The communist party disappointed with the speed of the assimilation of the estimated 160,000 Germans decided to use a different approach to settle the problem. The Central Committee Secretary for Nationality Affairs, Bruno Köhler, himself an ethnic German, decided that all remaining unassimilated Germans should be assimilated once and for all (Roucel, 1990: 204). It was now argued that their right to exist as a national minority in Czechoslovakia ceased as a result of the decisions of the Potsdam conference and the consequent confirmation of Prague's decision to expel all disloyal citizens. All rights and privileges given to the German minority since 1950 were abolished. This change in attitude appears to have come about for three reasons. The first was the aforementioned failure of previous policies. The second was that the GDR had recently reaffirmed the territorial integrity of Czechoslovakia, and as such had signalled that it had no interest in the fate of the remaining German minority. Finally, Prague's action can be interpreted as a reaction to the increasing influence of the *Sudetendeutsche Landsmannschaft* in the Federal Republic in general and especially in Bavaria.

The final shift in pre-1989 national minority policy came with the Prague Spring of 1968. In fact, an easing of the situation had become apparent from 1966, with a rise in the number of Germans who were permitted to leave Czechoslovakia, and the easing and partial abolition of anti-German statutes. A significant example of this changing attitude came with the transformation of the German *Volkszeitung* (People's Daily) from an uninspired governmental bulletin to a discussion platform for Germans. With the accession to power of the Dubceck regime, such changes were complemented by efforts to establish official contacts with Germany. Most notable among these efforts were an interview in the Czechoslovak press with the future German Chancellor Helmut Schmidt and the publication of an exchange of letters on themes of common interest between the SPD in the Federal Republic and the Czechoslovak Communist Party. This correspondence was itself shadowed by correspondence in the Czechoslovak press, which condemned the national minority policy of the Czechoslovak Communist Party and especially Bruno Köhler and Josef Lenk, who had, although being of German origin, supported and devised the party line with respect to the German minority. In June 1968 the government established a Commission on Constitutional Regulations in which the German and other minorities were represented. In the same month a preparatory commission for a Cultural Association of the Germans in Czechoslovakia was founded in order to secure minority rights for the German minority. Similar organizations were also established for the Hungarian and Polish minorities. The most significant event of this period came on 27 October 1968, with the passing of the Constitutional Law on the Legal Status of National Minorities. Its main points included the right to mother-tongue education, the right of ethnic minorities to establish independent cultural activities, the right of individuals to use their mother tongue in correspondence and communication with public agencies and institutions, and the right of ethnic minorities to establish sociocultural associations.

In August 1968 the Soviet-led invasion led to the fall of the Dubcek regime. One of the aspects of the regime which had most alarmed them was a perceived uncontrolled desire to repair relations with a government in Bonn which Moscow did not trust. However, this did not mean that Moscow did not wish to improve relations with Bonn. Rather, the watchword was that the process of change should be controlled, and preferably with the German CDU/CSU in opposition, and with the SPD firmly in control. So as a testament of good faith, Dubcek's minorities policy was by and large continued by the regime of his successor, Gustav Husak. Neither should we forget that, as ethnic Slovaks, both were probably slightly more sensitive to the question than were their Czech counterparts. Among other things in June 1969 this led to the establishment of the Cultural Association of Citizens of German Nationality in Czechoslovakia. For good measure, similar organizations for Hungarians and Poles were also established.

Although the Prague Spring was short-lived, it had a tremendous influence on the long-term situation of the ethnic minorities, as their role within the state and society had been freely discussed for the first time since 1968. The various problems faced by the national minorities had been brought to the attention of the wider public. In Poland and the other socialist states, public comment was muted. In Germany opinion was divided between those who like the government saw the changes as being a step in the right direction, and the condemnatory comments of the *Sudetendeutsche Landsmannschaft* that this law had no effect on the situation of the Germans in Czechoslovakia as it did not address the question of rehabilitation and property restitution (Böse and Eibicht, 1989: 115). Although ideological purges were carried out, the Germans remained formally represented on the local and regional level. Within the context of Husak's policy of 'normalization', we should not be surprised to learn that minority organizations reassumed their previous role of being transmission belts for the communist party. As for the opposition which coalesced around Charter 77, although it was prepared to discuss the process of expulsion, the fate of remaining minority populations barely featured in the dissidents' discourse (Riese, 1979). Of course the overall struggle against 'really existing socialism' was more important. On the other hand such silence also serves to indicate the extent to which the minorities themselves had become invisible to wider Czechoslovak society.

Just prior to the downfall of communism in 1989 there were an estimated 60 German cultural societies with a total of around 7,000 members. Their main function seems to have been lending support to the government 'on behalf of the wider German minority' as and when needed. In addition they engaged in non-political cultural activities. No German schools were in existence, no state-wide cultural festival was held in 1989, and the German-language press had collapsed. The official explanation, which carried an element of truth, was that territorial dispersal and a disproportionately elderly community precluded a more proactive set of activities. However, whereas a survey carried out by the author in 1998 reinforced this picture it also revealed discrimination and negligence on the part of both the government and wider society as having been contributory factors to the creation of this state of affairs.

Concluding remarks: resolution through emigration

The fate of ethnic minorities in communist Czechoslovakia followed different phases. These ranged from initial policies of mass expulsion to Stalinist suppression, post-Stalin toleration, the intermezzo of the Prague Spring and finally grudging tolerance of the Husak regime. With regard to Czech Silesia, it is important to mention the influence of Czechoslovakia's relationship with Poland, and Stalin's absolute refusal to allow either side to press maximal demands. It is therefore no wonder that writers such as Ulc could refer to the Polish population of Czech Silesia as being a 'spillover' from Poland (Ulc, 1974: 12). The post-1945 situation of the Poles of Czech Silesia was difficult due to the burden of historical memory, but it did ease with the downfall of the Benes regime. With respect to the German minority in Czech Silesia, their position was overshadowed and complicated by the overall pattern of bilateral relations between Prague and Bonn, and later by the attitude of the *Sudetendeutsche Landsmannschaft*, which catered for a much wider constituency. The best indicator of how those Germans who remained felt is perhaps to be found through a glance at the emigration statistics. Between 1950 to 1987, every year between 63 (1953) and 15,602 (1969) Germans left Czechoslovakia for Germany, reducing the number of ethnic Germans by 98,125 (Roucek, 1990: 214.). Having completed our survey of the area during the years of communism, we must now turn to post-communist developments, and note the radical changes that have occurred in the area since 1989.

Bibliography

Adamczuk, L. and Zdaniewicz, W. (eds), *Kosciol katolicki w Polsce 1918–1990: Rocznik statystyczny*. Warsaw, GUS and Zaklad Socjologii Religii SAC, 1991.

Auslandskurier 17, June 1996.

Bahlcke, J., *Schlesien und die Schlesier*. Berlin, Langen Müller, 1996.

Barcz, J., *Opcja integracyjna konstytucji RFN*. Warsaw; Polski Instytut Spraw Miedzynarodowych, 1989.

Barcz, J. (ed.), *Historyczne, polityczne I prawne aspekty tez RFN o niemieckiej narodowej w Polsce*, pt 2. Warsaw, Glowna Komisja Badania Zbrodni Hitlerowkisch, n.d.

Belzyt, L., *Miedzy Polska a Niemcami: weryfikacja norodowosciowa i jej nastepstwa na Warmii, Mazurach i Powislu w latach 1945–1980*. Torun, Adam Marszalek, 1996.

Berdychowska, B., et al. (eds), *Mniejszosci narodowe w Polsce w 1993 roku*. Warsaw, Biuro do Spraw Mniejszosci Narodowych przy Ministerstwie Kultury i Sztuki, 1994.

Berlinska, D., 'Narodowo-etniczne stosunki miedzygrupowe na Slasku Opolskim: ciaglosc i zmiana', in K. Frysztacki (ed.), *Polacy, Slazacy, Niemcy: Studia nad stosunkami spoleczno-kulturowymi na Slasku Opolskim*. Cracow: Universitas, 1998.

Bielski, J., *Emigranci ze ze Slaska Opolskiego do Republiki Federalnej Niemiec. realizacja zapisu protokolarnego z Helsinek w wojewodztwie opolskim (1975–1979)*. Oplole, Instytut Slaski, 1986.

Blasiak, W., 'Slaska zbiorowosc regionalna I jej kultura w latach 1945–1956', in M. Blaszczyk-Waclawik et al., *Gorny Slask. Szczegolny przypadek kulturowy*. Kielce, Wydawnictwo Naukowe Jan Szumacher, 1990.

Boda-Krezel, Z., *Sprawa volkslisty na Gornym Slasku. koncepcje likwidacji problemu i ich realizacja*. Opole, Instytut Slaski, 1978.

Böse, O. and Eibicht, R.-J. (eds), *Die Sudetendeutschen. Eine Volksgruppe im Herzen Europas*. Munich, Langen Müller, 1989.

Brügel, J. W., *Tschechen und Deutsche, 1939–1946*. Munich, Nymphenburger, 1974.

Burcher, T., *The Sudeten German Question and Czechoslovak–German Relations since 1989*. London, Royal United Services Institute for Defence Studies, 1996.

Cordell, K., 'Retreat from Ethnicity? Upper Silesia and German–Polish Relations', *Plymouth International Papers*, 1995.

European Commission, *Agenda 2000: Commission Opinion on the Czech Republic's Application for Membership of the European Union*. Brussels, EC, 1997.

Gilbert, T., 'State Policy, Ethnic Persistence and Nationality Formation in Eastern Europe', in P. Sugar (ed.), *Ethnic Diversity and Conflict in Eastern Europe*. Oxford, Clio Press, 1980.

Görlich, J. G., 'Als Deutscher unter Polen', in H. Hupka (ed.), *Meime Heimat Schlesien. Erinnerungen an ein geliebtes Land*. Augsburg, Weltbild, 1990.

Hajduk, R., 'Problem Polakow bylych zolnierzy armii niemieckiej na posiedzeniach Komisji Wojskowej Rady Narodowej Rzeczypospolitej Polskiej w Londynie', *Studia Slaskie* 40, 1982.

Hauner, M., 'The Czechs and the Germans: A One Thousand Year Relationship', in D. Verheyen and C. Soe (eds), *The Germans and Their Neighbors*. Boulder, Westview Press, 1993.

Hoskova, M., 'Der Minderheitenschutz in der Tschechischen Republik', in P. Mohlek and M. Hoskova, *Der Minderheitenschutz in der Republik Polen, in der Tschechischen und in der Slovakischen Republik*. Bonn, Kulturstiftung der deutschen Vertriebenen, 1994.

Hyde-Price, A., *The International Politics of East Central Europe*. Manchester, Manchester University Press, 1996.

Jaworski, M., *Na piastowskim szlaku. Dzialalnosc Ministerstwa Ziem Odzyskanych w latach 1945–1948*. Warsaw, Wydawinictwo Ministerstwa Obrony Narodowej, 1973.

Jaworski, W. L., *Prawa panstwa polskiego*. Cracow, Krakowskaj Spolka Wydawnicza, 1973.

Jonderko, F., 'Stereotypy etniczne na Slasku Opolskim. Czy generacyjna zmiana?' in K. Frysztacki (ed.), *Polacy, Slazacy, Niemcy. Studia nad stosunkami spoleczno-kulturowymi na Slasku Opolskim*. Cracow, Universitas, 1998.

Kamusella, T., 'Geneza i anatomia wysiedlen przeprowadzonych na Gornym Slasku w koncowym stadium i po zakonczeniu II wojny swiatowej', in E. Nycz (ed.), *Historyczne i wspolczesne problemy miasta i jego mieszkancow*. Opole, Instytut Slaski, 1996.

Korbel, J., *Polska-Gorny Slask-Niemcy: Polityczny bilans 50-lecia Poczdamu*. Opole, Wydawnictwo Uniwesytetu Opolskiego, 1995.

Lempinski, Z., *Przesiedlenie ludnosci niemieckiej z wojewodztwa slasko-dabrowskiego w latach 1945–1950*. Katowice, Slaski Instytut Naukowy, 1979.

Linek, B., 'Oddzwiek polemik wokol sposobu rozwiazania problemu ludnosci slaskiej na Opolszczyznie w latach 1955–1957 w owczesnej prasie wojewodzkiej', *Studia Slaskie* 52, 1993.

Linek, B., *'Odniemczanie' wojewodztwa slaskiego w latach 1945–1950 w swietle materialow wojewodzkich*. Opole, Instytut Slaski, 1997.

Linek, B., 'Obraz mieszkancow Slaska Opolskiego na lamach prasy regionalnej: tozsamosc grupowa, relacje miedzygrupowe, modele wspolistnienia', in K. Frysztacki (ed.), *Polacy, Slazacy, Niemcy. Studia nad stosunkami spoleczno-kulturowymi na Slasku Opolskim*. Cracow, Universitas, 1998.

Lis, M., *Ludnosc rodzima na Slasku Opolskim po II wojnie swiatowej (1945–1993)*. Opole, Instytut Slaski, 1993.

Madajczyk, P., *Na drodze pojednania. Wokol oredzia biskupow polskich do biskupow niemieckich z 1965*. Warsaw, PWN, 1994.

Madajczyk, P., *Przylaczenie Slaska Opolskiego do Polski, 1945–1948*. Warsaw: Instytut Studiow Politycznych Polskiej Akademii Nauk, 1996.

Magocsi, P., *Historical Atlas of East Central Europe*. London, University of Washington Press, 1995.

Marczak, T., 'Od Poczdamu do Zgorzelca (1945–1950)', in W. Wrzesinski (ed.), *W strone Odry i Baltyku. Wybor zrodel (1795–1950)*. Wroclaw and Warsaw, Oficyna Wydawnicza Volumen, 1991.

Misztal, J., *Weryfikacja narodowosciowa na Slasku Opolskim 1945–1950*. Opole, Instytut Slaski, 1984.

Moldawa, T., *Ludzie wladzy 1944–1991*. Warsaw, PWN, 1991.

Morison, J., 'The Road to Separation: Nationalism in Czechoslovakia', in P. Latawski (ed.), *Contemporary Nationalism in East Central Europe*. New York, St. Martins Press, 1995.

Nitschke, B., 'Pierwsze zorganizowane wysiedlenia ludnosci niemieckiej z Polski po konferencji poczdamski', *Sobotka* 3/4, 1997 (a).

Nitschke, B., 'Polozenie ludnosci niemieckiej na terenach na wschod od Odry I Nysy Luzyckiej w 1945 roku', *Przeglad Zachodni* 3, 1997 (b).

Osekowski, C., *Spoleczenstwo Polski zachodniej i polnocnej w latach 1945–1956: procesy integracji i dezintegracji*. Zielona Gora, Wyzsza Szkola Pedagogiczna, 1994.

Pater, J., 'Kominek B', in M. Pater (ed.), *Slownik biograficzny katolickiego duchowienstwa slaskiego XIX i XX wieku*. Katowice, Ksiegarnia sw. Jacka, 1996.

Pawlak, W. (ed.), *Atlas Slaska Dolnego i Opolskiego*. Wroclaw, Uniwersytet Wroclawski,1997.

Polityka, 14 June 1997.

Reichling, G., *Die deutschen Vertriebenen in Zahlen*, pt. i: *Umsiedler, Verschleppte, Vertriebene, Aussiedler 1940–1985)*. Bonn, Kulturstiftung der deutschen Vertriebenen, 1986.

Rhodes, M., 'National Identity and Minority Rights in the Constitution of the Czech Republic and Slovakia', *East European Quarterly* 29 (3), 1995.

Riese, H. (ed.), *Since the Prague Spring*. New York, Vantage Books, 1979.

Roucek, L., *Die Tschechoslowakei und die Bundesrepublik Deutschland 1949–1989*. Munich, tuduv, 1990.

Ruszczewski, J., 'Polskie obozy I miejsca odosobnienia dla ludnosci slaskiej I niemieckiej na Slasku Opolskim w latach 1945–1949', *Kwartalnik Opolski* 4, 1993.

Ryback, T. W., 'Dateline Sudetenland: Hostages to History', *Foreign Policy* 105, 1996.

Sakson, A., *Stosunki narodowosciowe na Warmii i Mazurach 1945–1997*. Poznan: Intytut Zachodni, 1998.

Satava, L., *Narodnostni mensiny v Evrope*. Prague, Ivo Zelazny, 1994.

Schlesische Nachrichten. 5, Mar. 1996.

Stoll, C. T., *Die Rechtsstellung der deutschen Staatsangehörigen in den polnisch verwalteten Gebieten: Zur Integration der sogenannten Autochthonen in die polnische Nation*. Frankfurt/Main, Metzner, 1968.

Strauchold, G., *Polska ludnosc rodzima zien zachodnich I polmocnych: opinie nie tylko publiczne lat 1944–1948*. Olsztyn, Osrodek Badan Nauk, 1995.

Strauchold, G., 'Zagadnienie repolonizacji ludnosci rodzimej w pracach ministerstwa oswiaty (1945–1948)', *Sobotka* 3–4, 1997.

Ther, P., 'Wypedzeni w Brandenburgii i na Slasku Opolskim w latach 1945–1952. Proba historycznego uporzadkowania', *Studia Slaskie* 54, 1995.

Ther, P., 'Dzieje poszukiwania identyfikacji narodowej I regionalnej w sowieckiej strefie okupacynej I NRD w latach 1945–1953', in B. Linek et al. (eds), *Fenomen nowoczesnego nacjonalizmu w Europie Srodkowiej*. Opole, PIN-Instytut Skaski, 1997.

Tyrmand, L., Dziennik 1954. Warsaw, Res Publica, 1989.

Ulc, O., *Politics in Czechoslovakia*. San Fransisco, Freeman, 1974.

Wanatowicz, M., *Historia spoleczno-polityczna Gornego Slaska i Slaska Cieszynskiego w latach 1918–1945*. Katowice, Wydawnictwo Uniwersytetu Wroclawskiego,1994.

Wiskemann, E., *Czechs and Germans: A Study of the Struggle in the Historic Provinces of Bohemia and Moravia*. London, Macmillan, 1967.

Wolf, A., *Der Status des Spätaussiedlers nach dem Kriegsfolgenbereinigungsgesetz*. Wiesbaden, Kommunal-und Schul-Verlag,1996.

Wrzesinski, W., *Polska-polacy-mniejszosci narodowe*. Wroclaw, Zaklad Narodowy, 1992.

Zycie 66, 19 Mar. 1998.

Notes

1. Bernard Linek wote the section on Polish Silesia, and Karl Martin Born that on Czech Silesia.
2. To this day, discussion on the process of expulsion and on the situation of the expellees is riddled with nationalist hubris which hinders the creation of any consensus on how best to describe these events. For the Allies the expulsions were 'population transfers'. German historians tend to use the phrase *Vertreibung* (expulsion). Since 1989 Polish scholars have begun to look beyond the mere technical and legal side of the expulsions. The terms *wysiedlenie* (displacement/expulsion) and *wypedzenie* (driving out/expulsion) have been used alongside the long-established *transfer* (transfer). Although the two Polish terms are very close, Polish scholars prefer to use the former, as it is less emotionally laden than the latter. For their part, German researchers would prefer it if their Polish co-workers employed the latter term, as it conveys the human tragedy of what happened. Unsurprisingly, a similar debate exists between the Czech academic community and their German counterparts.
3. The House of Piast was the first Polish dynasty. The Piast Kingdom contained some of the *Deutsche Ostgebiete* incorporated by Poland in in 1945. Piast rule over these areas was fairly short-lived, and their successors, the Jagiellonians, were so fixed upon eastward expansion, that in 1356 they renounced claim to (formerly Piast) Silesia for all time.
4. For years after the war, German Upper Silesians continued to refer to the Federal Republic as the Reich, which apart from anything else indicates how little they actually knew about postwar Germany.
5. Following intervention from the Allies, the expulsion of ethnic Hungarians was restricted to some 100,000 individuals.
6. The attitude of these people toward the National Socialist regime, coupled with any family ties to Czech culture, may well explain why members of this group chose to stay behind.

7

The Articulation of Identity in Silesia since 1989[1]

The years of consolidation

With the rise of Solidarity in Poland, and their eventual triumph, came the project finally to establish the notion of civil society and a notion of individual civil and collective human rights. Fundamental to this reappraisal of the relationship between state and society was a reassessment of nation and citizenship and a move away from the idea that Polish society was almost exclusively composed of ethnic Poles. Thus as Solidarity moved toward the attainment of political power it had to confront the position of indigenous ethnic minorities in Poland. Apart from anything else, it would be impossible finally to jettison the legacy of Yalta without acknowledging all of the human consequences that had stemmed from it. The role of the first post-communist prime minister Tadeusz Mazowiecki was particularly important at this time. Not only was he instrumental in repairing Polish–German inter-state relations, he was also supportive of the attempts of the German minority to organize itself both politically and culturally (Bingen, 1994).

When it came to the position of ethnic Germans, such a reappraisal also fairly obviously contained an element of Realpolitik on the part of Solidarity. It was inevitably intertwined with relations between Poland and united Germany and a definitive recognition of Poland's western border. The first post-communist government in Poland became actively engaged in the 'two-plus-four' negotiations on German unification. After much soul-searching on both sides and not a little disagreement, two treaties eventually emerged which sought to redefine bilateral inter-state relations, and in addition sought to promote reconciliation between the two peoples. The first of these treaties was the German–Polish Treaty of 14 November 1990. This treaty finally granted to the Poles recognition of Poland's western border by the government in Bonn in international law and not merely in accordance with the norms of international law, as had the Warsaw Treaty of 1970 (Johannes, 1994). The second of these treaties was the Treaty on Good Neighbourly and Friendly Cooperation of 17 June 1991, and is that which most directly concerns us. The basic trade-off was that in return for definitive German recognition of Poland's western border, Poland would not stand in the way of German unification and would undertake to recognize the existence of an indigenous German minority. In return the German government would further distance itself from those elements among the *Landsmannschaften* who demanded the right of return to their places of origin and/or compensation from the Polish government for material and emotional harm suffered as a result of their expulsion. Of greater importance however, was the fact that Germany agreed to act as Poland's de facto ambassador with regard to Polish membership of the EU and NATO.

By signing the treaty of 1991 Poland recognized that an ethnic German minority resided in Poland and granted official recognition to that minority. The inability since then of parliament to pass a Law on National Minorities has contributed to a situation where no single ministry has overall responsibility for minority questions. A Commission for National and Minority Rights was established in 1988, under the ambit of the Ministry of the Interior. With the completion of the first phase of the post-communist transition in 1990, the Commission was transferred to the more appropriate Ministry of Culture, and was upgraded to the status of Bureau in 1992. To complicate matters further, the Ministries of Education and Foreign Affairs quite obviously become involved in the affairs of ethnic minorities from time to time. Thus it was noticed as early as 1995 that a negative consequence of a laudable endeavour was to muddy accountability and to encourage buck-passing (*Dialog* 2/3, 1995).

Clearly if the Sejm were able to pass a National Minorities Law, this rather confusing situation might be rectified. In the summer of 1998 a draft was finally laid before parliament. Importantly, for the *Verband der deutschen sozial-kulturelle Gesellschaften in Polen* (VdG), an important concession has been made by the government. Under the terms of the draft, the government has agreed to the use of bilingual signage in areas of minority settlement. It has also agreed that in areas of substantial minority residence, minority languages will be accorded a degree of official status (*Schlesisches Wochenblatt*, 28 August 1998). Whether or not the draft will ever be passed and in what form is another question. The governing Solidarity electoral Alliance (AWS) possesses large and voluble nationalist factions to whom the idea that concessions be granted to Poland's ethnic minorities, especially the Germans, is anathema. As in the case of voivodeship reform (see below), the government will be dependent upon the goodwill of the president and the parliamentary opposition. Having said that, the fact the current government is willing to honour its international obligations on this particularly delicate matter is encouraging.

Organizational structures

Having mapped out some of the key developments which have affected Poland's German minority since the late 1980s, we now need to establish just who these measures are designed to serve, and make some observations about the organizational structures and activities of the German community in Upper Silesia, and where appropriate elsewhere in Poland. The response of the emerging leadership of the German community in Upper Silesia to the wider process of political change in Poland was to press forward with a series of political and cultural demands. We have already noted that as early as 1988 Johann Kroll and others attempted to register a DFK with the courts (Kroll, 1994). Although their initial attempt was unsuccessful, they met with positive results when in January 1990 such societies were registered with the courts in Katowice. Following the treaties of 1990 and 1991 any remaining legal obstacles to the registration of German cultural societies were removed. The immediate consequence was that a plethora of such societies appeared throughout Poland, even in such cities as Radom and Gdansk, where the German population had been reduced to a mere remnant of its prewar size. The objective of the societies in Upper Silesia as elsewhere was to secure the support of both governments for a series of activities which were designed to maintain the collective existence and cultural cohesion of the German community.

These societies operate in a majority of Poland's 16 voivodeships. Their activities are coordinated by a ten-person national executive, which is turn is led by the former Opole senator Gerhard Bartodziej. Beneath the executive exists a number of departments each of which has responsibility for specific issues such as education, culture and links with the *Landsmannschaft Schlesien*. Individuals are organized into a network of local DFKs whose activities are coordinated by the aforementioned VdG. The VdG's seat is in the small town of Gogolin in rural Upper Silesia. Given that Gogolin is neither on a main railway line nor on a main road, and that telecommunications in Poland do not correspond to Western European standards, communication with other parts of Upper Silesia, and more especially other parts of Poland can be problematic. Having said that, the restructuring of regional and local government in Poland has led to the consolidation of the overwhelming majority of Upper Silesian Germans, and therefore the great majority of Poland's German minority, within the Opole voivodeship. It is claimed that in the Opole voivodeship around 200,000 individuals adhere to the German sociocultural societies, with there being a further 80,000 in the Silesian voivodeship.

The role of the DFKs, of which there are around 500, is to provide a common forum through which Germans can collectively express their identity; to put it more prosaically, they act as social clubs and meeting-places for Germans (Ministry of the Interior, 1994). Similar organizations exist throughout the whole of Poland, but are much more common in Upper Silesia than elsewhere in the country. On the social side, the DFK's organize fêtes, choirs, dance groups, exhibitions of local history and sporting competitions. They also liaise with former residents who now live in Germany and who not only provide additional income but also help organize youth exchanges and holiday camps for young Upper Silesians. The DFKs above all provide a forum where Germans, and the older generation in particular, can meet, reminisce and provide mutual solidarity (Urban, 1994: 102 ff).This latter point is of particular importance for such people as former Wehrmacht veterans, whose pensions are low, and who only started to receive a war pension in the mid 1990s.

As for the youth there is in existence *Die Bund der Jugend der deutschen Minderheit* (The Federation of German Minority Youth, BJdM). Organizationally it is distinct from the VdG. As its name suggests, it is supposed to cater for German-oriented youth. Although it met with some success immediately after its inception, it quickly degenerated into a series of factional disputes, which ostensibly centred around the extent to which the youth of the Opole voivodeship were being catered for at the expense of young Germans elsewhere in Poland. In the summer of 1998 a new executive committee was established with a brief to revive the fortunes of the organization.

Probably the most important issues for German activists regardless of age are those of language and the provision of a German language education, together with the dissemination of a German language media. If we first examine the educational sphere, we may identify three areas of activity. The first concerns the provision of education for the German minority as a minority within the state schools system, and as such is seen to be of primary importance (Rostropowicz, ND). Unsurprisingly, it is also a bone of contention with the authorities. The VdG constantly accuses the authorities at all levels of dragging their feet on this issue. Bilingual and mother-tongue (i.e. German language) schools have been established throughout Upper Silesia. However, in the latter schools the bulk of instruction is actually given in Polish, with only three hours a week of German-language instruction being available. Both sides are agreed that there are not enough qualified teachers. For its part, the government claims that it is doing its best with limited resources. The predictable response from the VdG is that the government is doing the necessary minimum. Whereas at the local level the VdG may have a point, we should not lose sight of the following: first, the educational needs of German Upper Silesians are not the most pressing item on the government's agenda. Secondly, the VdG itself has a localist perhaps parochial view of the world, and represents a community that in essence turned in on itself in order to survive the period of communist rule. Thirdly, the policy of filling the gaps by importing teachers from Germany has had only limited success. For a number of complex reasons, unemployed German teachers, are reluctant to relocate to Poland, although older retired teachers particularly those of Silesian origin, tend to find the option more attractive. Finally, the extent to which the demand for such provision actually corresponds to the aspirations of the VdG is another matter, as was demonstrated in 1997 in the town of Kedzierzyn-Kozle, where the take-up of places to a newly established bilingual school was much lower than the local activists had anticipated.

In addition to seeking to revive the use of German in the educational and thus in the everyday sphere, the VdG also promotes seminars and workshops and which are designed to promote Polish–German understanding, and are not necessarily aimed at the German minority itself. In addition it works closely with the *Bund der Vertriebene* (Federation of Expellees, BdV), to establish similar fora designed to inform both members of the minority and Poles of the cultural inheritance of formerly German areas of Poland. The hope here is that such gatherings contribute to the erosion of stereotypes. This is important because such stereotypes are still prevalent among both Poles and Germans who experienced the 'dictatorship of The Other'. Thus German expellees tend to be ill-informed of the experiences of the Poles who were resettled in former German areas after the Second World War, and in turn

Poles who were originally born outside their 'new' homelands, are often ignorant of the suffering visited upon ordinary German civilians in the aftermath of the National Socialist dictatorship and its defeat.

In order further to re-establish the use of German, the language is disseminated through both the printed and broadcast media. There is a German-language press in Poland, and in the Opole and Silesian voivodeships, there are now weekly radio broadcasts in German. In the Opole voivodeship where the greatest number of Germans live, there is also a fortnightly German-language TV programme (*Schlesisches Wochenblatt*, 11 April 1997). Once again, German activists complain about lack of access to the broadcast media and official obstructionism, but as usual this may only be part of the story. For example, in 1997 a radio station in Lower Silesia offered the Wroclaw DFK the opportunity of a weekly programme in German. The purpose was to allow the local DFK to publicize its activities to the remaining 4,000 or so Germans who live in Wroclaw and its environs. The DFK for its part rejected the offer on the grounds that it lacked the technical expertise (Petrach, 1997). The response of the local DFK to this offer serves to indicate that in this area, as in many others, the German minority is reluctant to take up offers of help from Poles.

Another key objective was that the practice of ensuring that the religious clergy of (Upper) Silesia is bilingual begun in the nineteenth century, and terminated by the Nazis be restored. German Upper Silesians are overwhelmingly Catholic and deeply religious. The right to hold services either wholly or partially in their mother tongue was one of the original demands of the activists in the late 1980s. By 1991, and mainly thanks to the endeavors of Bishop Nossol of the Silesian diocese and despite opposition from Cardinal Glemp, the situation had changed and such church services are once again a regular occurrence. In addition to masses in Polish, bilingual services are available in over 200 parishes in Upper Silesia, and priests are once again required as far as possible to be bilingual. Similarly, Bishop Nossol was instrumental in gaining permission for bilingual services to be held for the Moravian, Ukrainian and Armenian communities of Upper Silesia (Kandzia, 1995).

Political issues and constitutional reform

Local and parliamentary elections have shown that German candidates have had their greatest success in the rural areas in the eastern half of the Opole voivodeship, in the westernmost communes of the former

Silesian voivodeship and, prior to the reorganization of the voivodeships, in the south-eastern corner of the former Czestochowa voivodeship. They have also had some success in the run-down old worker residential areas in the Upper Silesian industrial basin, primarily in Katowice, Gliwice and Bytom. The inferior spatial locations (most often than not shared by *Szlonzoks*, *Slonzaks* and local Upper Silesian Poles) indicate the disadvantaged social status of the (German) population under communist rule.

We must also be aware of the fact that at general elections the share of the vote received by German candidates has fallen with each successive election, as has the number of individuals who actually pay their subscriptions to the various DFKs. At the general election of 1997, voter participation was lowest in precisely those electoral districts where the number of ethnic Germans was highest. In fact, in the Opole voivodeship only 19,000 electors voted for German candidates. This in turn provoked a furious debate among German activists as to why this was the case and a thorough review of organizational structures, objectives, activities and membership lists.

The apparently spontaneous appearance of Germans in Upper Silesia was graphically symbolized at a by-election to the Senate in 1990. Following the death of the incumbent, the subsequent contest pitched Henryk Kroll an Upper Silesian German, against Dorota Simonides, an Upper Silesian Pole. Although the latter won, the election launched the German minority into the political and social life of Poland. Kroll campaigned on behalf of the Germans of Opole Silesia, whose sociocultural societies, as we noted earlier, first received legal recognition in January 1990 in the Katowice courts.

In the 1991 general election, the Germans of Upper Silesia won seven mandates to the *Sejm* and one to the Senate. In the subsequent election of 1993 the number of German representatives dwindled to four in the Sejm, together with the single senator. Following the 1997 election, representation fell to a mere two for the *Sejm* with the Senate representation also being lost. This steady decline in support is due to a number of factors. First, in the early 1990s there were unrealistic expectations on the part of many Upper Silesians of the German government. Berlin has not secured and does not wish to secure, any special privileges or status for Upper Silesia. Acutely aware of its own budgetary restraints and that Upper Silesia is in a foreign country, neither does it accord Upper Silesia the level of funding demanded by the VdG. Secondly, voter apathy was highest in precisely those constituencies in which Germans reside. In part the first-mentioned factor plays a role here. However, we should not forget that many who voted for German candidates in 1991 subsequently emigrated, that many German passport-holders are in fact absent voters, that the German community is disproportionately elderly and that younger Germans do not necessarily vote on the basis of national identity. The German government's increasingly restrictive policy on granting German passports may also be a factor (*Schlesisches Wochenblatt*, 26 June 1998).

Prior to the general election of 1997 VdG used both houses of parliament as a means of publicizing its grievances, and in reality confines itself to a rather parochial range of issues. Not only did the VdG lose its seat in the senate in these elections, it lost two of its four seats in the Sejm (it had already lost three in the 1993 elections), and with them the privileges accorded to political parties (*Schlesisches Wochenblatt*, 21 September 1997). Its two remaining representatives, Henryk Kroll and Helmut Pazdzior, lobby the Parliamentary Committee for National and Ethnic Minorities (Kroll is actually a member of this committee) and the relevant sections of the Ministries of Interior and Culture on behalf of their constituents. Significant gains have been made in recent years, although the party claims that areas of discrimination still exist. It has been claimed that because (collective) minority rights which guarantee equality before the law to all ethnic minorities in Poland have not yet fully been enshrined within Polish law, the various minorities do not necessarily receive equal treatment. This is held particularly to apply to the German community, whose existence prior to 1990, unlike that of the Ukrainian and other minorities, was never officially recognized (*Dialog* 2/3, 1995).

Following the general election of 1997, the post-communist SLD (Democratic Left Alliance) and their Peasant Party allies lost power to a coalition of the right-wing Solidarity Electoral Action (AWS) and the liberal Freedom Union (UW). The main criterion for the formation of this government seems to have been to deny power to the post-communist SLD. The UW is secular, neo-liberal on social issues, in favour of classical liberal economic policies, pro-European and tolerant of diversity. For its part, the much larger AWS is in fact an amorphous collection of over 30 organizations; which are riven by factionalism and are to varying degrees nationalist, conservative and Catholic-traditionalist, as well as being suspicious of both the EU and those who are not 'True Poles'. Despite being rhetorically committed to privatization, sections of the AWS are beholden to special interest groups in the coal and steel industries, and are equally opposed to selling state assets either to 'communists' or foreigners. Quite how this government intends to take Poland 'into Europe' is as yet unclear.

Yet the AWS/UW coalition has succeeded in breaking the impasse on constitutional reform, a theme which was of utmost concern to German activists in Upper Silesia and elsewhere. In the immediate phase of post-communism, a series of amendments was passed to the 1952 constitution which struck out all clauses which pertained to the leading role of the communist party, and were incompatible with the transition toward liberal democracy. Subsequently numerous drafts were proposed but none was actually laid before parliament. In the winter of 1996/97, the constitutional committee finally reached agreement on a draft which was submitted for ratification at the end of March 1997 and came into force on September of that year. Although, as we shall see, the constitution was bitterly opposed by Polish integralists from within the AWS and the Polish Peasants Party (PSL), the constitution was eventually approved in the *Sejm* by 450 votes to 40. For our purposes it is important note that the German parliamentarians are reasonably satisfied with the new constitution. They were particularly pleased that the constitution was promulgated 'in the name of the Polish people and all Polish citizens'. In other words, the constitution recognizes that all Polish citizens are not ethnic Poles. They also are satisfied that the constitution goes as far as it can in providing for the maintenance of minority languages and cultures, in securing the overall situation of national minorities and in creating a society that is based upon the rule of law (*Schlesisches Wochenblatt*, 2 December 1996).

The importance of this wording and the clauses which guarantee such rights cannot be overstated. However, after the constitution was approved by parliament, the wider issue was not one of whether or not the constitution suited the German minority, but whether it would ever be enacted. After the draft received the requisite two-thirds majority in both houses of parliament, it was submitted to popular referendum on 25 May 1997. Given the fractured state of society, this was a huge obstacle. The results of the referendum can best be described as mixed. On the one hand, 53 per cent of those who voted approved the constitution, and the president subsequently approved the constitution without any fuss. On the other hand, only 42 per cent of the population bothered to vote in a campaign that became increasingly ugly and xenophobic in tone, and in which elements of the Catholic clergy were prominent in criticizing the input of 'aliens' and 'atheists' into the constitution itself.

Another arena of contestation has been that of the reform of regional and local government. The complexity of the process of restructuring, has been neatly illustrated by the government's hapless attempt to promote such reform in order to render Polish practice more compatible with EU norms. The original proposals centred around combining the previous 49 voivodeships into a total of 12 larger units with increased decision-making powers. The new voivodeships are governed by directly elected politicians, unlike as is presently the case. Beneath the voivodeships a number of counties and county boroughs with directly elected councils have been established. At the bottom, the communes remain. It is argued that such an amalgamation is in keeping with EU standards, will promote efficiency and greater economies of scale, as well as enhancing the overall process of democratization. In most parts of Poland, although the proposals provoked furious debate, they did not lead to the outbreak of near-hysteria that occurred in the Opole voivodeship.

The original plans would have entailed the integration of the Opole voivodeship into a new Upper Silesian voivodeship. There was wide cross-party and inter-ethnic opposition to these plans from within the Opole region. The attitude of the VdG, however, speaks volumes for the mind set, background and experiences of its members. The VdG seemed convinced that the main purpose of liquidating the Opole voivodeship was to destroy both the sociocultural and political cohesion of the German community (*Schlesisches Wochenblatt*, 13 March 1998). No doubt a sizable number of Poles, particularly older less educated people from rural areas, would not be unhappy at such an outcome. However, to argue that this a majority of Polish society desires this outcome, or indeed has any more than a passing interest in the area, is highly questionable. It is also quite frankly ludicrous to believe that, for all its faults, the government is so preoccupied with Poland's German minority in general, and the Germans of Upper Silesia in particular.

The reaction of the VdG speaks volumes for the nature of its own elderly, poorly educated and rural membership, and the degree of alienation and residual fear that still exists. By way of an alternative, the VdG proposed that the Opole voivodeship be expanded to include areas of the neighboring voivodeships of Katowice and Czestochowa, which contain a sizable German population (*Schlesisches Wochenblatt*, 13 February 1998). Although there was widespread support for this within the affected area of the Czestochowa voivodeship, the picture in the corresponding areas of the Katowice voivodeship was more blurred. Indeed, Prime Minister Buzek (himself a Protestant Upper Silesian from Czech Silesia) bluntly told Henryk Kroll that in his opinion such proposals were a barely veiled attempt on the part of the VdG to increase its regional influence. For its part the VdG argued that the disappearance of the Opole voivodeship (the population of which is perhaps one-third German) might lead to a deterioration in inter-ethnic relations, and would not bring any of the aforementioned benefits. With regard to the former point, there is little evidence to suggest that Germans would have faced increased discrimination in an Upper Silesian voivodeship. However, at present they constitute the largest single grouping in the Opole voivodeship *Sejmik* (regional assembly), and under the original proposals they would have constituted but a small minority in an all-embracing Upper Silesian voivodeship, and that perhaps is the rub.

In light of recent electoral setbacks, an ageing electorate, an increasingly assimilated younger and middle generation, particularly the latter, the VdG found itself at a crossroads. It chose to ignore the fact that under the proposals there would be every possibility of it taking control of county councils and wielding more power than it does today in the communes it governs. Instead, it made its stand over the issue of the voivodeship. That it has been able to work so closely with ethnic Poles shows that the situation on the ground is by no means bad. It has also been argued by (Opole) senator Dorota Simonides that the creation of a single Upper Silesian voivodeship would strengthen the hand of Silesian autonomists (*Schlesisches Wochenblatt*, 29 May 1998). In recent months there has been something of a revival in the Silesian national movement, and it must not be forgotten that until the last quarter of the nineteenth century Upper Silesian identification with Poland was extremely weak.

In the event, the government's original proposals were destroyed for a number of reasons. In part this defeat was due to the cross-party and inter-ethnic opposition from within the Opole region itself. Also, the AWS leadership was unable to impose discipline upon many of its own members, for whom any form of decentralization was anathema and who sought to wreck the plans on the basis that they were endangering Polish sovereignty. As a result the government was forced to turn to the post-communists for help. In turn the SLD demanded that 16 voivodeships, including an Opole voivodeship, be created. Given the lack of alternatives the government agreed to the SLD's demands and the Opole voivodeship was saved (*Schlesisches Wochenblatt*, 12 June 1998). The political representatives of the German community are more than pleased with this turn of events. Not only did they and their Polish allies at regional and national level force the government to back down, most of the 'German' areas of the Czestochowa voivodeship were transferred to the newly expanded Opole voivodeship.

On the surface, this strategy paid off handsomely at the local and regional elections of October 1998. In Opole Silesia the regional branch of the VdG captured 13 seats on the *Sejmik* and emerged as the second strongest part behind the SLD (*Gazeta Wyborcza*, 23 October 1998). Whether or not this will lead to German participation in regional government is another question. However, given the hostility that exists between the AWS and SLD, it seems that an AWS/UW regime will be at the very least dependent upon the votes of the German minority.

Success at the aforementioned level was also repeated at the lower levels. The VdG has taken control of a large number of *gminy* (communes) mainly in the south and east of the voivodeship and in addition now controls the Opole, Krapkowice and Strzelce Opolskie counties. For the first time since the Second World War, there is also German representation on the Opole city council. However, the VdG did not fare well in the neighbouring (Upper) Silesian voivodeship, except in the town of Raciborz, and to a lesser extent in the Gliwice area. Each branch of the VdG was left to make its own decision on whether they contested the elections on their own or together with a Polish party. That most decided to run joint lists with their Polish counterparts is encouraging. What was less encouraging for the VdG was that, the aforementioned examples apart, German candidates did not fare well, and nowhere in the voivodeship do the Germans have a majority at county level.

A question of numbers

It should be clear from the above that for a whole raft of reasons the appeal of German minority candidates to their putative electorate is limited, as is the electorate itself. Just how many Germans remain in Poland is a matter of some conjecture. Estimates vary from Polish nationalist estimates of a few thousand to German nationalist claims of over one million. Both are certainly wrong. In an interview in 1998, Herbert Hupka, the chairman of the *Landsmannschaft Schlesien,* shed some light on how this latter figure was arrived at. He quite simply asserted that according to his interpretation all indigenous Upper Silesians were members of the *Deutschtum*, and that approximately one million Germans reside in Poland. This claim, which would have mystified any Polish Upper Silesians who read it, let alone the wider Polish population, was based on claims that over 700 years of German rule had resulted in (all) Upper Silesians having become Germanized (*Schlesische Nachrichten*, 15 February 1998). Such claims, made as they were by a professional historian, are as staggering as they are revealing. They demonstrate an adherence to primordial theories of nationality, a dubious set of precepts which during the nineteenth and parts of the twentieth century have been utilized by those Polish nationalists who lay equal claim on all Upper Silesians as Poles, some of whom who had acquired a German veneer, on the basis that (Upper) Silesia was Polish prior to 1335. The intellectual absurdities of both arguments apart, Hupka's assertion may well reveal that those Upper Silesians who do not see themselves as Germans are an audience which the *Landsmannschaft Schlesien* would like to reach by virtue of its activities in Poland.

Regardless of the interminable debates about numbers, it is claimed that a total of 420,000 adults are affiliated to the VdG through their membership of individual DFKs. The overwhelming majority of these people live in Upper Silesia.[2] Only around one third of the claimed total membership actually pays its membership dues. This in turn raises a whole host of questions, such as why the initial rush of enthusiasm, and why the equally sudden waning of interest? Inevitably, answers to these questions are complex, and space does not permit anything other than a cursory examination In Poland the years 1989/91 were a time of hope, especially for groups which had previously been marginalized. Given that the Germans of Upper Silesia did not officially exist until 1989, it is reasonable to assume that their hopes and expectations were possibly the greatest among any similar group in Poland. Unfortunately, their knowledge of geopolitical realities and of Germany had been mediated by three equally unrepresentative sources: the communist media, *Landsmannschaft* activists, and contacts with relatives in Germany. Consequently their expectations of what was possible were unrealistic, and the progress that has been made since 1989 is sometimes lost sight of.

In effect no one knows just how many Germans reside in Poland. There are no official figures, because the census contains no question on ethnic/national allegiance. In part this is a hangover from communist times, when the party/state tried to create an ethnically homogeneous country. On the other hand, it is probably not in the interest of any party to establish an 'official' number. Minority activists, whether German, Ukrainian, or from any other such community, have a vested interest in maximizing the number of supposed co-nationals, and the (overwhelming) Polish majority and Polish state almost certainly underestimate the number of Polish citizens who are ethnically non-Polish. In the event, both sides have a vested interest in letting sleeping dogs lie.

To recapitulate, although we cannot be certain of exact figures, there is nothing like one million Germans in Poland. Poles from Masuria, Ermland and Kashubia, and Upper Silesians who could theoretically lay claim to adherence to the *Deutschtum,* are not Germans by virtue of the fact they choose not to be. The same applies to those who designate themselves simply as Mazurs, Kashubes or Silesians, just as it does to people of mixed descent who have opted for a Polish identity. The claim of there being one million Germans in Poland is based on a rather dubious and largely discredited theoretical precept. Whatever the case, out of this definitional tangle it is normal for German academics to offer a figure for the community in the region of 500,000 (Bingen, 1994). Polish academics tend to offer figures of between 350,000–400,000, which as much as anything else are a reflection of different methodologies and, the nationalist fringes, aside, causes no real dispute at the academic, public or official levels.

The aforementioned local election results might just shed some light on the matter. We have noted that the VdG was successful in reestablishing itself as a major player in the Opole voivodeship. However, there is a sting in the tail. VdG candidates succeeded in obtaining 26, 21, and 20 per cent of the votes in the *gminy, powiaty*, and *Semjik* elections respectively. The Opole voivodeship has a population of 1,092,000. Even if we take the *gminy* results as our benchmark, take into account that some voters were working in Germany and did not vote, and make the highly dubious assumption that no Poles voted for VdG candidates, we can estimate the size of the German population as being in the region of 280,000. No matter which way you look at it, the claim that there are at least 500,000 Germans living in Poland is difficult to substantiate, and the estimates of Polish scholars are probably nearest the mark.

Of the German minority, around 190,000 now possess dual Polish–German nationality. The extent to which Polish-German relations have improved in recent years is evidenced by the fact that both governments turn a blind eye to this phenomenon, which is technically illegal in both countries. Polish citizens of German descent acquire German passports under the terms of the *Kriegsfolgenbereinigungsgesetz* (War Consequences Consolidation Act) of 1993. Among other things, this law limited the grounds on which ethnic Germans living in Eastern Europe, and the former Soviet Union, could claim a German passport on the basis of Article 116 of the German constitution, and reduced the assistance available to such Germans should they decide to move to Germany (Cordell, 1995: 20; Wolf, 1996). Moreover, the German government also demands a higher standard of proof than in the past of an individual's claim to be a German. Not only is it aware of the fact that the previous system was open to abuse, but it also points out that Germans in most former communist countries are no longer subject to (official) discrimination by virtue of their ethnicity. In Poland, the matter is complicated by the fact that the Polish authorities do not issue copies of the DVL, or of 'rehabilitation' or 'verification' documents to the interested parties, which makes it extremely difficult for many applicants to provide proof to the German authorities of their eligibility for a German passport.

In other words, of the hypothesized 500,000 Germans living in Upper Silesia and elsewhere in Poland, well under half have received German passports. Many of those who were admitted onto the DVL have very slim chances of obtaining such passports, as have their descendants. Thus, although according to some estimates almost 400,000 inhabitants of the Opole voivodeship consider themselves to be German, the fact that the majority cannot obtain a German passport may in the coming years, together with the ageing process, serve to reduce the size of the German community. Self-evidently, this pattern will also be repeated throughout the rest of Upper Silesia, as well as in other parts of Poland. Those unable to obtain German passports face two alternatives; either to assume a fully Polish identity, or to retreat into a regional identity. Interestingly enough, there is increasing evidence to show, that the latter alternative is becoming of increasing relevance to Upper Silesians irrespective of ethnic provenance.

Regionalism in post-communist upper Silesia

What then of ethnic provenance and its relationship, if any, to regional identification in an area which claims to have a specific identity which marks it out as being different from the rest of the country? In 1990 a number of regionalist organizations were established. They included the Opole-based *Zwiazek Gornoslazakow* (Union of the Upper Silesians, ZG), the Katowice-centered *Zwiazek Gornoslaski* (Upper Silesian Union, ZGr) and the *Ruch Autonomii Slaska* (Movement for the Silesian Autonomy, RAS) in Rybnik. In 1996 they were joined by the *Stowarzyszenie Patriotyczne 'Slask'* (Patriotic Association 'Silesia', SPS), based in Kedzierzyn-Kozle. The ZG numbered a few hundred and sought recognition of the Szlonzoks of Opole Silesia as an ethnic group distinct from both Poles and Germans. Today it is virtually defunct, primarily because in the crucial years of the early 1990s it could not compete with the better-resourced German associations. The ZGr, which has several thousand members in the Silesian voivodeship, and its own *Fundacja Gornoslaska* (Upper Silesian Foundation), has remained quite influential in that part of Upper Silesia. Its objective is to construct and sustain the regional identity of all the inhabitants of Upper Silesia regardless of their ethnic background, as an integral Silesian ingredient of a civic Polish nation. The RAS has a membership of 10,000, and has a similar programme to that of the ZGr, although it emphasizes the 'intrinsic link' between Silesia and the Polish nation-state. The RAS advocates the re-establishment of Upper Silesian autonomy as practised within the pre-war Polish voivodeship. Its espousal of Christian democracy places it close to Korfanty's thinking on Upper Silesia. As for the anti-German SPS, it has approximately 20 members, and as such is an irrelevance (Lis, 1993: 99–103).

The ZG may also be destined for the dustbin of history. It has difficulty in attracting members in the Opole voivodeship, where those looking for institutional expression of attachment to their region are well served by a network of well-organized and financed (with the assistance of the German government) German associations. On the other hand, the ZGr and the RAS are an option for those in the Katowice voivodeship who cannot obtain or do not want German citizenship and who identify with the region. What is more, the needs of these two groups are also served by the *Niemiecka Wspolnota Robocza 'Pojednanie i Przyszlosc'/Deutsche Gemeinschaft 'Versöhnung und Zukunft'* (the German Society 'Reconciliation and Future', NWR/DG). This organization came into being in 1991 and, with 10,000 members, aims to serve as the interface between the German and Polish populations of Katowice Silesia, as well as to save the region from 'civilizational, cultural and social collapse' (Berdychowska, 1994: 31). In terms of parliamentary representation, the RAS and the ZGr managed to have two deputies elected to the *Sejm* in 1991, but they fell foul of the 5 per cent threshold in 1993 and have since failed to win any mandates. Yet we should be aware of the presence of a political space available to such movements. There are constant complaints in Upper Silesia that the 'national parties' hardly serve the needs of this element of the *Szlonzakian* population, which regards itself as first and foremost Silesian.

National minority candidates are exempted from the 5 per cent threshold, which accounts for the survival of the German minority in the *Sejm*. With that in mind, in 1997 Jerzy Gorzelik, a leader of the *Slaski Zwiazek Akademicki* (Silesian Academic Union, SZA), supported by the RAS and the ZGr, filed a request for the registration of the *Zwiazek Ludnosci Narodowosci Slaskiej* (Association of the People of Silesian Nationality, ZLNS) with the courts in Katowice. The ZLNS succeeded in attracting a lot of initial interest even within the Opole voivodeship. Although the Katowice voivodeship court registered the ZLNS in June 1997, the Polish supreme court overturned the ruling in March 1998 on the basis that, although there might well be Silesians who exist as members of the wider Polish nation, there was no such thing as a separate Silesian nation. As a result, the ZLNS was not able to claim exemption from the 5 per cent clause, decided not to contest the 1997 elections and is now faced with trying to appeal the decision at the Court of Human Rights at Strasbourg. Even if any appeal were to be successful, there is no guarantee that the Polish government would recognize the validity of such a decision.

The ZLNS assumes the existence of a Silesian/*Szlonzokian* nation, and wishes to develop national consciousness among *Szlonzoks* as well to preserve the *Szlonzokian* culture and language. In true nationalist fashion it seeks to establish a standardized and codified Silesian language from among the various Slavic-German creoles and West Slavic dialects still spoken in some rural areas, which in turn would become the medium of education at *Szlonzokian* minority schools. This *Szlonzokian* nation would embrace not only ethnic *Szlonzoks* but also those non-*Szlonzokian* inhabitants of Upper Silesia who have over the years become *Szlonzokized*. As evidence for the existence of such a nation, the ZLNS points to the fact that in the 1991 Czechoslovak census in addition to 1,400,000 declared Moravians, 44,000 people described themselves as Silesians[3] (Dziadul, 1997; Satava, 1994: 50). If the ZLNS were to persevere, and actually succeed in forcing Warsaw to recognize the existence of a Silesian nation, the consequences could be quite dramatic. The capital also faces pressure from Kashubes and *Lehmke* activists for official recognition of these groups as national minorities. Given that such recognition flies in the face of deep-seated Polish traditions, and is seen as endangering the (national) fabric of society, such concessions are hardly likely to be easily won, if they are to be won at all.

The *kresy* expellees, settlers from central Poland, together with Polish repatriates from Germany and elsewhere who settled in the former *Deutsche Ostgebiete*, strongly identified themselves with Poland as they had understood it before 1939. The settlers from central Poland maintained links with their towns and villages of origin, while many of the expellees from the *kresy* continued to hope that they might be allowed to return to their former homes. The older generation especially did not identify with their new homeland, precisely because they recognized it as being obviously German.

Such emotions faded somewhat with the birth of a new generation who came of age in the 1980s and 1990s. They do not feel any emotional attachment to the central and former eastern Polish regions where their parents and grandparents were born. After the German threat which had been assiduously cultivated in communist times disappeared with the signing of the German–Polish border treaty, many young people expressed their identification with their regions of birth by establishing various regional associations and delving into local history. Thus they have come to accept the multicultural past of Silesia.

This has been particularly so in Lower Silesia, where the German population numbers only a few thousand, consists mainly of migrants from Upper Silesia and is limited to a few cities such as Wroclaw, Walbrzych, Swidnica and Legnica (*Schlesisches Wochenblatt*, 17 July 1998). In fact the German population may even be outnumbered by Ukrainians and Lemkos.[4] The physical absence of the 'Other' may in fact facilitate the process of regional identification. The process is more complicated in the case of Upper Silesia because the local Germans and *Szlonzoks* refer to themselves as (Upper) Silesians and to 'incomers' as Poles. The fact that numerous Upper Silesian Germans and *Szlonzoks* are holders of German passports, and as such can work in Germany, creates an economic cleavage between them and ethnic Poles. Consequently, the rate of unemployment is higher among the latter. Thus even the younger generations still have problems with identifying with their region of birth and choose Poland as the main locus of their identity.

Further evidence that inter-communal tensions are waning is evidenced by the fact that since the 1980s many ethnic Poles born in Upper Silesia have contracted marriages with Germans and *Szlonzoks*, and that many identify with traditional local culture. This process of socialization is facilitated by the fact that German organizations with assistance from Germany, secure better hospital equipment, infrastructural improvements and the like, not only for themselves but for whole communities irrespective of the ethnic origin of any of the inhabitants. In fact such aid is conditional upon it being at the disposal of everyone and not just for Germans. This integrative process develops on the basis of growing acceptance of the idea that possession of multiple identities does not automatically signal disloyalty to Poland. Hence despite everything, in Upper Silesia one can still be a Pole/German/ *Szlonzok*/*Moravec*.

However, due to the aforementioned qualifications, it does not appear likely that these identities will merge into a common Upper Silesian whole. The cleavage which arose in the nineteenth century with development of industry in eastern Upper Silesia was deepened by the division of this region between Poland and Germany. It was worsened during the second World War, and was reaffirmed by the establishment of the two separate Upper Silesian regencies of Oppeln and Kattowitz, the DVL, the post-war 'verification' and 'rehabilitation' processes and since 1950 by the division of Upper Silesia into two or more voivodeships.

This cleavage is manifested by the use of the names Opole Silesia and the *Opolszczyzna* for denoting the Opole voivodeship, and by reserving the use of Silesia for the former Katowice voivodeship. Hence, in the near future, after the completion of the process of regionalization of Poland in anticipation of the state's accession into the EU, Opole Silesia may become the locus of Opole Silesian identity. As such, it would be reinforced by the Catholicism of almost all the region's members and the fact that Opole Silesia largely coincides with boundaries of the Opole diocese.

The prospect of developing a corresponding regional identity is not so obvious in the case of the Katowice voivodeship. The main cleavage in the Katowice voivodeship runs between the area of the interwar Silesian voivodeship and the non-Silesian Dabrowa industrial basin. The ethno-regional identity of the *Szlonzoks* in the voivodeship is often pitted against that of the *Zaglebiaks*, the inhabitants of the Dabrowa industrial basin. Moreover, the Dabrowa basin is not part of historical Silesia and in the past was separated from Silesia by the Prussian/German–Russian border. The old border is reflected at the ecclesiastical level to this day: the Dabrowa basin with the western areas of the Kielce voivodeship constitutes the Sosnowiec diocese, which is part of the Czestochowa ecclesiastical province. The new Silesian voivodeship includes most of the former Bielsko-Biala voivodeship, which has had the effect of further distorting the relationship between ecclesiastical and secular administrative boundaries, as the boundaries of the latter voivodeship coincided with those of the Bielsko-Zywiec diocese of the Cracow ecclesiastical province. For its part, the Silesian voivodeship, apart from the Dabrowa basin, is split into the Katowice archdiocese and the Gliwice diocese.

Thus many obstacles would have to be removed to make it possible for Silesian regional identity to emerge in the Silesian voivodeship. The coming into being of such an identity would additionally be hindered by the low percentage of the *Szlonzokian* and Upper Silesian German population in comparison to the overall population of the voivodeship, which with enlargement rose rise to five million. The voivodeship is also differentiated at the spatial and social level: with the center highly industrialized, the north agricultural and the south reliant on agriculture and tourism. In sum, any moves toward the development of regional consciousness in this area depends upon events in the region itself, in the rest of Poland, and increasingly in the EU.

The future of Czech Silesia

The consolidation of communist rule in Czechoslovakia after the Prague Spring affected the minorities only slightly. The minority rights provisions of the previous regime were not abolished but the influence of minority organizations was severely reduced as a consequence of their integration within the National Front. During this time, the German minority was constantly reminded of the GDR's part in the invasion of 1968. As for the Polish minority during the last years of communism, it actually played host to members of Solidarity who fled to Czech Silesia following the declaration of Martial Law in December 1981. Apart from that, both minorities continued their rather shadowy existence. They didn't bother the authorities, and in return the authorities didn't bother them.

Although some of the dissidents continued to discuss the postwar expulsion of the Germans, it was clear even before the Velvet Revolution that there was increasing alienation between Czechs and Slovaks. Federalism, albeit within a one-party state, had not solved these issues, and this inter-ethnic fissure was also evident within the dissident movement (Pithart, 1995: 215). Following the Velvet Revolution in the autumn of 1989, a tendency to form ethnically based parties became almost immediately observable. In fact the campaign against communist rule had been dominated by separate Czech and Slovak movements, Civic Forum in Prague and Public Against Violence in Bratislava (Whightman, 1995: 60). It soon became clear that the main line of cleavage in post-communist Czechoslovakia would be that between Czechs and Slovaks, allowing much smaller groups such as the Poles or Germans to remain hidden from public view.

As we noted in Chapter 2, the census of 1991 revealed there to be 59,383 Poles, 48,556 Germans, and 44,446 thousand Silesians resident in the country. Respectively this amounted to 0.6, 0.5, and 0.4 per cent of the entire population. The figures also revealed that in Czech Silesia Poles constituted 20 per cent of the population, and that Silesians accounted for a further 18 per cent of the population. They also revealed that declared Germans only made up 1.3 of the population (calculated from Bricke, 1994).

Although the accuracy of these figures can be doubted, as many members of ethnic minorities, especially the Roma, still did not dare to confess their ethnic origin, it is remarkable that in this census the formerly Czech sub-groups of Silesians and much more numerous Moravians were classified as nationalities. Official acknowledgment of this status is also reflected in the opening sentence of the Czech constitution, which begins: 'We, citizens of the Czech Republic in Bohemia, Moravia, and Silesia'; and in a gesture to history the Silesian coat of arms has formed part of the state coat of arms since the downfall of the communists.

At this point it is useful to attempt to define what the term 'ethnic minority' actually means in the Czech Republic. Although President Havel and Prime Ministers Klaus and Zeman have all pronounced themselves to be in favour of territorial-administrative reform, they have all been wary of undertaking any action which might foster the growth of autonomous movements. They have argued, no doubt with an eye on the past, that no Czech government should do anything which might either precipitate or sponsor such movements. Rather, they argue that the government should aim to act in the interest of all citizens and to ensure administrative efficiency (Rhodes, 1995: 362). It could be argued that the Czech government in applying the 'civic principle' to all decisions concerning minorities and minority rights has contributed to the absence of any major separatist movement appearing within the country. This principle, which is built upon notions of *jus soli* as opposed to *jus sanguinis,* dominates the various documents which outline the rights of minorities in the Czech Republic.

The protection of minorities, both in domestic law and through the incorporation of international law in the Czech Republic, has been analysed earlier in the volume. Let us now examine some of their practical ramifications of this policy. Under the various statutes, minority rights have been incorporated within the law on schools, enabling local school boards to provide non-Czech classes or even non-Czech schools, the law on the registration of names which allows individuals to reassume a previously Czechisized name, through the provision of minority language media, and by allowing the minorities to form their own political parties. Hoskova states that the catalogue of minority rights reaches the international standards and that the rights of members of these minorities are evenly protected even without a specific minority law (Hoskova, 1994: 103). Hoskova may well be right as regards the letter of the law; however, the extent to which such laws are honoured, especially with regard to the Roma, is a matter of the utmost doubt.

The contemporary situation

Shortly after the Velvet Revolution a test case for the minorities policy of the new government emerged when the 'Movement for Self-governing Democracy-Society for Moravia and Silesia' (MSD-SMS) was founded (Rhodes, 1995: 352 ff.). The main aim of the party was to strengthen the position of these former Austrian provinces of Czechoslovakia by demanding autonomy and a fairer distribution of funds from Prague. Although relatively successful at the 1990 elections, with a share of 8.5 per cent of the vote in Moravia, their desire for a federalization of the Czech Lands into constituent Bohemian, Moravian and Silesian provinces failed, not only due to the absolute refusal of President Havel and Prime Minister Klaus to countenance such demands but due also to internal conflicts between extremist and moderate sub-groups within the party. With a power base mostly in the southern parts of Moravia, and with the withdrawal of some of its most radical activists, the party became more centrist. However, this strategy of moderation failed, and in the 1992 elections the MSD-SMS obtained only 4.57 per cent of the votes in Moravia. The support for autonomy in Silesia also underwent significant changes. In 1990, the party gained nearly 25 per cent of the votes in Silesia, a success which could not be emulated in 1992, when only 11 per cent of the vote was obtained (Kostelecky, 1995: 101 ff.). In the wake of this failure the MSD-SMS split in 1993, with the bulk of its members joining either the newly founded Czech-Moravian Centre Party or the Moravian National Party, neither of which has had any impact at the national level. Whatever the original stimulus behind the demand for autonomy, it has proved ephemeral, and the fact that Slovakia is now an independent state, and no longer a 'drain' on Moravian resources, may well be a factor in explaining the decline in the movement.

In Czech Silesia the Poles and the Germans were granted administrative and financial support for their collective activities. It must be emphasized that the attitude of Prague toward these two groups was governed by three factors. The first was a recognition of the needs of the communities. The second was an acknowledgment of the historical sensitivities of the Czech population in the area. Additionally, the political relationship between the Czech Republic and Poland and Germany also had an impact upon how Prague proceeded.

The Poles of Czech Silesia, who constitute approximately 20 per cent of the entire population, intensified their organizational efforts by creating the Congress of Poles in 1992. Its 18 sub-groups have the role of coordinating the work of the numerous local organizations. Their main demands cover the much needed improvement of their schools and compensation or property restitution to Poles who migrated to Poland shortly after the war. There are approximately 60 Polish schools in Czech Silesia, all of which are in urgent need of repair as well as financial assistance for the purchase of teaching materials. Neither the Czech nor the Polish government supplies them with the necessary funds. The close contact of the minority organization with the Confederation for an Independent (KPN) in Poland does not help the situation, and would seem to preclude the possibility of the growth of any inter-communal regional identity (Bricke, 1994). To make things more difficult, irritants in Czech–Polish inter-state relations do nothing to ease the situation. The refusal of Czechoslovakia fully to open its border with Poland until 1991, recriminations about Polish behaviour in 1938 and the growing competition for western European investment have all soured bilateral cooperation and have had an adverse affect on the Polish minority in Czech Silesia (Hyde-Price, 1996).

The position of the German minority in Czech Silesia as well as in the remainder of the country is strongly influenced by the past and the different interpretations placed upon it by the German government, the *Sudetendeutsche Landsmannschaft*, the Czech government and Czech public opinion. The process of reconciliation between the two countries has been far more complicated and difficult than Franco-German or German–Polish reconciliation. The discussion has been dominated by questions concerning who should apologize to whom and for what concerning events during the years 1938 and 1949. The situation has been further complicated the deliberate omission of any reference to this period in the Treaty on Good Neighbourly Relations and Cooperation of 1993 and the German–Czech

Declaration on Mutual Relations and Their Future Development of 1997. Neither has it been helped by accusations from the *Landsmannschaft* that Czechs did not suffer during the period of German occupation, or the Czech Prime Minister's comparison of the *Landsmannschaft* with both extremes of right and left in Czech politics. Although the German government stated in 1993 that the situation of the German minority in the Czech Republic was generally satisfactory and that the support from Bonn and Prague met the needs of the minority (*Deutscher Bundestag*, 1993) the *Bund der Vertriebene*, in one of its very rare statements about the remaining German minority in the country, later complained about insufficient funds, a hostile Czech administration and a general decrease in German self-awareness (Bund der Vertriebene, 1994).

In 1998 a questionnaire carried out by the author of this section revealed that most German organizations were established between 1990 and 1995.[5] In 1997 they received no funds from the Czech Republic but between 10,000 and 267,000 Czech crowns each from Germany. Among their activities are the publication of newspapers and the organization of cultural events. The German centres cooperate very closely with one another and take advantage of a strong communal spirit, especially in Silesia. When asked about their living conditions they confirmed that Germans are now allowed to speak German in public and that they participate in the political administration at local and regional level, although there are no German political parties. German as a medium of instruction is, however, only provided in Plzen, which demonstrates just how old the minority is, as much as it does a reluctance on the part of the Czechs to provide such an education. There is a widespread feeling of discrimination, especially in the field of property purchase. The majority of answers evaluated the attitude toward them held by their Czech neighbours generally as being 'distant' or 'neutral', and far from 'friendly' or 'neighbourly'. However, they agreed that it is now possible publicly to admit to having regional Sudeten Silesian identity. These observations must be evaluated against the pre-1989 situation, which was also investigated in the questionnaire. The only major improvements that were observable were in the use of German, financial aid from Germany and a reduction in the level of discrimination. On the other hand, it was claimed there had been no improvement in relations with their Czech neighbours. It should also be mentioned here that the percentage of the German population speaking German is on the decrease. The participants in the survey estimated that 70 per cent of all those over 70 years of age,

45 per cent of the 51–60 year olds but only 15 per cent of the generation up to 40 years of age speak German. The obvious gap between official portrayals of harmony and the of Czechs and Poles living in Czech Silesia toward one another, and to their German co-nationals, can be explained in two ways. First, historical memory of the years 1938–1945 still lingers. Secondly, there remains a fear one day the German expellee organizations will get their way and have their claims for property restitution granted (see Frank, 1998; Glauber, 1998; Huemer, 1998). To 'western eyes' such fears may seem groundless. However, as we shall see in the next chapter, the burden of history is a factor with regard to the envisaged eastward expansion of the EU. It is to this envisaged future, and its ramifications for Silesia, that we shall now turn.

Bibliography

Adamczuk, L. and Zdaniewicz, W. (eds), *Kosciol katolicki w Polsce 1918–1990: Rocznik statystyczny*. Warsaw, GUS and Zaklad Socjologii Religii SAC, 1991.

Auslandskurier 17, June 1996.

Bahlcke, J., *Schlesien und die Schlesier*. Berlin, Langen Müller, 1996.

Berdychowska, B., et al. (eds), *Mniejszosci narodowe w Polsce w 1993 roku*. Warsaw, Biuro do Spraw Mniejszosci Narodowych przy Ministerstwie Kultury i Sztuki, 1994.

Berlinska, D., 'Narodowo-etniczne stosunki miedzygrupowe na Slasku Opolskim: ciaglosc i zmiana', in K. Frysztacki (ed.), *Polacy, Slazacy, Niemcy: Studia nad stosunkami spoleczno-kulturowymi na Slasku Opolskim*. Cracow, Universitas, 1998.

Bingen, D., 'Bundesinstitut für Ostwissenschaftliche und Internationale Studien', interview with Karl Cordell, 8 Nov. 1994.

Bundesministerium für des Inneren, *Minderheit in Polen*, Internal Report. Bonn, 1994.

Cordell, K., 'Retreat from Ethnicity? Upper Silesia and German–Polish Relations', *Plymouth International Papers*, 1995.

Dialog 2/3, 1995.

Gazeta Wyborcza, 23 Oct. 1998.

Hajduk, R., 'Problem Polakow bylych zolnierzy armii niemieckiej na posiedzeniach Komisji Wojskowej Rady Narodowej Rzeczypospolitej Polskiej w Londynie', *Studia Slaskie* 40, 1982.

Johannes, B., Ministry of Foreign Affairs, in conversation with Karl Cordell, 25 Oct. 1994.

Jonderko, F., 'Stereotypy etniczne na Slasku Opolskim. Czy generacyjna zmiana?' in K. Frysztacki (ed.), *Polacy, Slazacy, Niemcy. Studia nad stosunkami spoleczno-kulturowymi na Slasku Opolskim*. Cracow, Universitas, 1998.

Kamusella, T., 'Geneza i anatomia wysiedlen przeprowadzonych na Gornym Slasku w koncowym stadium i po zakonczeniu II wojny swiatowej', in E. Nycz (ed.), *Historyczne i wspolczesne problemy miasta i jego mieszkancow*. Opole, Instytut Slaski, 1996.

Kandzia, C., Member of the BJDM, interview with Karl Cordell, 9 Nov. 1995.

Kroll, H., Member of the Polish *Sejm*, interview with Karl Cordell, 16 Nov. 1994.
Linek, B., *'Odniemczanie' wojewodztwa slaskiego w latach 1945–1950 w swietle materialow wojewodzkich*. Opole, Instytut Slaski, 1997.
Linek, B., 'Obraz mieszkancow Slaska Opolskiego na lamach prasy regionalnej: tozsamosc grupowa, relacje miedzygrupowe, modele wspolistnienia', in K. Frysztacki (ed.), *Polacy, Slazacy, Niemcy. Studia nad stosunkami spoleczno-kulturowymi na Slasku Opolskim*. Cracow, Universitas, 1998.
Lis, M., *Ludnosc rodzima na Slasku Opolskim po II wojnie swiatowej (1945–1993)*. Opole, Instytut Slaski, 1993.
Madajczyk, P., *Na drodze pojednania. Wokol oredzia biskupow polskich do biskupow niemieckich z 1965*. Warsaw, PWN, 1994.
Magocsi, P., *Historical Atlas of East Central Europe*. London, University of Washington Press, 1995.
Moldawa, T., *Ludzie wladzy 1944–1991*. Warsaw, PWN, 1991.
Nossol, A., Pastoral Address, 3 Nov. 1992.
Pawlak, W. (ed.), *Atlas Slaska Dolnego i Opolskiego*. Wroclaw, Uniwersytet Wroclawski, 1997.
Pater, J., 'Kominek B', in M. Pater (ed.), *Slownik biograficzny katolickiego duchowienstwa slaskiego XIX i XX wieku*. Katowice, Ksiegarnia sw. Jacka, 1996.
Petrach, F., *Verband der Deutschen Gesellschaften in Polen*, in conversation with Karl Cordell, 10 Nov. 1997.
Reichling, G., *Die deutschen Vertriebenen in Zahlen*, pt. i: *Umsiedler, Verschleppte, Vertriebene, Aussiedler 1940–1985*. Bonn, Kulturstiftung der deutschen Vertriebenen, 1986.
Rostropowicz, J., *'Die Oberschlesier in Oberschlesien-eine Brücke zwischen Polen und Deutschen'*, undated conference paper.
Satava, L., *Narodnostni mensiny v Evrope*. Prague, Ivo Zelazny,1994.
Schlesische Nachrichten, 15 Feb. 1998.
Schlesisches Wochenblatt, 11 April 1997; 21 Sept. 1997; 13 Feb. 1998; 13 Mar. 1998; 29 May 1998; 26 June 1998; 17 July 1998; 28 Aug. 1998.
Urban, T., *Deutsche in Polen*. Munich, Beck, 1994.
Wanatowicz, M., *Historia spoleczno-polityczna Gornego Slaska i Slaska Cieszynskiego w latach 1918–1945*. Katowice, Wydawnictwo Uniwersytetu Wroclawskiego,1994.
Wolf, A., *Der Status des Spätaussiedlers nach dem Kriegsfolgenbereinigungsgesetz*. Wiesbaden, Kommunal- und Schul-Verlag, 1996.
Zycie 66, 19 Mar. 1998.

Notes

1. The early sections of this chapter which deal with Polish Upper Silesia were written by Tomasz Kamusella and completed by Karl Cordell. The sections on Czech Silesia were written by Karl Martin Born.
2. The next greatest concentration of Germans is in the Warmia and Mazury voivodeship, i.e. former East Prussia, where perhaps 50,000 Germans/German-oriented Mazurs still live.
3. Moravian identity is more regional than ethnic. A few activists dream of creating a Moravian nation, some who declare themselves to be Silesians and who often could equally be classified as *Slonzaks*, Germans or Czechs who

identify with historical Austrian Silesia, and hope for its re-creation within the planned re-organization of Czech local government.

4. Several hundred thousand Ukrainians and ethnically related *Lemkos* were deported to former German areas of Poland in the late 1940s in order to break armed Ukrainian resistance to the Polish and Soviet authorities.
5. In July 1998, questionnaires were sent to the German *Begegnungszentren* in Brno, Cheb, Chomutov, Havirov, Horni Slakov, Liberec, Moravska Trebova, Opava, Plzen and Sumperk. Eight organizations replied. There is no significant regional variation between answers, and as such the responses are taken to be representative of the community as a whole.

8
The Future of Silesia

Contemporary perspectives

As we noted in the previous two chapters, for years the position and existence of Germans in Upper Silesia and other parts of Poland was one of the issues which dogged bilateral relations between Warsaw and Bonn. After the two sides eventually established formal diplomatic relations in 1970, one of the fruits of this tentative rapprochement was that between 1970 and 1988 over 550,000 people claiming adherence to the Deutschtum were allowed to leave Poland. From 1988 the changed political climate in Poland resulted in recognition on the part of the government that Poland did in fact possess an ethnic German minority. However, we also need to note that the fall of communism prompted a further exodus of Germans from Poland to Germany, and that this exodus coupled with the changed political climate in Poland prompted a rethink in Bonn of its policy toward (the future of) this minority.

As a consequence of the above factors and the general disquiet in Germany over the huge number of immigrants that west Germany absorbed in the late 1980s, from 1990 the German government changed its position on the German minorities in Poland and elsewhere in Eastern Europe. In the wake of the passing of the War Consequences Consolidation Act by the German parliament, (descendants of) ethnic Germans resident in Eastern Europe and the former Soviet Union born after 1 January 1993 are not entitled to receive German passports. This has had an important impact on the role of the German diplomatic corps in Poland, who do not see it as their primary task to facilitate the emigration of German passport holders from Poland to Germany. In addition, the German government now requires more documentary evidence than in the past from individuals who wish to claim German passports. The objective of this policy is dual: on the one hand the German government wishes, even if it does not officially admit it, to stem the flow of *Spätaussiedler* (late resettlers). On the other, it wishes to minimize abuse of the law on the part of those who wish to better their life chances by emigrating to Germany. This creates a problem for would be German citizens living in Poland and elsewhere in Eastern Europe. For various reasons they often lack the requisite documentation which might prove their entitlement to a German passport. For instance people may simply have lost such documentation. In other cases German documents were confiscated by the Polish authorities, and in some instances those who possessed a German passport before 1945 passed themselves off as Polish after 1945, and destroyed any evidence which might have proved otherwise. To complicate matters even further, the Polish government rarely issues copies of 'rehabilitation' or 'verification' documents to those who request them.

Germany now has a large diplomatic presence in Poland. Apart from the embassy in Warsaw, there are consulates in Wroclaw, Szczecin, Gdansk, Opole and elsewhere. With regard to the minority itself, members of the German diplomatic corps in have made it clear that the role of the German government is to aid in the process of post-communist consolidation, and that in turn this involves economic and political initiatives aimed at Polish society as a whole, as well as supporting activities which facilitate the self-expression of the German minority in Poland itself. As a result, embassy staff actively involve themselves in the cultural activities of the VdG, and in addition work closely with the organization's political leadership. The VdG often claims that they receive insufficient financial and material support from the federal government. For its part the federal government sees itself as a facilitator of aid and rarely involves itself in issues which it considers to be solely within the competence of the Polish state. It has also made it crystal-clear to the nationalist fringe which inevitably inhabits various of the German societies that any activities which might lead to disturbance in Polish–German relations, or within Polish society, will not be tolerated (Kroll, 1994). In light of the above, it could be argued that sometimes the VdG forgets that the German government's first obligation is to Germany itself, and that the situation of Poland's German minority is but one element of the general pattern of German–Polish relations.

Future trends

It now remains for us in the light of our findings to make some assessment of the future of the German community in Upper Silesia. The pattern of migration to Germany has temporarily at least, been broken. In fact in recent years more people have left Germany for Poland than the other way round. Despite the uncertainty over exact numbers, the German community appears now to be the largest ethnic minority in Poland, and certainly is the best organized (Sakson, 1993: 7). We have already noted that the leadership of the VdG is not always enamoured with Berlin. There are also complaints that the wider population of the Federal Republic has insufficient interest in the fate of the Germans of Upper Silesia. Here they have a point. Although there is no reason to expect that every German should have an interest in Poland, a relatively narrow circle of enthusiasts, specialists, Germany's Polish minority, the *Vertriebene*, and *Spätaussiedler* to one side, for the rest of the German population Poland might as well be Mars.

In a sense such attitudes should come as no surprise, given the nature of Polish–German relations from the mid-eighteenth to the mid-twentieth century. They also help explain why the German minority in Upper Silesia and elsewhere in Poland from time to time expresses disappointment with both the German government and wider population. Despite the years of isolation from Germany, the Federal Republic always served as a point of reference and role model for those Germans who remained in Poland. It goes without saying that Poland did not fulfil a similar role in Germany, east or west. Indeed, years of isolation from Germany contributed to the creation in Germany of a community which finds it difficult to comes to terms with the fact that the experiences and orientations of postwar Germans, and particularly postwar west Germans, are very different to those Germans who have remained in Poland (Bingen, 1994).

As should be clear by now, despite the progress of the past few years, the hubris of distrust still lingers, as was shown in the thorny issue of pension rights of former members of the German armed forces living in Poland. As we noted in Chapter 7, a bilateral agreement had been initialled in 1975. Yet the question of pension rights for those who served in the German armed forces up until 1945 was settled only in the autumn of 1995. This settlement, for which time spent as a prisoner of war, or in the *Landarmee* or as civilian forced labour (either in Poland, Germany or the Soviet Union), is not reckonable, has proved to be something of a disappointment for many members of the minority. Quite simply, they regard it as insufficient compensation for both their years of military service, and the subsequent discrimination they had to endure because of it. In addition, as mentioned earlier, one encounters complaints that the German minority does not enjoy the same privileges as the Ukrainian and other minorities in Poland. This is a claim which both the Polish and German governments refute, having jointly stated that in their opinion the treaty of 1991 conforms to the United Nations Charter on Human Rights, the Closing Act of the 1975 Helsinki Agreement, the Paris Charter for a New Europe of 1990 and the Copenhagen Document on the Human Dimension of 1990. In fact, given that the Law on National Minorities, if passed in its draft form, will allow both bilingual signage and the use of minority languages for official business in areas of minority residence, it is quite simply wrong to claim that in this field liberal democratic Poland has made no real break with communist practice.

In the late 1980s and early 1990s the 'Grand Design' of the VdG was to develop (Upper) Silesia as a bridge between Poland and Germany on the one hand and Western Europe and Eastern Europe on the other (Sakson 1993: 19–20). In fact, this idea was also widely touted by an unheard-of coalition of the CDU/CSU in Germany, the *Landsmannschaft Schlesien* and large sections of the Polish political class (Koschyk, 1993). Although bilateral cooperation has improved out of all recognition, there is no sign that Silesia is about to become some kind of 'Super-Euroregion'. Under Article 24 of the Basic Law, German *Länder* are empowered to transfer functions to Euroregions. The idea that in the short or even medium term Polish voivodeships will acquire similar rights is pure fantasy. We have already remarked how difficult was the process of reform of regional and local government, and the extent to which a significant minority of Polish nationalists sought to play 'the German card'. This aside, the success of such schemes is of course contingent upon Polish admission into the EU and a continued strengthening of the EU's regional policy. Discounting the vagaries of the latter, we can say that not only is the former contingent upon a continued strengthening of the Polish economy, it is also contingent upon a specific programme aimed at radically restructuring the economy of Upper Silesia. As if that were not enough, such designs are also predicated upon the process of constitutional reform. Given the ambiguities of the situation, German (Upper Silesian) anxieties are understandable, if at times exaggerated. According to the new constitution, where Polish law conflicts with international law, the latter takes precedence.

However, as we have seen, the matter is much more complex than is suggested by such a bald statement.

People and politics today

In terms of ethnic composition, Lower Silesia is now almost exclusively ethnically Polish. West and especially central Upper Silesia are mixed, and eastern Upper Silesia is overwhelmingly Polish. The current Silesian voivodeship boundaries mirror that fact. In many ways, the current boundaries represent the culmination of a process which began in 1945, when hardly anything was certain and final. This process was most decisive in Lower Silesia where the German University of Breslau was replaced with its Lwow (Lviv) counterpart. As the cultural and academic centre of Polish Lower Silesia, Wroclaw became something of in postwar Polish terms, a meeting place of various ethnic and regional traditions brought from the *kresy* and elsewhere with what was left of German Lower Silesia. Today Poles, remaining Germans, Ukrainians, *Lehmke*, together with the members of much smaller communities such as the Jewish minority, by and large a share a common affinity with their region.

Despite postwar ethnic cleansing, large-scale emigration and the accompanying Polonizing campaigns, a similar process has developed since 1989 in the much more heterogeneous Upper Silesia, despite of the best efforts of the Polish communists. Their campaign of ethnic cleansing/ethno-homogenization was complemented by the establishment of a number of academic institutes. The *Slaski Instytut Naukowy* (Silesian Scholastic Institute, SIN), established at Katowice in 1958, and the *Instytut Slaski* (Silesian Institute, SI), re-established at Opole in 1957 on the lines of its prewar counterpart originally founded in Katowice in 1934, were aimed at lending academic credence to the Polonization of Upper Silesia rather than at encouraging any interest in matters regional or German. As a supplement to the activities of these institutes, the government decided in 1967 to establish the University of Silesia as a model socialist university. The university which was located in several different centres, did not allow development of a student community which could engage in any coherent anti-communist actions, and the PZPR's generosity turned it into the creature of party ideologues who supported the party line on all matters Silesian regardless of the social and environmental costs (Kamusella, 1998: 118).

Yet after 1989 the university became an intellectual centre of Upper Silesian regionalism, both producing and supporting the leadership of the ZGr and the ZLNS. Actually the first post-communist Katowice voivode, Czech, was sympathetic to the ZGr, and toyed with the idea of re-creating Upper Silesia within its historical boundaries. To that end he closed the SIN, and started propagating his aforementioned vision. With the victory of the post-communist SLD at the 1993 parliamentary elections he was replaced by a succession of nondescript individuals who were content to let matters rest as they were. However, with the coming to power of the AWS and the Freedom Union UW in 1997, came the plans for territorial administrative reform dealt with in the previous chapter.

The successful campaign to save the Opole voivodeship not only demonstrates the weakness of the government, it also shows the strength of regional identity in Opole Silesia. Such societal cohesion should ensure the effective functioning of the region on the basis of a non-ethnically based loyalty to the region. As for the new (Upper) Silesian voivodeship, given its sub-regional and structural differences, as well as with the widespread degradation of the environment and the social costs of having to shut down numerous mines and metallurgical works which are predicted to result in 200,000 people losing their jobs, the future is much more uncertain.

An interim report

It is important for us now to acknowledge the gains that have been made in Upper Silesia in the past few years. The German minority now has its own voice in both national and local politics in Poland. Their existence is no longer denied by the Polish state, and both the Polish and German governments have sponsored a range of initiatives aimed at preserving the distinct nature of this society. It must be noted that there is tendency on the part of the VdG and its affiliates to look to Bonn rather than Warsaw in this respect, and to lobby Bonn through the *Landsmannschaften* (Liedtke 1994). This is a situation, given the latter's preoccupation with the question of property rights in Poland for the *Vertriebene,* that neither government is happy with. However, this has not led to real disruption to either inter-state relations or inter-communal relations, which at present are good.

The greatest change has perhaps been in the matter of citizenship and ethnicity. What we have witnessed in Poland since 1945 is the creation of a German community in Upper Silesia which is more certain of its identity than it was prior to 1939. This has come about not because of the success of German nation building strategies, but because of the failure of Polish equivalents. The failure of communist authoritarianism shows that identity cannot be forced upon people, even at the point of a gun. Since 1988 the presence of a declared and substantial German minority has not proven to be the major political issue in Poland that some feared it might have become, although their 'discovery' did come as something of an initial shock to a people who for years had been told that virtually no Germans resided in Poland.

The incorporation of the Germans and their peak organizations into the new Polish political culture demonstrates that there is increasing acceptance that Poland as a state is host to a number of national minorities. Both sides have made concessions. The greatest of these concessions has been to recognize that not every citizen of a state has ipso facto to possess the nationality of the titular nation. Citizenship has become detached from nationality, thereby challenging the idea that only 'True Poles' can be Polish patriots. Given the terrible legacy of German–Polish relations in this century, the continued toleration and flourishing of a German minority in Poland is the best indication we have of the strength of Polish liberal democracy.

Silesia in modern Germany

What then of the westernmost part of Lower Silesia east of the Oder–Neiße line, which remained with Germany after 1945? The GDR authorities prohibited to use such terms as 'Silesian', 'East Prussian', *Deutsche Ostgebiete* or 'expellee'. When referring to the former *Deutsche Ostgebiete*, they used Polish place names and discouraged any discussion on the expulsion. In addition they split the westernmost tip of Silesia between the districts of Dresden and Cottbus in 1952, and in 1968 purged the noun Silesia from the name of the Evangelical Church of Silesia. Yet the memory of Silesia lingered on in various ways, for example in the form of the truncated Breslau archdiocese with the seat at Görlitz. In 1972 it was transformed into the Görlitz apostolic administration, and simultaneously the Pope allowed the Breslau archdiocese clergy and faithful to establish the Breslau apostolic visitature in the FRG. The visitature cooperated with the FRG's various organizations of the Silesian expellees in developing and sustaining a feeling of Silesian identity among a group of people most of whom will never be able to return to live in Silesia, and most of whom, rhetoric aside, would never want to anyway.

Although the *Landsmannschaft Schlesien* had been busy for over 30 years creating a 'virtual Silesia' in the Federal Republic, only with unification did the synergy come to allow for the explicit reconstruction of Silesian identity in what little remains of German Silesia. The German fragment of Silesia now lies within the re-established Land of Saxony and the *Landsmannschaft Schlesien* has extended its activities to this region. Requests by the *Landsmannschaft Schlesien* that the Land be renamed Saxony-Silesia, however, got absolutely nowhere. In 1993 the former Evangelical Church of Silesia was renamed the Evangelical Church of Silesian Upper Lusatia (*Evangelische Kirche der schlesischen Oberlausitz*), and next year the apostolic administration was transformed into the Görlitz diocese. For its part, in its 1992 constitution Land of Saxony permitted not only the expression of Silesian culture and identity, but also allowed the indigenous west Slavic Sorb minority of around 60,000 persons the right to use of traditional symbols, and the Sorbian language and culture.

It should also be noted that, despite the foundation of Silesian Electoral Federation, the low level of support it enjoys indicates that few people vote according to a parochial 'Silesia First' agenda. Nevertheless, Görlitz advertises itself as the 'largest Lower Silesian city in Germany', and Lower Silesian regional elements remain part of and parcel of Saxony (Bahlcke, 1996: 213–16). The area around Görlitz has become a centre of activity for the *Landsmannschaft Schlesien*, whose roots go back to 1947. Together with similar associations the *Landsmannschaft Schlesien* seeks to provide a common voice for former German residents of former areas of German settlement in Central Europe and Russia. Since 1952 All *Landsmannschaften* have been grouped together under the common roof of the *Bund der Vertriebene* (Federation of Expellees) (Weiß, 1995: 125–44). Although the Landsmannschaft Schlesien claims to represent the interests of all Silesian Germans, including those who still live there, it tends to be dominated by the attitudes of expellee generation. As a result, it has not proven to be very effective in recruiting *Spätaussiedler*. For years the BdV in general, and in particular, the leader of the *Landsmannschaft Schlesien* Herbert Hupka, were portrayed in Poland as crypto-Nazis. Although the leadership of the *Landsmannschaft* was, and sometimes still is, hidebound and obstinate, this epithet was ill-merited, especially in the case of Hupka, whose mother was Jewish and who died in the Theresienstadt concentration camp.

In recent years, something of a paradox has occurred in their fortunes: whereas in Germany the *Landsmannschaft Schlesien* along with all others finds itself increasingly at the political margins, in Poland it is taken seriously as a legitimate albeit prickly political actor. In fact, unlike other *Landsmannschaften*, the *Landsmannschaft Schlesien* has showed a willingness to compromise on such questions as property rights, and the circumstances under which expellees and pre-1976 emigrants could return to their former areas of residence.

The *Landsmannschaft Schlesien* now operates legally in both countries. In Germany the base organizations are formed by exiles who gather together according to their former places of residence. Their activities are not exactly typical of contemporary life in modern Germany. They centre around the preservation of folklore, custom and a way of life that has all but vanished in Silesia itself. At the national level, the executive committee, seeks to coordinate these activities and engender a sense of community among those of Silesian descent, including the post-1945 generations. It has its own newspaper, the *Schlesische Nachrichten*, and continues to lobby Berlin both directly and through a small band of CDU/CSU parliamentarians who themselves are members of the Silesian and other *Landsmannschaften*.

Members are also increasingly active in Poland. Together with local DFKs they organize cultural festivals, engage in seminars, and channel funds to towns and villages in which Germans still live. Their entry into Polish politics understandably caused something of a stir in the late 1980s. After all, the Polish press had for years denigrated the *Landsmannschaften* as little more than Nazis. Of course, many Polish people have anxieties over such organizations, and Poland's desire to enter the EU cannot be separated from such concerns. Yet in the past few years, the *Landsmannschaft Schlesien* has organized joint seminars with the Department of German at the University of Wroclaw, in 1998 Hupka, received a distinguished service medal from the council of his home town of Raciborz, and in the same year, the BdV held talks in Warsaw with representatives of the Polish government. All of which demonstrate the extent to which the climate has changed in recent years (*Schlesische Nachrichten*, 1 September 1998).

What then of the future of expellees and *Aussiedler* who now live in Germany? There is in fact little interest among the postwar generations for the *Heimat* of their parents and grandparents. This is evidenced by the ageing membership of the *Landsmannschaft Schlesien*. The renewed contact between those who were expelled and who emigrated and those who remained behind in Poland reinvigorated both groups in the early 1990s. However, the euphoria which greeted the collapse of communism, and the failure on the part of the German government to demand some kind of special status for Polish Silesia to press the claims for compensation and the *Recht auf Heimat*, has alienated the

Landsmannschaft even further from the political mainstream in Germany. In essence, the Lower Silesian section of the *Landsmannschaft* in particular is ageing. There is little recruitment from among the younger generation, and given the lack of Germans in Polish Lower Silesia, there is no potential pool of recruits, nor indeed much scope for continued cooperation in that part of Poland, once the current generation of pensioners is gone. The same process is also to a lesser apparent with the Upper Silesian branch of the *Landsmannschaft,* where there has been more of an influx of members since the late 1950s, given the continuous emigration to Germany. However, once again the younger generation tends to steer clear of the organization. This is in itself hardly surprising, given that the *Landsmannschaft*, rightly or wrongly, often gives the impression that it is more concerned with rescuing the past than it is with understanding the present.

European futures

What then of the future? If the European project continues in its present direction, destructive antagonisms bred by petty ethnic/national differences may well abate, and public acceptance of various religious, regional and ethnic/national identities will increase. Hence Silesia may survive in the form of the five separate regions of Lower Silesia, Opole Silesia, (Upper) Silesia, German Lower Silesia and Czech Silesia. However, for the foreseeable future they will remain constituent parts of their respective nation-states and eventually of the EU, and with accession to the EU, so the shadow of history should cease to cast its shadow of those who live in Silesia today. Although this is an optimistic scenario, it is not altogether unrealistic. Of course, the examples of Bosnia and Kosovo serve as alternative models. However, given the progress that has been made at all levels of Polish–German and indeed Czech–German relations since 1990, combined with progress made with regard to the accession of Poland and the Czech Republic to Nato and the EU, the Balkan alternative is fortunately by far the less likely.

The sweeping changes of 1989 not only marked the end of communism, but simultaneously redefined Poland's relationship with Germany and the other states of the EU. This new and novel situation hopefully denotes a decisive break with past political practice. Unfortunately, such an assumption does not match the experiences of the average Silesian, or for that matter anyone else who has lived in Central Europe during this century. The EU, which in part bases its political programme on the doctrine of personalism, supported by the principle of subsidiarity, has since the signing of the Maastricht Treaty, sought to create a Europe which operates on three political levels.

These are at the level of the EU as a series of institutions, the level of the nation-state and the level of the region. This approach recognizes and encourages the articulation of multiple identities whose constituents are not necessarily contradictory, and may be mutually complementary and fortifying. According to this view, multiple loyalties are preferable to their monistic national counterparts, as the former contribute to the creation of a multi-layered Europe, and are conducive to strengthening of civil society at the micro and macro levels. The multiple interlocking loyalties made tangible by increasing mobility hold together the three levels of the EU, as do the constituent elements themselves. This is in contradistinction to loyalty based solely around membership of a nation-state, which absolutizes the nation-state as the ultimate entity of governance and locus of identity.

This move away from the paradigm of nationalist conflict in European relations was made possible above all by Franco-German reconciliation, which produced the political core of the movement toward European union. It firmly contained Germany within the framework of European structures, transforming it from being a strategic risk into a key factor for European stability. This wider process of reconciliation has now been extended to Central Europe, and most significantly to Poland; the largest country in the region whose postwar nationalism, as we have noted, was based on virulent anti-Germanism (Kinsky, 1997: 115–24).

This means that a new beginning for Silesia and its inhabitants may be created. All Silesians, due to their living in a borderland, have since 1918 learned to expect rapid reversals of nationalistic campaigns of assimilation. Should Poland become part of the EU, unidimensional Polish–German relations would become a thing of the past. As German nationalism was softened and to some extent rendered obsolete through the revitalization of the federal principle both at home and abroad, so Polish statecraft could follow the same route. Eventually, the German–Polish border would no longer carry the same political and emotional significance as in previous decades of the century.

If this optimistic scenario prevails (Upper) Silesians would be more ready to leave the protective cocoon of their variegated ethnicity. Hence, the expression of the traditional regionalism of the *Szlonzoks* and other Upper Silesians would not be only tolerated but would come to be encouraged by the Polish majority who would increasingly look favourably upon the regionalization of the country. However, it must be stressed that any form of decentralized government has traditionally been anathema in Poland since the foundation of the modern state. We should also note that it is still almost impossible for foreigners to buy land in Poland, and that there are increasing signs of reluctance on the part of the Polish government to change the law either in this area or in the sphere of residence and employment rights for foreigners.

The land ownership law dates back to before World War Two. However, this issue and the question of residence and employment rights for foreigners are beginning to reopen old wounds in some sections of Polish society. The *Landmannschaft Schlesien* has moderated its stance on property restitution, unlike some of its sister organizations. Instead, it calls for compromise on the issue and argues that, as a member of the EU, Poland will have to change its those laws which deal with residency, employment, and property ownership rights. In that way, as far as the *Landsmannschaft* is concerned, the legacy of Yalta and Potsdam will finally be disposed of.

Increasingly, this is not how it looks from the Polish perspective. Quite rightly, the Poles point out that the superior purchasing power of Germans could lead to their buying up chunks of Poland at bargain prices. For some this would simply be the precursor to a renewed wave of German migration which would change the ethnographic balance of areas such as Silesia, and eventually lead to demands that the borders once again being redrawn. No matter how far-fetched this may sound to non-Polish ears, unfortunately it makes sense to sizeable sections of the Polish electorate, especially older, ill-educated and poor people living in rural areas. Matters are not helped by tiny numbers of *Vertriebene* launching hopeless petitions in the Polish courts for the restoration of property. Just for the record, in 1997, foreigners were allowed to purchase a total of 2,942 hectares. Of this amount, 120 hectares was sold to a total of 367 Germans, 296 of whom were of 'Polish descent'. These 367 individuals managed to construct a total of 18 flats between them (*Schlesiches Wochenblatt*, 4 September 1998).

Because of historically based anxieties, the widespread indifference toward Poland in Germany is not matched in Poland. The idea that possibly millions of *Vertriebene* would migrate to Poland is absurd. The idea that even if they did, they could do so in an uncontrolled manner, and live off the Polish state is even more ridiculous. Yet, as negotiations for Poland's entry into the EU become more intense, that is exactly the kind of scenario that the Polish nationalist right is painting. Although this group is much diminished, it is still much more part of the political mainstream than it is in Germany. Indeed, in the first decade of the new millennium it will be interesting to see the extent to which the right in Poland will be able to rally ordinary voters around a xenophobic 'strong state' campaign.

Forms of government which are felt to strengthen the periphery at the expense of the centre, are identified as one of the causes for the collapse of the Polish-Lithuanian Commonwealth in the eighteenth century. In other words, if a meaningful form of decentralization is to succeed in Poland it will only come about with a definitive change of the national psyche. From a practical point of view, the growth of regional structures could contribute to ending the difference in status between Upper Silesia's *Szlonzoks* and Poles, and especially of those Germans who possess German passports. This equalization of status with the concomitant acceptance of ethnic difference would facilitate construction of new regional identities in Silesia based on a common recognition of Silesia's past. However, it seems improbable that the process could lead to (re-)emergence of an all-Silesian identity, if indeed such a thing ever existed. In fact it probably did not, because even in the nineteenth century the term *Schlesier* (Silesian) usually denoted an inhabitant of Lower Silesia, and the term *Oberschlesier* (Upper Silesian) referred to the inhabitants of a much more ethnically and economically diversified Upper Silesia. Indeed, such a development would be seized upon by Polish nationalists as yet another reason to stay out of the EU. With our survey of Silesia almost complete, our remaining task is to make some comment about contemporary Czech Silesia.

Concluding remarks

What then does the future hold for Silesia as a whole after centuries of bitter struggle? In both Czech and Polish Silesia as well as in the countries with a former Silesian population, namely Germany and Austria, there are high expectations of what regionalization and Europeanization might bring. The concept of regionalization refers both to the creation of economic units of a similar size and population as well as to developing a strategy aimed at satisfying the demands of ethnically defined regions with a homogeneous historical and ethnic component (for a discussion of these concepts and their implications for Silesia see Born, 1998). With both the Czech Republic and Poland due to become full members of the EU in the first decade of the next century, it is more than likely that the positions of minorities will be secured and even strengthened. A first step for the Europeanization of Silesia has already been taken, as the EU has funded several bi-and trinational cross-border cooperation projects. All such projects still suffer from a lack of standardization, language problems and prejudice, not least from national administrations, but the advantages of introducing European project management standards and forcing cooperation through the selective granting of funds can be seen in the case of the cross-border cooperation between Upper Silesia and Czech Silesia. Competition for western investment, and different political orientations and the burden of the past, led Jan Olbrycht, mayor of the Polish part of Cieszyn, to analyze the situation as follows: 'Polish–Czech contacts have never been easy, the fact that we cooperate at the moment means that both sides are thinking openly and along rational lines to overcome certain negative attitudes' (Hyde-Price, 1996: 87). Whether the German population in any part of Silesia might also participate in this improvement can only be guessed at. An indication of changed attitudes might come with the Czech and Polish government using their German minorities as a positive investment factor, relying on the legendary German work ethic. In the final analysis the future of Silesia might depend on its the very multi-ethnic identity, forged as we have seen centuries ago.

Today's division of Silesia between Poland, Germany and the Czech Republic is in many senses the result of past events. They hark all the way back to the division of Silesia between Prussia and the Habsburg empire in 1740 on which the ever more complicated pattern of national and ethnic cleavage was superimposed in the nineteenth and twentieth centuries. No nation-state vying for possession of Silesia has managed to homogenize the resultant territorial-ethnic mosaic, if only because geopolitical and military realities stood in the way. Nazi Germany attempted to create a racially pure state through a policy of genocide, and failed at the cost of millions of lives. Poland, having gained most of Prussian Silesia after 1945, strove to Polonize the population by erasing all 'German traces', which included doing away with the region altogether by dividing it among ever smaller voivodeships which mixed Silesian with non-Silesian areas. The multi-cultural mix of Silesia, and especially Upper Silesia, changed and was weakened, but in the end it remained. The resilience of the region should serve as a warning to all who toy with schemes of ethnic purity.

Bibliography

Bahlcke, J., *Schlesien und die Schlesier.* Berlin, Langen Müller, 1996.

Berdychowska, B. et al. (eds), *Mniejszosci narodowe w Polsce w 1993 roku.* Warsaw, Biuro do Spraw Mniejszosci Narodowych przy Ministerstwie kultury i Sztuki, 1994.

—— *Mniejszosci narodowe w Polsce, informator 1994.* Warsaw, Wydawnictwo Sejmowe, 1995.

Bingen, D., Bundesinstitut für Ostwissenschaftliche und Internationale Studien, interview with Karl Cordell, 8 Nov. 1994.

Born, K. M., 'Regionen in Europa und der Fall Schlesien', *Europa Regional* 6 (3), 1998.

Borussia 16, 1998.

Bricke, D. W., *Minderheiten im östlichen Mitteleuropa. Deutsche und europäische Optionen.* Ebenhausen, Stiftung Wissenschaft und Politik, 1994.

Bronsztejn, S., *Z dziejow ludnosci zydowskiej na Dolnym Slasku po II wojnie swiatowej.* Wroclaw, Wydawnictwo Uniwersytetu Wroclawskiego, 1993.

'Bund der Vertriebenen, Stellungnahmen zu den im Rahmen des Mitarbeiterkongresses am 1./2. Oktober 1994 stattfindenen Anhörungen zur Lage der deutschen Volksgruppen und Erhaltung ihres kulturellen Erbes'. Unpublished, 1994.

Burcher, T., *The Sudeten German question and Czechoslovak–German relations since 1989.* London, Royal United Services Institute for Defence Studies, 1996.

Deutscher Bundestag, *Antwort der Bundesregierung auf die Große Anfrage der Fraktionen der CDU/CSU und F.D.P. (BT 12/5046) zur Unterstützung der Reformprozesse in den Staaten Mittel-, Südost- und Osteuropas (einschließlich der baltischen Staaten).* BT-Drucksache 12/6162, Bonn, 1993.

European Commission, *Agenda 2000: Commission Opinion on the Czech Republic's Application for Membership in the European Union.* Brussels, 1997.

EIPA, 'Subsidiarity: The Challenge of Change', Maastricht, 1991.

Frankfurter Rundschau, 6 Sept. 1998.

Hoskova, M., 'Der Minderheitenschutz in der Tschechischen Republik', in P. Mohlek and M. Hoskova, *Der Minderheitenschutz in der Republik Polen, in der Tschechischen und in der Slovakischen Republik.* Bonn, Kulturstiftung der deutschen Vertriebenen, 1994.

Hyde-Price, A., *The International Politics of East Central Europe.* Manchester, Manchester University Press, 1996.

Iwanicki, M., *Ukraincy, Bialorusini, Litwini i Niemcy w polsce w latach 1918–1990.* Siedlce, WSP, 1994.

Kimminich, O., 'Völkerrechtliche Bemerkungen zur deutsch-tschechischen Erklärung. Folgerungen für das Recht auf Heimat', in D. Blumenwitz, G. H.Gornig , and D. Murswiek (eds), *Der Beitritt der Staaten Ostmitteleuropas zur Europäischen Union und die Rechte der deutschen Volksgruppen und Minderheiten sowie der Vertriebenen.* Cologne, Verlag Wissenschaft und Politik, 1997.

Kinsky, F., *Federalism: A Global Theory. The Impact of Proudhon and the Personalist Movement on Federalism.* Nice, Presse d'Europe, 1995.

Kinsky, F., *L'Allemagne et l'Europe.* Nice, Presse d'Europe, 1997.

Kopstein, J. S., 'The Politics of National Reconciliation: Memory and Institutions in German–Czech Relations since 1989', *Nationalism and Ethnic Politics* 3 (2), 1997.

Koschyk, H. (ed.), *Schlesien als verständigungspolitisches Schlüsselgebiet in und für Europa: Fachtagung der Landsmannschaft Schlesiens, 9–12. Dezember*. Haus Schlesien, Königswinter, 1993.

Kostelecky, T., 'Changing Party Allegiances in a Changing Party System: The 1990 and 1992 Parliamentary Elections in the Czech Republic', in G. Whightman (ed.), *Party Formation in East-Central Europe*. Bodmin, Hartnolls, 1995.

Kroll, H., member of the Polish *Sejm*, interview with Karl Cordell, 16 Nov. 1998.

Nagengast, E., 'Coming to Terms with a "European Identity": The Sudeten Germans between Bonn and Prague', *German Politics* 5 (1), 1996.

Ociepka, B., *Niemcy na Dolnym Slasku w latach 1945–1970*. Wroclaw, Wydawnictwo Uniwersytetu Wroclawskiego, 1994.

Pithart, P., 'Towards a Shared Freedom, 1968–89', in J. Musil (ed.), *The End of Czechoslovakia*. Budapest, Central European University Press, 1995.

Pudlo, K., 'Polityka panstwa polskiego wobec ludnosci ukrainskiej (1944–1991)', *Sprawy Narodowosciowe* 1 (2), 1993.

Pudlo, K., 'Grecy i Macedonczycy w Polsce 1948–1993', *Sprawy Narodowosciowe* 1 (6), 1995.

Rhodes, M., 'National Identity and Minority Rights in the Constitution of the Czech Republic and Slovakia', *East European Quarterly* 29 (3), 1995.

Ryback, T. W., 'Dateline Sudetenland: Hostages to History', *Foreign Policy* 105, 1996.

Sakson, A., 'Die deutsche Minderheit in Polen: Gegenwart und Zukunft', conference paper (venue unknown), Aug. 1993.

Schlesische Nachrichten, 1 Sept. 1998; 4 Sept 1998.

Siebel-Achenbach, S., *Lower Silesia from Nazi Germany to Communist Poland, 1942–1949*. New York, St. Martin's Press, 1994.

Smith, A., 'The Politics of Culture: Ethnicity and Nationalism', in T. Ingold (ed.), *Companion Encyclopedia of Anthropology*. London, Routledge, 1997.

Der Standard, 15 Sept. 1998.

Süddeutsche Zeitung, 10 Aug. 1998.

Weiß, U., 'Die Organisationen der Vertriebenen und ihre Presse', in W. Benz (ed.), *Die Vertreibung der Deutschen aus dem Osten*. Frankfurt/Main, 1995.

Whightman, G., 'The Development of the Party System and the break-up of Czechoslovakia', in G. Whightman (ed.), *Party Formation in East-Central Europe*. Bodmin, Hartnolls Limited, 1995.

Zerlik, R., 'Mniejszosc ukrainska w polsce po II wojnie swiatowej', in Z. Kurcz (ed.), *Mniejszosci narodowe w Polsce*. Wroclaw, Wydawnictwo Uniwersytetu Wroclawskiego, 1997.

Zurko, J., 'Lemkowie – miedzy grupa etniczna a narodem', in Z. Kurcz (ed.), *Mniejszosci narodowe w Polsce*. Wroclaw, Wydawnictwo Uniwersytetu Wroclawskiego, 1997.

Notes

1. Karl Cordell wrote the opening sections and closing comments of this chapter. The remainder was written by Tomasz Kamusella.

Conclusion

Our survey is now almost complete. It is to be hoped that, for those for whom the subject matter was wholly new, the volume has stimulated an interest in the politics of this part of Central Europe, as well as in the politics of nation-building and ethnicity. For the more experienced reader, we hope that we have added to the existing stock of knowledge. Perhaps the only task which remains is to identify and comment upon the more important of the volume's findings.

The first finding is this: as the introductory chapters show, in the attempt to render the idea of the nation-state real in Central Europe, nation-building elites have employed a series of fairly common strategies. These strategies have involved an often mutually exclusive competition for human resources, an attempt to establish a sense of continuity between past and present state forms, and attempts to homogenize sometimes rather disparate population groups. Whereas all of the above is true, we should, however, avoid falling into the trap of stereotypical thinking. These phenomena have been by no means confined to Central Europe. On the contrary, they appear, to one extent or the other, to be integral elements in any project to create a nation-state. In other words they are universal. This is not to say that hitherto unsuspecting people are always forced into assuming national identities against their will. Rather it is to acknowledge that in any such project, nation-builders will inevitably encounter resistance from the periphery, established pre-national interests or indeed other nation-builders. In fact, the 'national' perspectives of nation-builders often result in them acting in an insensitive manner toward members of the putative nation-state, especially when the given population resides in an ethnographic borderland.

Our second finding is this: in Central Europe the attempt to implement such abstract notions as national self-determination was particularly problematic. In the latter part of the nineteenth and early part of the twentieth century, the subjects of the various European and Eurasian empires rarely possessed a collective consciousness that could be described as national. This is not to claim the modern states of Central Europe are simply the products of will and imagination. Rather it is to point out that in the absence of mass literacy, mass communication, mass media, and mass transportation, national identification was ill-placed to replace older, entrenched forms of such identification in a smooth an orderly manner.

Thirdly, as industrialization spread and the imperial units became increasingly dysfunctional, so the new order gained wider currency and came to replace the old. It is the circumstances within which this change took place, as well as the nature of the change itself, which help explain why this transition was so problematic. Crisis often precipitates change. However, the crisis which East-Central Europe found itself in at the beginning of the twentieth century was uniquely profound. Indeed it could reasonably be argued that the area is only just beginning definitively to emerge from a crisis which culminated in the Second World War.

The evidence that the effects of the crisis have finally ceased to be a major factor in the politics of the area, is the collapse of Europe's last empire, the Soviet Union in 1991, and the nature of the transition from secularized neo-imperial rule. That Poland, Hungary, and Czechoslovakia were able to achieve a transition from Soviet-style communism to liberal-democratic rule bears witness to that statement. The fact that Slovakia was able peacefully to secede from Czechoslovakia re-enforces that claim. As we saw in Chapter 2, problems still remain in the area, particularly over the treatment of the Roma, but it would be scandalous to suggest that even the Meciar administrations in Slovakia attempted to solve Slovakia's 'nationality problem' with a repetition of the tactics of the 1920s, 1930s, and 1940s. Had such tactics been adopted, and there is no reason to assume they were actually contemplated, there is little chance they would have succeeded. Not only does constitutional protection exist for minorities in each of the states under examination, but, more importantly, those who would rather not enforce it, or would indeed scrap such protection, are well aware of both internal checks and balances, and of the fact that if they wish to take part in the long march of European integration, a policy of overt and officially sanctioned discrimination is unacceptable. In fact, such policies are likely to bring far more costs than benefits.

Turning to Silesia, with which the bulk of this work has been concerned, the large majority of the above observations also apply. All the issues raised in the initial stages of the volume have found expression in Silesia. Indeed, they are given added poignancy given that Auschwitz lies in Upper Silesia. That Upper Silesia in particular encapsulated the general struggle for hearts and minds demonstrates why Silesia as a whole was chosen as the case study through which to examine in more depth the themes and issues raised in the earlier part of the work. Although for centuries ruled by German-speaking elites, Slavic influence in Upper Silesia as opposed to Lower Silesia was never completely eradicated. 'As in Danish German borderland of Schleswig-Holstein, ethno-national identification was not an issue until the Prussians, spurred by their desire to create a modern German society, began the process of national homogenization. That counter-claims concerning the national provenance of Upper Silesians then emerged is no more an accident than it was a consequence of this process. On the contrary, it was an integral ingredient of a much wider phenomenon, that of nation-building, and the consequent competition for hearts and minds.

The case of Silesia was indeed tragic. Yet despite the fact that the specific course of national competition was unique, once again the general phenomenon was not. It occurred throughout the region, has occurred, and continues to occur elsewhere throughout the globe. Two examples will suffice. The first is the United Kingdom, where the triumph of the idea of the Britishness was achieved, among other means, by repeated attempts to destroy the Welsh language, the mass deportations of Jacobite Scots, under the guise of 'Highland Clearances', and repeated attempts to destroy Irish Catholic culture. The second example comes from the United States, the 'first new nation', where the new nation-builders sought to destroy the culture of the original inhabitants and in its place erect a society in their own image. The reader may protest that this is all in the past, and that like is not being compared with like. There is of course much merit to such an argument. The point is that these events contributed to the foundation of new nations and nation-states, and we should not for one minute believe that what occurred in Silesia and elsewhere in Central Europe was or is a phenomenon specific to that part of the globe.

In Silesia today the topics dealt with in this volume are discussed with more honesty than in the past. As a classic borderland, where different cultures and traditions met and coexisted within another, nation-building was always likely to be especially problematic. The aforementioned crisis of the early twentieth century served to magnify these problems to monstrous proportions. As the century draws to a close, Poles, Germans, Czechs and others once again coexist in Silesia, and the vast majority of the area is an integral part of the Polish state. Indeed, the overwhelming majority of Silesia's population readily identifies itself as Polish. As a new century dawns, it appears that the Czech Republic and Poland together with Hungary are about to join Germany as members of the European Union. It is to be hoped that accession to a supranational Europe will finally lay the ghosts of the past to rest, not only in Silesia but in the region as a whole.

Index